POSTCARD HISTORY SERIES

Shaver, Huntington, and Hume Lakes

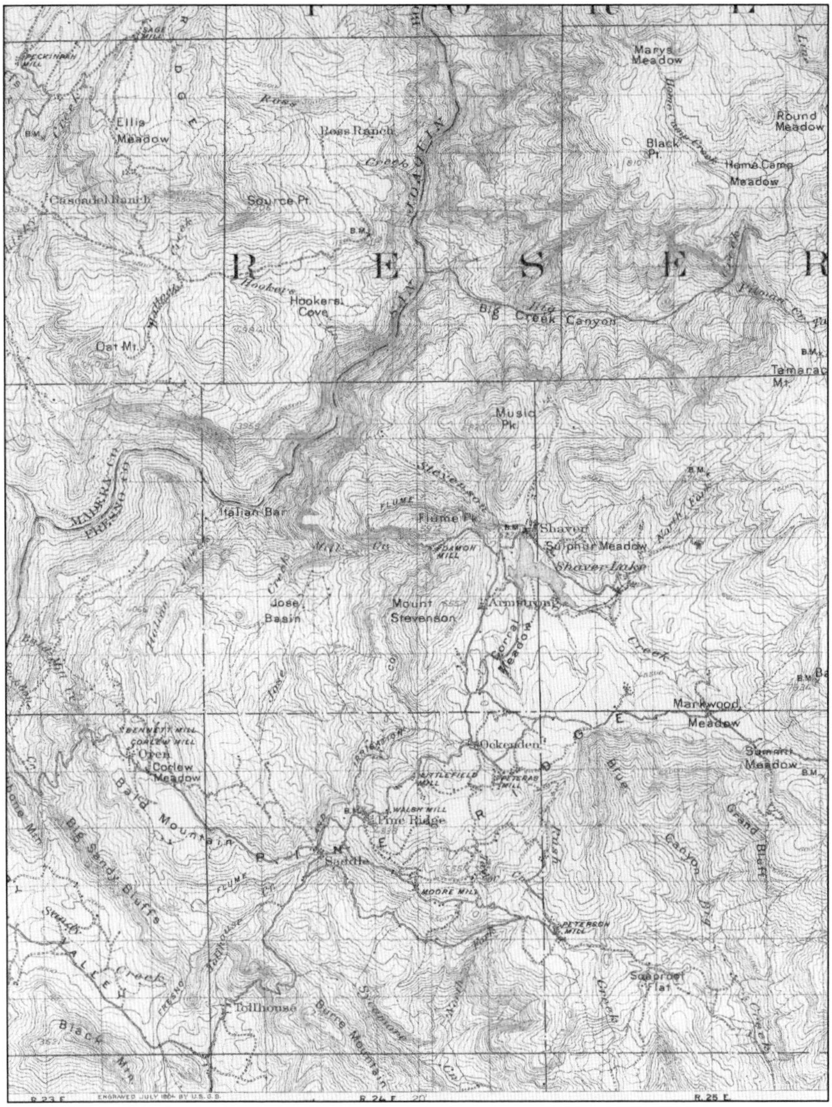

This portion of a 1904 topographic map shows the Shaver Lake area with some of the place names used in this book. (Michael J. Semas collection.)

On the Front Cover: A crowd of loggers and millhands poses around 1910 as they prepare to send these huge logs through the second Converse Basin sawmill. These are logs from giant sequoias, the largest trees on earth and just one of several species logged in the Sierra Nevada. Converse Basin held one of the largest groves of giant sequoias; nearly all were cut down, but the logging company made little profit. In response to such wasteful logging, federal and state governments protected many of the giant sequoia groves in parks, including Kings Canyon National Park, Sequoia National Park, and Yosemite National Park. (Michael J. Semas collection.)

On the Back Cover: Moving large logs from the forest to the sawmill was not easy. Initially, horses and oxen were used, but the development of the steam donkey engine eventually made animals obsolete in most logging operations. (Michael J. Semas collection.)

POSTCARD HISTORY SERIES

Shaver, Huntington, and Hume Lakes

Steven D. Harrison and Michael J. Semas

ARCADIA PUBLISHING

ISBN 978-1-4671-3143-8

Published by Arcadia Publishing
Charleston, South Carolina

Printed in the United States of America

Library of Congress Control Number: 2013948953

For all general information contact Arcadia Publishing at:
Telephone 843-853-2070
Fax 843-853-0044
E-mail sales@arcadiapublishing.com
For customer service and orders:
Toll-Free 1-888-313-2665

Visit us on the Internet at www.arcadiapublishing.com

This book is dedicated to my parents, Al and Betty Harrison, for instilling in me a love of the Sierra Nevada and a respect for history.

—SDH

This book is dedicated to my wife, Christine, who has supported my obsession with local history and is willing to travel with me to out-of-the-way places to see if "that building still stands."

—MJS

Contents

ACKNOWLEDGMENTS

The commercial activity and development in the central Sierra Nevada that is presented in this book occurred at the turn of the 20th century, when postcards boomed as an inexpensive and easy way to communicate. Most postcards were printed on presses and published by large companies. However, it was easy for anybody with a camera to make their own postcards on preprinted photographic paper. These images, referred to as real-photo postcards, are rarer because they were made in small quantities.

Steve's involvement in this began when he purchased a large collection of Manley Freeman White (1882–1953) photographs at an estate sale in 1974. White worked in the logging camp at Shaver as a millhand and took photographs in his spare time. Steve quickly realized the photographs were from Fresno County, which is where he was born and raised. While working in Yosemite National Park during the 1970s, Steve met author Hank Johnston, who generously gave him some postcards and photographs from the central Sierra Nevada. Hank had already published several books about the area, including *The Railroad That Lighted Southern California* and *They Felled the Redwoods.*

Michael has been collecting antique imagery of Central California for over 15 years and has amassed a collection of over 1,000 images of the central Sierra Nevada. He concentrates on acquiring images from specific local photographers, such as Riggs, Besaw, Eddy, Parker, Roberts, and Mudge. These photographers took thousands of images of the Shaver, Huntington, and Hume Lake areas and the industries that were developed there. The combination of the best of Michael's collection with the best of Steve's imagery allows a unique story to be told.

Nearly all of the postcards presented in this book are from the personal collections of the authors. Cards from other collections are appropriately credited.

We would like to thank Melissa Scroggins of the Fresno County Public Library for assisting us in locating specific images from the library's collection. We also would like to thank the Fresno County Public Library, the Central Sierra Historical Society, and John Reynolds for the use of images from their collections.

INTRODUCTION

The central Sierra Nevada of Fresno County is rich in natural resources, including timber, water, minerals, and scenery. As a result, the Shaver, Huntington, and Hume Lake areas have a rich and colorful history that is well documented with photographs.

Starting in the late 19th century, the timber resources began to be exploited. Numerous small, independent logging operations came into existence, especially on Pine Ridge, which was as rich in timber as the name implies. Due to the difficulty of logging, milling, and transporting logs and lumber in the rugged Sierra, the small logging operations were gradually integrated into larger lumber companies. One such company was the Fresno Flume & Lumber Company, originally called the Fresno Flume & Irrigation Company and later known as the Shaver Lake Lumber Company. The company logged around Shaver Lake for more than 20 years starting in the 1890s, built the Shaver Lake Railroad to haul logs to their millpond and large sawmill, and built a 42-mile-long flume to transport the boards from the sawmill to Clovis in the San Joaquin Valley.

To the south of Shaver, in the Kings River canyon, large-scale logging was begun by the Kings River Lumber Company, organized by Austin Moore and Hiram Smith in 1888. A reservoir was created at Mill Flat Meadow, two sawmills were built, and a flume was constructed. They also built the Sequoia Railroad to move logs and lumber. When the national economic depression of the early 1890s severely decreased demand for lumber, the company reorganized as The Sanger Lumber Company. Even with a cut of 22 million board feet of lumber in 1896, they could not meet expenses. Undeterred, the company operations moved over a ridge into Converse Basin, where it began to cut one of the largest known stands of giant sequoias, a tree that only grows on the western slope of the Sierra Nevada. The company even invested in a new sawmill in Converse Basin. Logging continued in Converse Basin for nearly a decade, and few giant sequoias were spared the axe and saw. Among the few remaining trees is the Boole Tree, one of the largest giant sequoias, which continues its solitary life in the basin to this day. Thousands of others were cut for lumber, but there was little profit for The Sanger Lumber Company, which was sold in 1905 to the newly incorporated Hume-Bennett Lumber Company, founded by Thomas Hume and Ira Bennett. In 1907, the company moved out of Converse Basin and into Long Meadow, about four miles east. In 1908, a new sawmill was constructed at Long Meadow. At the same time, a multiple-arch dam, designed by John S. Eastwood, was constructed. The 87-acre millpond was named Hume Lake after Thomas Hume. Full production at the new Hume site began in 1910. Ira Bennett was forced out of the company in 1912, and he quickly negotiated the purchase of a neighboring competitor, the Fresno Flume & Lumber Company. However, that firm became inactive in 1915. In 1917, the corporate name was changed from

Hume-Bennett to Sanger Lumber Company. This was the same year that the United States entered World War I, and many of the loggers and millhands, who worked in the sawmills, left the mountains to join the military. In November 1917, shortly after operations ceased for the season, the Hume sawmill and surrounding buildings burned to the ground; only limited logging occurred after that catastrophe. In 1927, after years of inactivity, the Sanger Lumber Company, with its few remaining assets, was sold.

The very name *Sierra Nevada*, which is Spanish for "snowy range," suggests heavy winter snow. When the Sierra snows melt in spring and summer, the water runs off the western slope into the Central Valley, a rich agricultural area that includes the Sacramento Valley and the San Joaquin Valley. This water is not only important for irrigation and domestic uses, it also has great power that is used to generate electricity. Most of the dams and hydropower plants are located in the foothills of the Sierra Nevada. However, eastern Fresno County is a major exception.

The hydroelectric story directly involves Los Angeles, over 200 miles south of Fresno. At the beginning of the 20th century, Henry E. Huntington developed extensive electric interurban railroad lines throughout Southern California. He also owned the Pacific Light & Power Company, which provided power for his interurban railway. As the Los Angeles–area population quickly grew, interurban railroads expanded, and the need for electricity increased beyond the capacity of the numerous but small Southern California power plants.

The Big Creek Hydroelectric Project was a very ambitious and grand plan, much larger than anything attempted until then. It was based, in part, on the hard work and vision of John S. Eastwood, who years earlier had recognized the hydroelectric power potential of the San Joaquin River in eastern Fresno County. In 1912, the 56-mile-long San Joaquin & Eastern (SJ&E) Railroad was built to carry construction materials into the mountains. The railroad ended at Cascada, renamed Big Creek in 1926. Completed in only 157 days, it was the most crooked railroad ever built in the world and soon had the nickname "Slow, Jerky, and Expensive."

In 1912, the Pacific Light & Power Company also started work on the three dams that would form Huntington Lake from Big Creek and began construction of Powerhouse No. 1 at Cascada. About 2,000 workers were hired by the contractor as construction commenced in earnest. In 1917, the Pacific Light & Power Company merged with Southern California Edison.

Over the years, other large lakes were created to impound snowmelt for power generation. Southern California Edison bought the idle Shaver property from the lumber company and built a new dam to enlarge the millpond, thus creating the current Shaver Lake. A multiple-arch dam on the South Fork of the San Joaquin River, also designed by John S. Eastwood, created Florence Lake. A later dam created Lake Thomas A. Edison. Construction on the Big Creek Hydroelectric Project was basically completed in 1929—only a few later additions, such as Mammoth Pool, would be made. In 1933, the San Joaquin & Eastern Railroad ceased operations. There were eventually nine power plants, five storage dams, four forebay dams, and 19 diversion dams in the Big Creek Hydroelectric Project.

As the 20th century moved along and roads improved, people from communities like Fresno in the San Joaquin Valley used the lakes for recreation, including fishing and boating. Vacation homes were built, as were numerous summer camps. Today, the area even has winter sports, with cross-country skiing and downhill skiing at China Peak.

The human story of the central Sierra Nevada is as big as the mountains. There are many wonderful photographs to document the history of the area. However, this book is limited in scope by what the authors have available in their extensive personal collections. Although we believe this provides a good representation of images that capture the wide range of activities in the mountains, we do not represent this as a definitive work on the central Sierra Nevada.

One

Logging

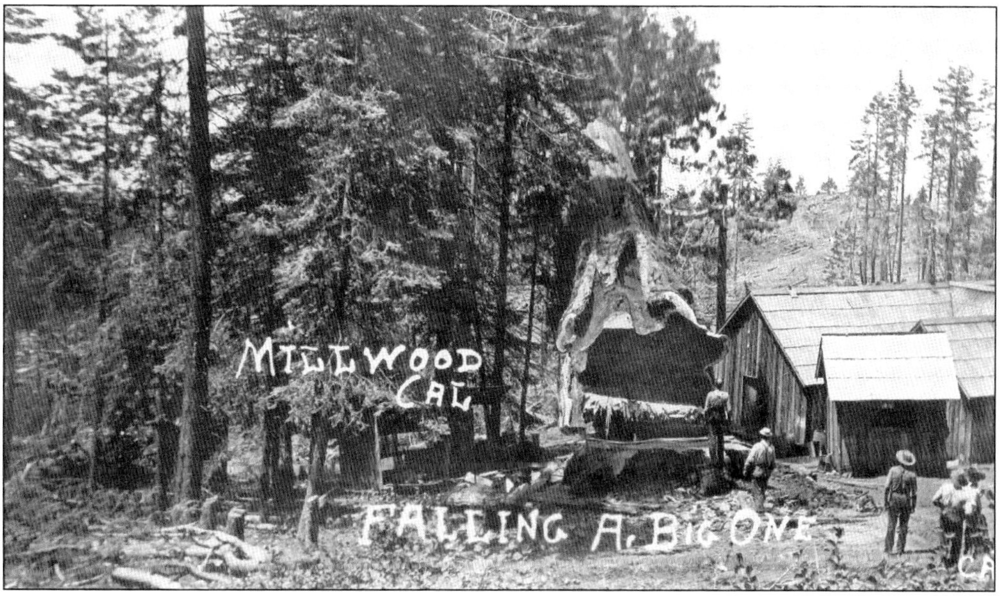

"Falling a Big One" may be an understatement. The Sanger Lumber Company, after constructing a sawmill at Millwood in the Kings River drainage of Fresno County, began to log giant sequoias. These onlookers are undoubtedly wondering if the falling tree will miss the camp buildings. This is proof of the skill of the loggers who worked in the Sierra Nevada at the turn of the 20th century.

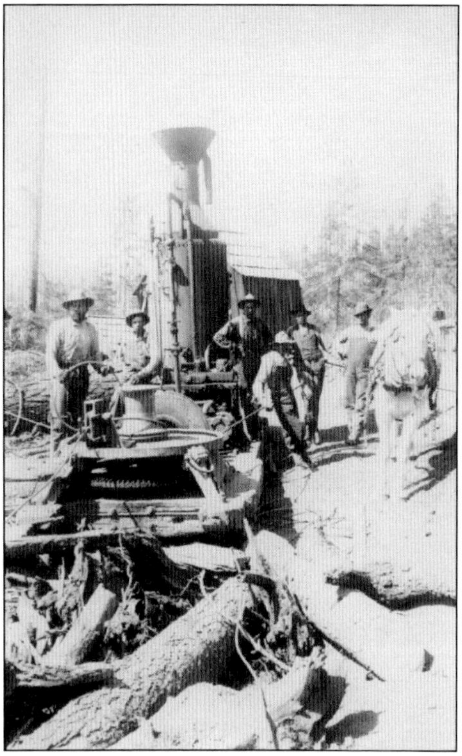

A group of six loggers pause from their hard work skidding logs to pose with a steam donkey near Shaver. This is a vertical-spool Dolbeer donkey. John Dolbeer, a founding partner of the Dolbeer & Carson Lumber Company in Eureka, California, invented the steam-powered logging engine in August 1881. The donkey was a winch used to move logs from where they were felled to the landing where they would be loaded for transport to a millpond or sawmill. Over the years, there were different designs made by different manufacturers. Steam donkeys originated on sailing ships, where the donkey engine was a small engine used to load and unload cargo, raise the larger sails, or power pumps. The lone horse shown in this photograph is probably a line horse that pulled the cable (or line) out to a log in the woods. The cable would be attached, and the steam donkey would then drag, or skid, the log toward it.

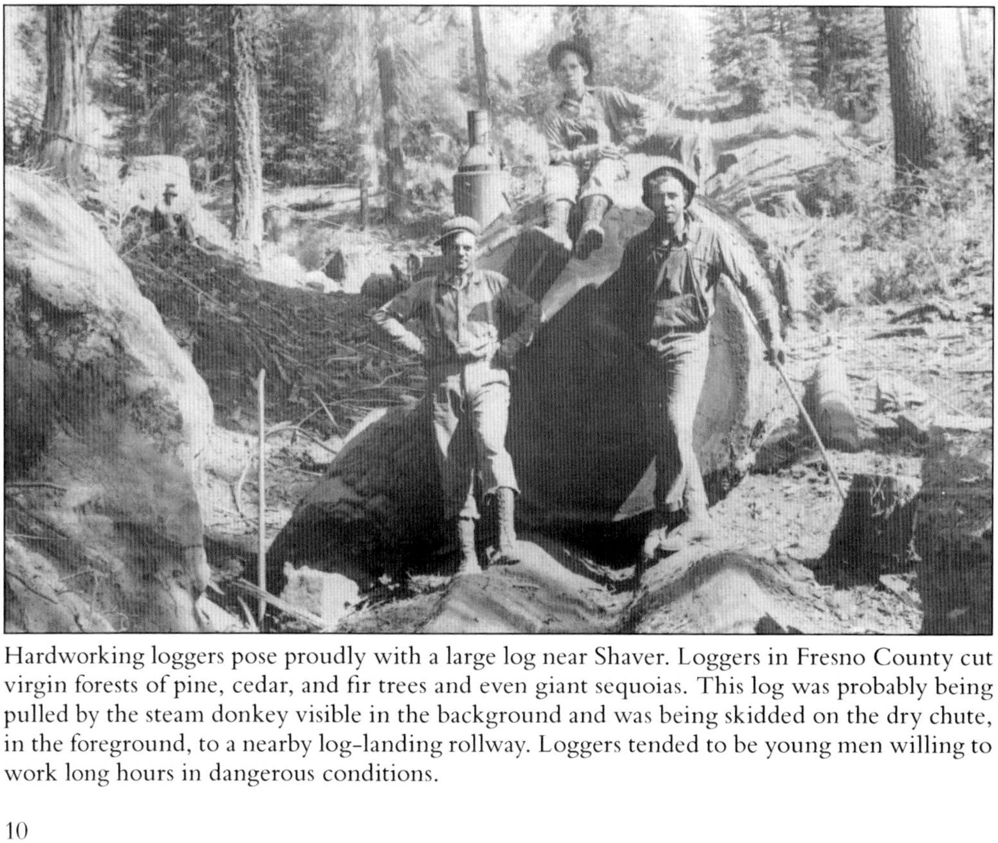

Hardworking loggers pose proudly with a large log near Shaver. Loggers in Fresno County cut virgin forests of pine, cedar, and fir trees and even giant sequoias. This log was probably being pulled by the steam donkey visible in the background and was being skidded on the dry chute, in the foreground, to a nearby log-landing rollway. Loggers tended to be young men willing to work long hours in dangerous conditions.

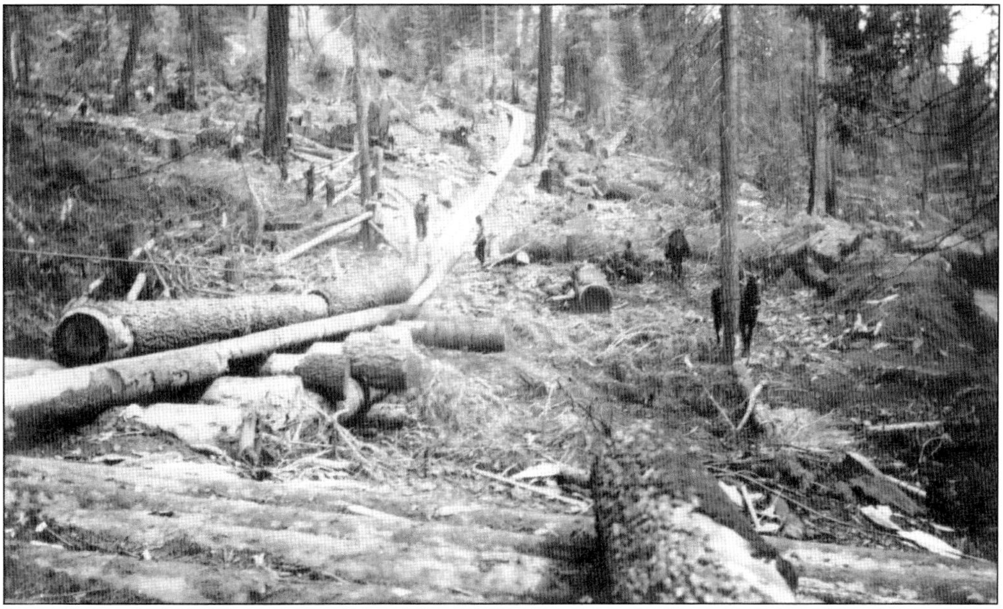

This photograph by Manley White shows several aspects of chute logging near Shaver. A number of men and a few horses are visible near the chute. The cable visible to the left suggests a steam donkey, out of view, is pulling the two logs along the chute. In the foreground, a log rests on the log-landing rollway, awaiting a railcar that would load to the right, out of view.

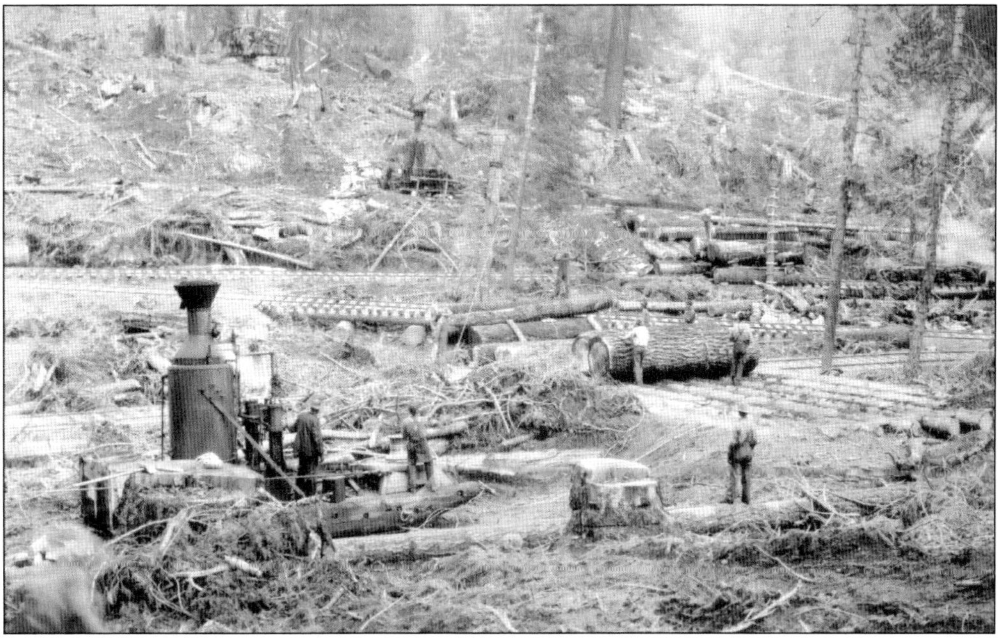

Manley White captured this busy scene in the woods with loggers hard at work near Shaver. A vertical-spool Dolbeer donkey in the foreground pulls logs to the rollway, at right, that leads down to a spur in the railroad. The logs are awaiting flatbed railcars that will take them to the millpond. In the distance are another steam donkey and rollway.

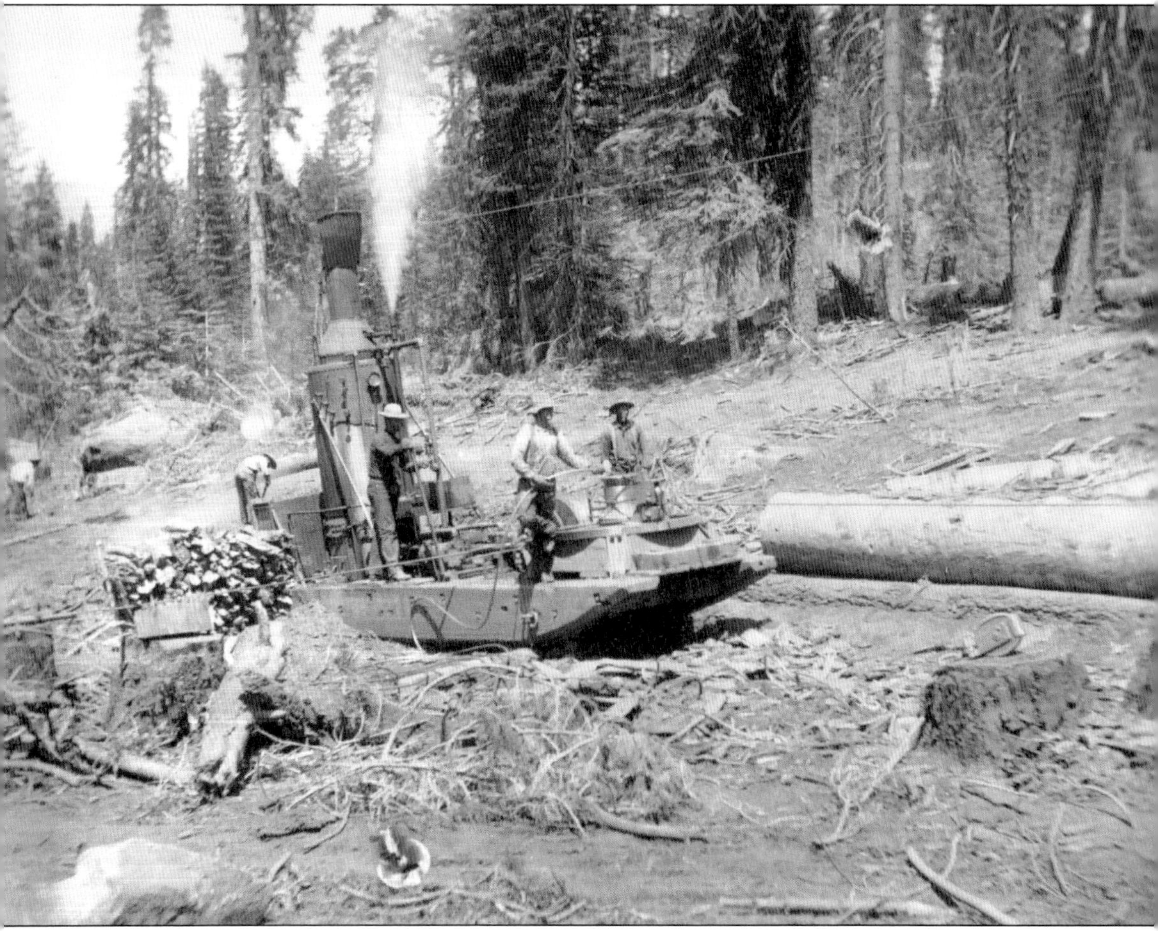

A vertical-spool Dolbeer steam donkey pulls the log at right on a chute toward a distant log rollway. The large stack of firewood to the left of the donkey was used to fire the boiler to generate steam. The sled under the donkey allowed the heavy equipment to be moved as logging progressed through the forest.

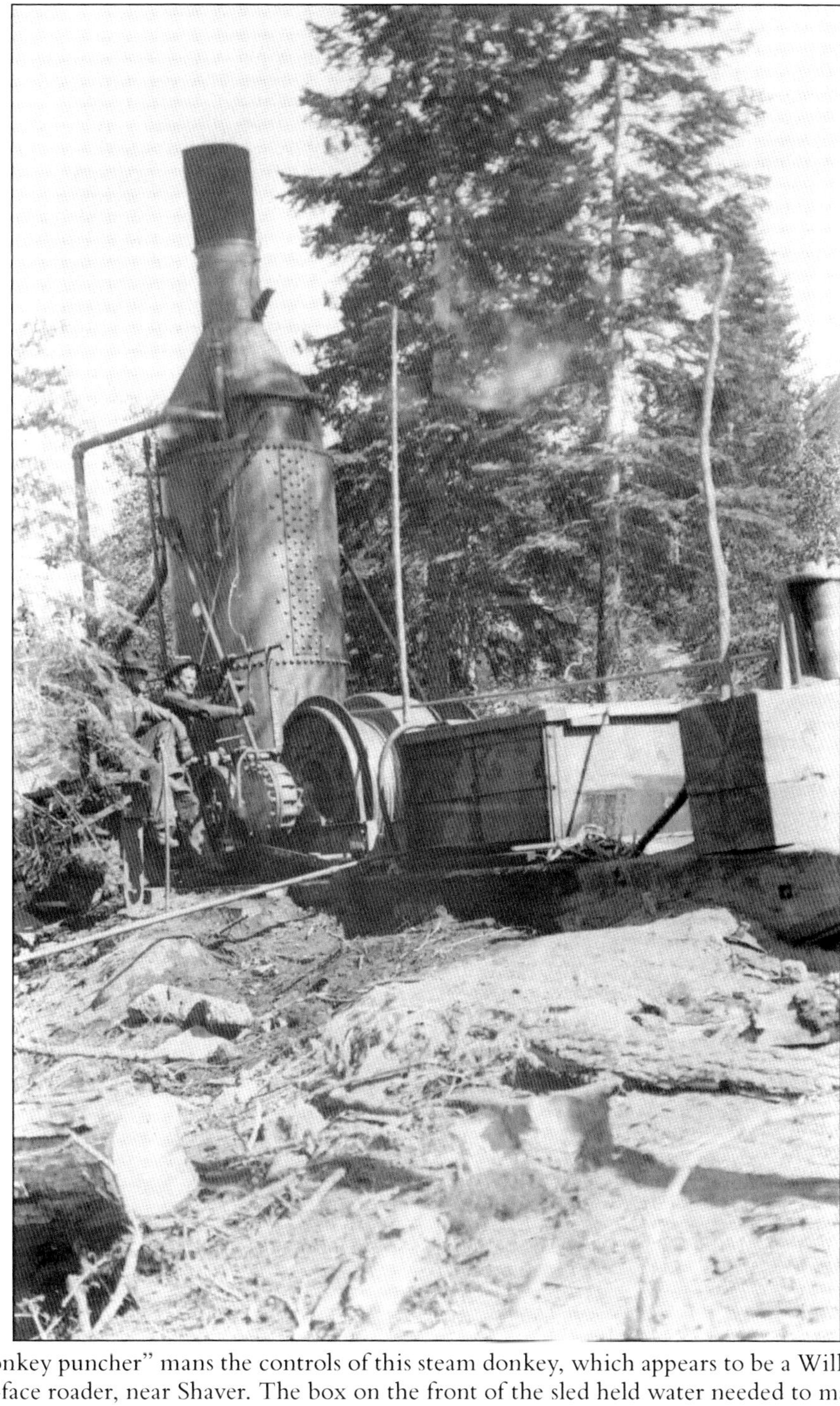

A "donkey puncher" mans the controls of this steam donkey, which appears to be a Willamette wide-face roader, near Shaver. The box on the front of the sled held water needed to make the steam that powered the engine. Maintaining and operating a steam donkey required a crew that was not afraid of hard work or noise. Just keeping a steam donkey supplied with water and wood required several men. Each steam donkeys had a whistle that was used by the operator as a signal to the rest of the crew.

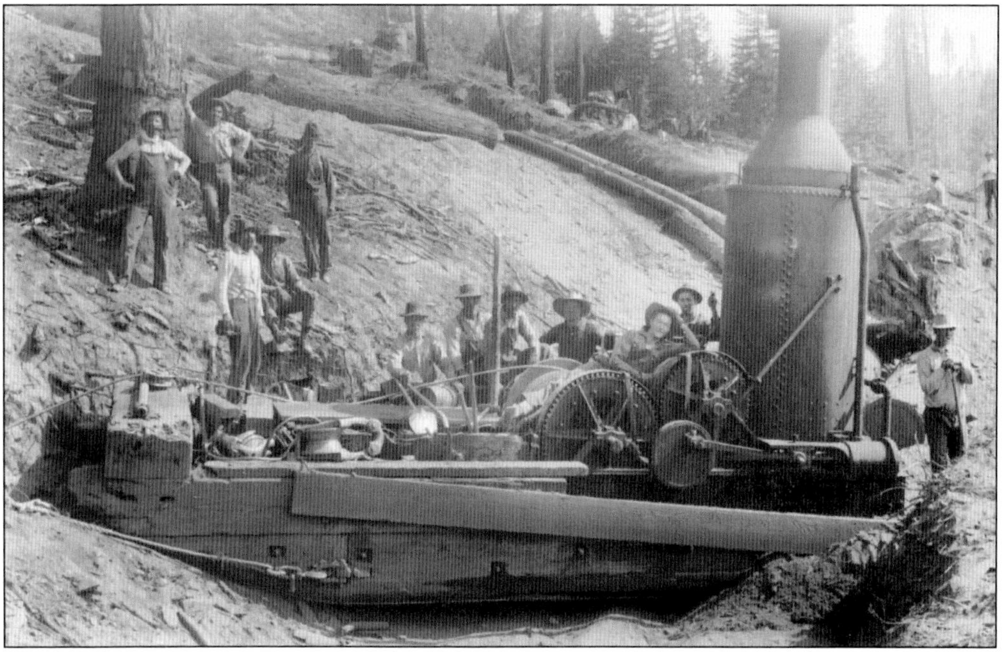

A large logging crew poses with a wide-face steam donkey for photographer Manley White in the sugar pine forest near Shaver. The heavy donkey engines were mounted on large wooden sleds so they could be moved around the forest under their own power. Visible beyond the donkey is the chute used to move logs to the Shaver Lake Railroad for transport to the millpond.

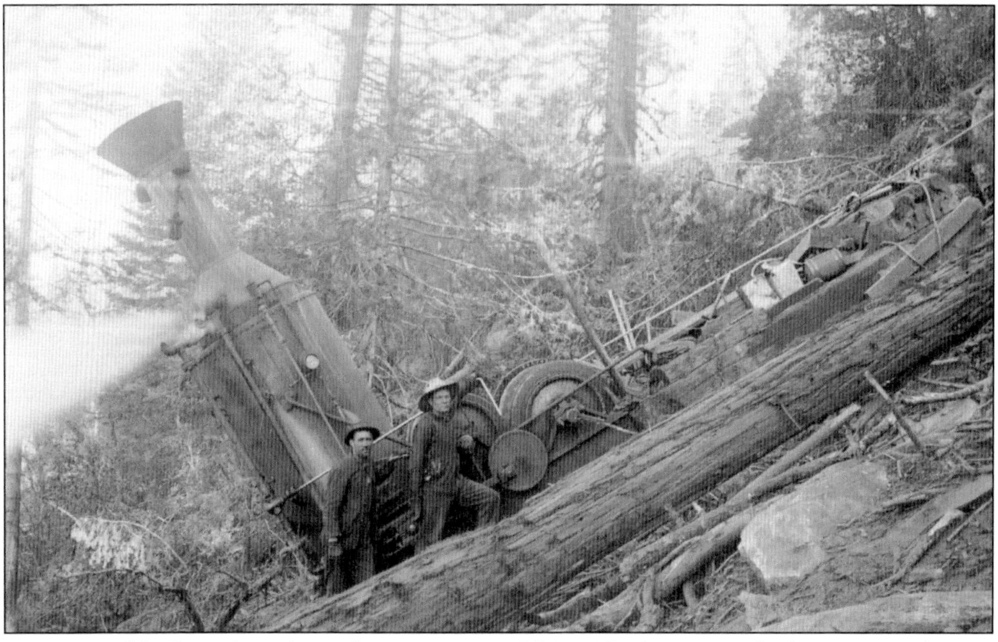

Steam, possibly from the safety valve, pours out of this wide-face steam donkey as it works on a very steep slope in the sugar pine forest near Shaver. The steam-powered donkey engine, which was cheap, reliable, and fast, quickly replaced horses and oxen as the preferred means of moving logs in the forest for larger-scale operations like the Fresno Flume & Lumber Company.

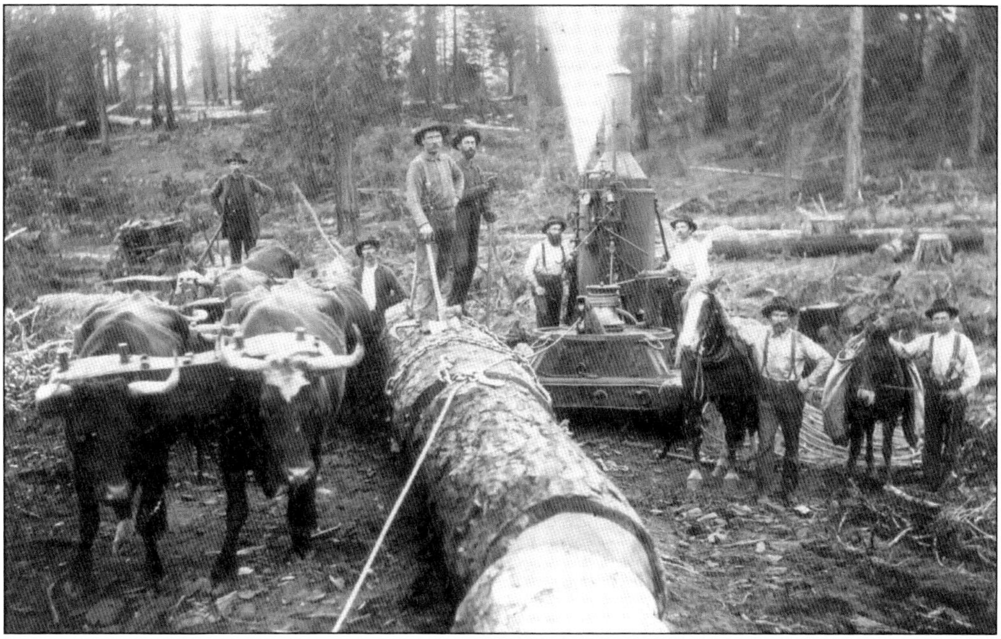

This steam-hissing vertical-spool Dolbeer donkey is busy moving logs in the woods. The logging crew poses with a horse, a mule, and a team of oxen. Oxen were generally replaced by steam engines in Western logging operations. This photograph, taken near Shaver in 1898, also shows one of the loggers standing on the log with his double-bit axe.

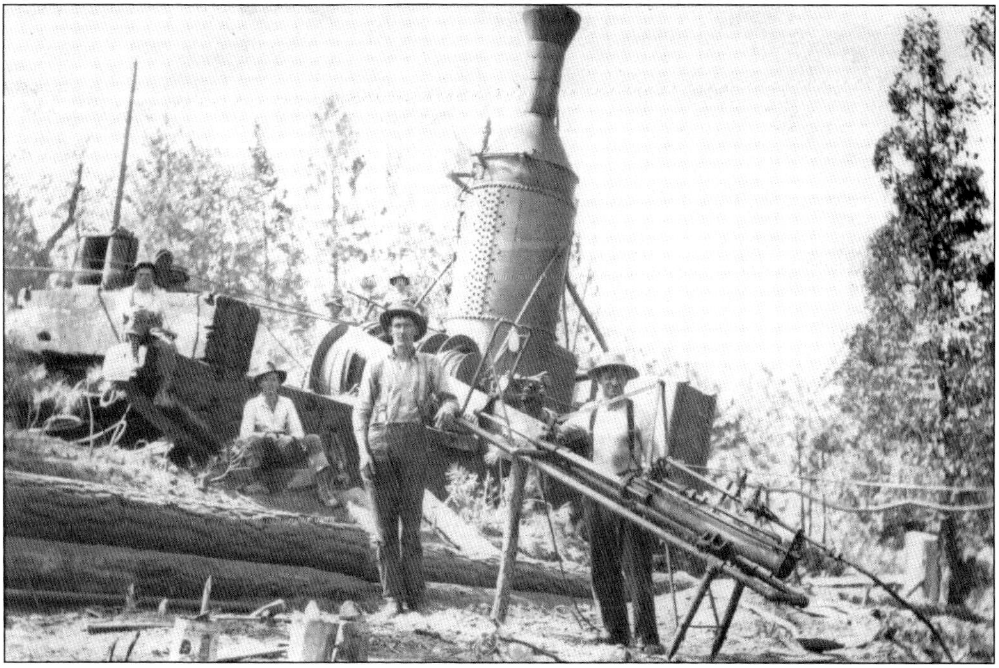

A logging crew takes a break to pose with a large Willamette steam donkey. These wide-face donkeys were made by the Willamette Iron & Steel Works in Portland, Oregon. The company built over 2,500 steam donkeys between 1901 and 1931. In the foreground is a dragsaw, a steam-powered, portable saw used to cut logs in the forest.

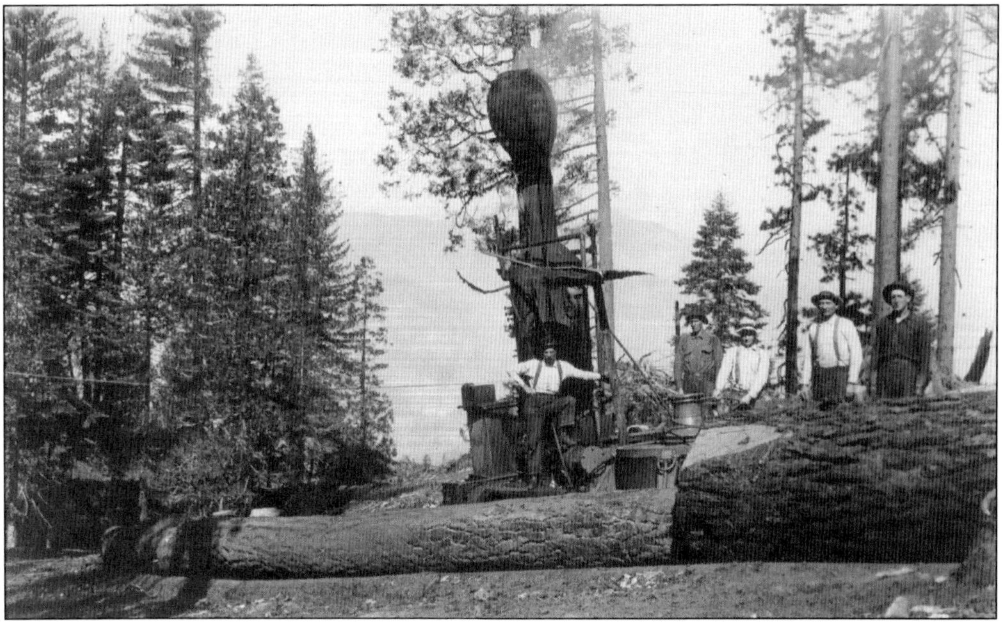

The crew poses with their Dolbeer vertical-spool steam donkey in the Sierra Nevada. This donkey has a spark arrestor on the stack to avoid starting a forest fire. The logs in the foreground are being moved along a chute, probably to a nearby logging railroad. The thinned forest suggests that a good deal of logging has already occurred in this area.

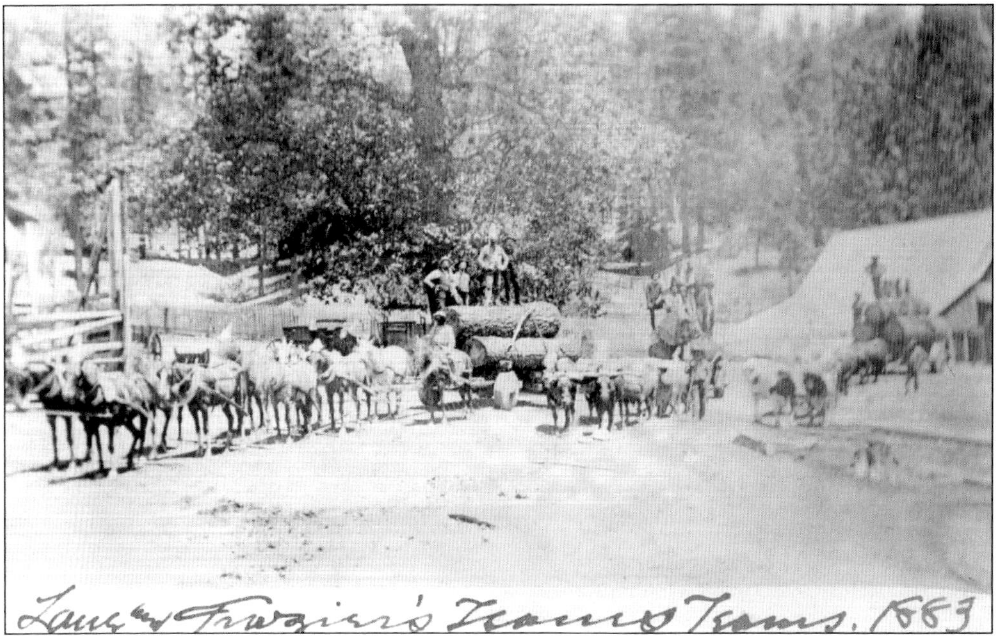

At the time this logging was being done in the Pine Ridge area in 1883, animals, not steam, were used to move logs to the sawmill. This photograph shows a team of horses pulling one wagon, while teams of oxen pull the others. Note the large wooden wheels on the wagons.

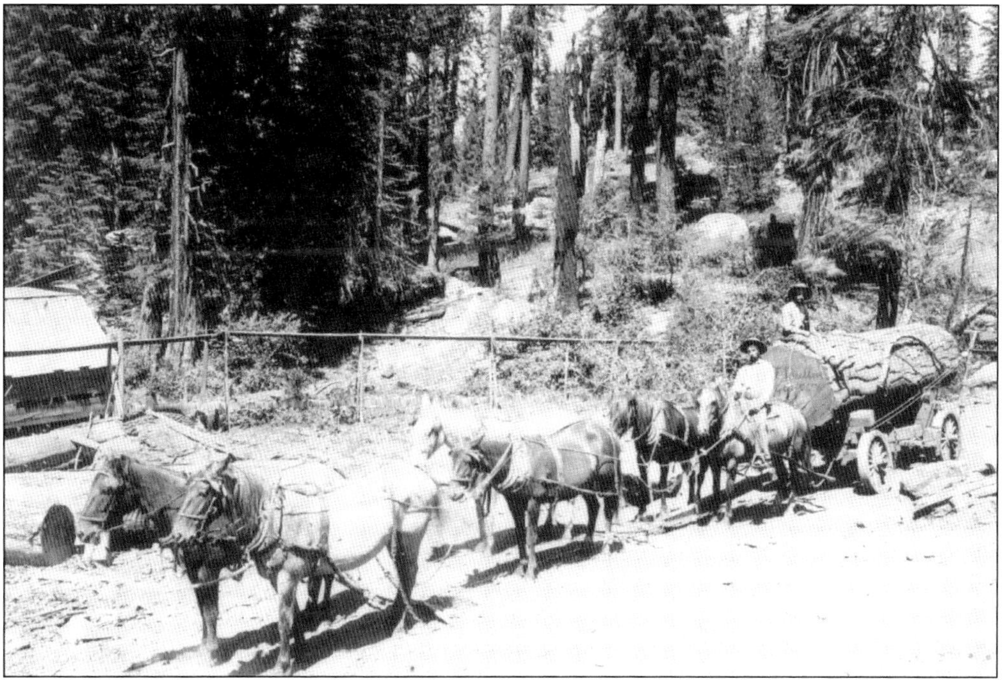

This log truck and six-horse team hauls a large log near Sage's Mill in 1897. John Sage built a double-circular steam-driven mill just south of the current Shaver Lake in 1893. The mill could cut about 15,000 board feet per day, and during the years it was in operation, about 100 acres were logged. It was one of many smaller mills on Pine Ridge.

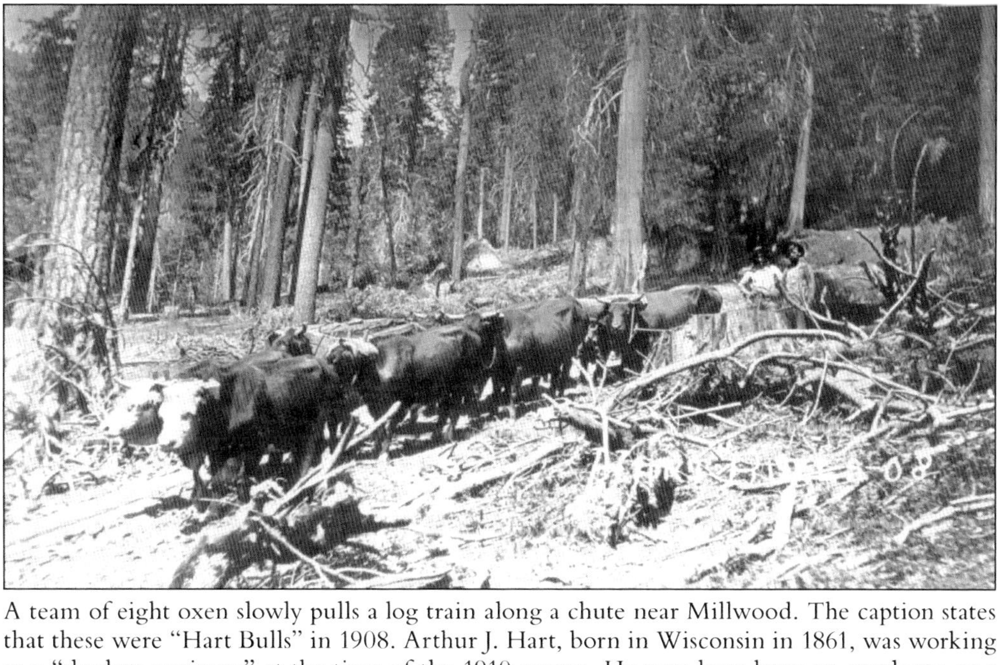

A team of eight oxen slowly pulls a log train along a chute near Millwood. The caption states that these were "Hart Bulls" in 1908. Arthur J. Hart, born in Wisconsin in 1861, was working as a "donkey engineer" at the time of the 1910 census. He may have been an employee or a contractor doing work for the Hume-Bennett Lumber Company.

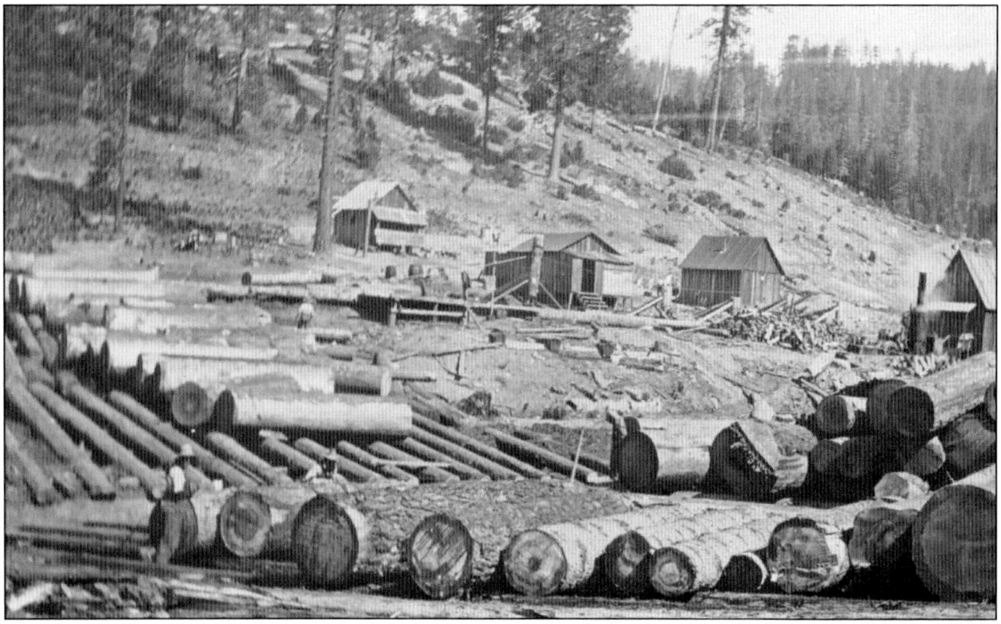

Stumps dot the mountain slope beyond the camp buildings at this loading area, probably near Shaver. The rollway is getting a lot of use as a donkey engine, to the right by the cabin, continues to pull logs from the woods. The presence of loggers in this image provides a scale for the size of the trees that were being logged.

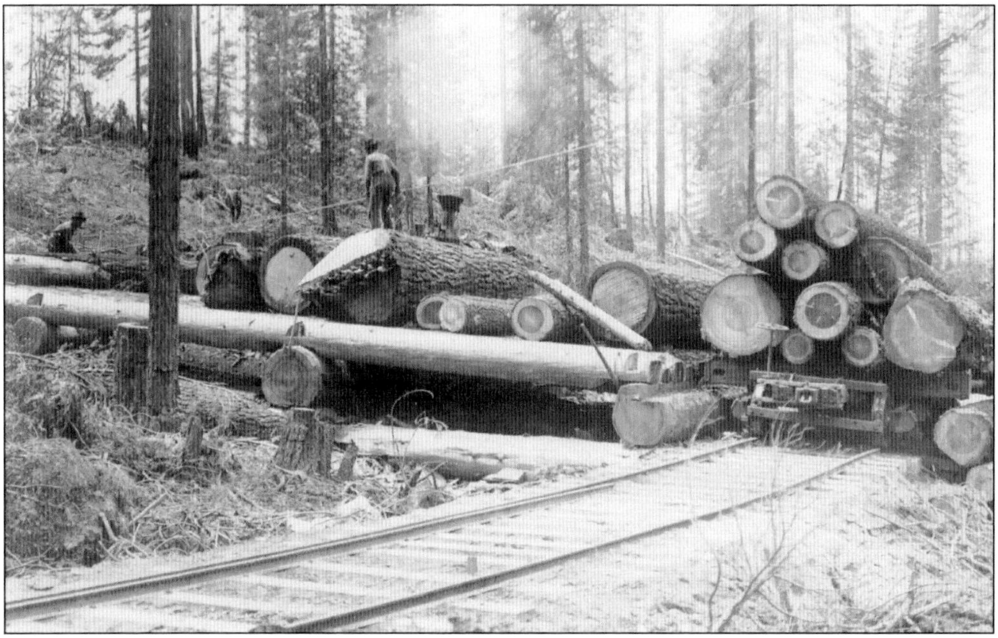

The thinned forest in the Shaver area is plainly visible in the background of this photograph of loggers loading a log car. Although a substantial load is already on the railcar, more logs are waiting on the log-landing rollway that gently slopes down to the railroad. The use of gravity slightly lessened the work for the loggers but did little to reduce the danger.

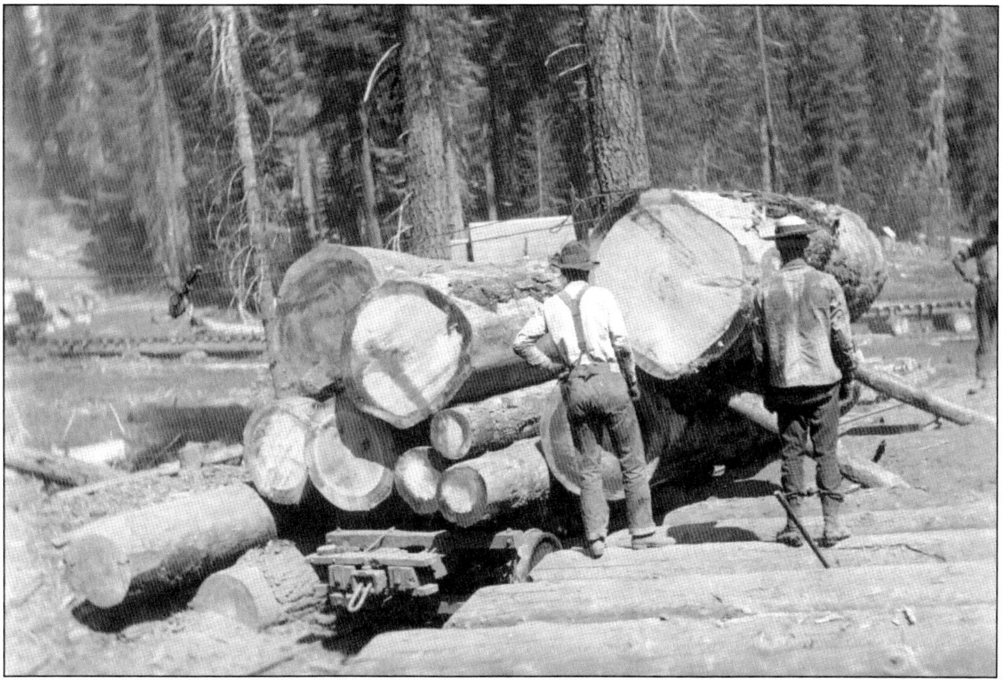

Photographer Manley White described this photograph as "loading logs on car with a cable line." The logging term for this procedure is "cross hauling." The logs were rolled down the log-landing rollway, at right, and then pulled by cable up the two small, inclined logs onto the railroad flatcar. The cable doing the pulling is attached to a steam donkey.

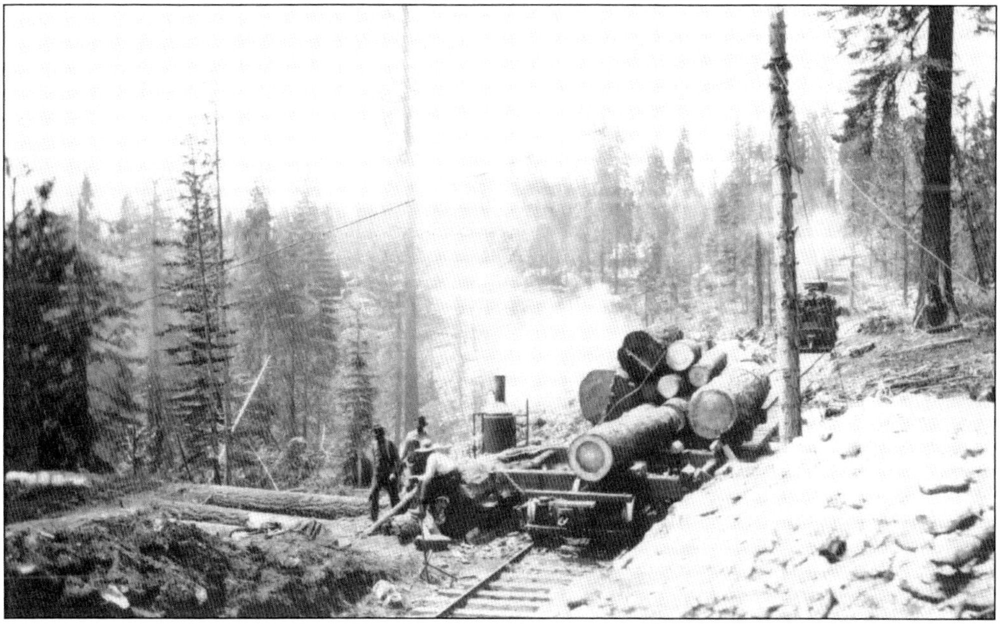

These loggers are busy loading a flatcar with logs as the Shay locomotive No. 1 *Sierra* backs down the track. There is no rollway visible in this Manley White photograph, so the donkey engine just beyond the flatcar provided power to help hoist logs onto the railcars. *Sierra* was delivered new to the Fresno Flume & Irrigation Company in 1902.

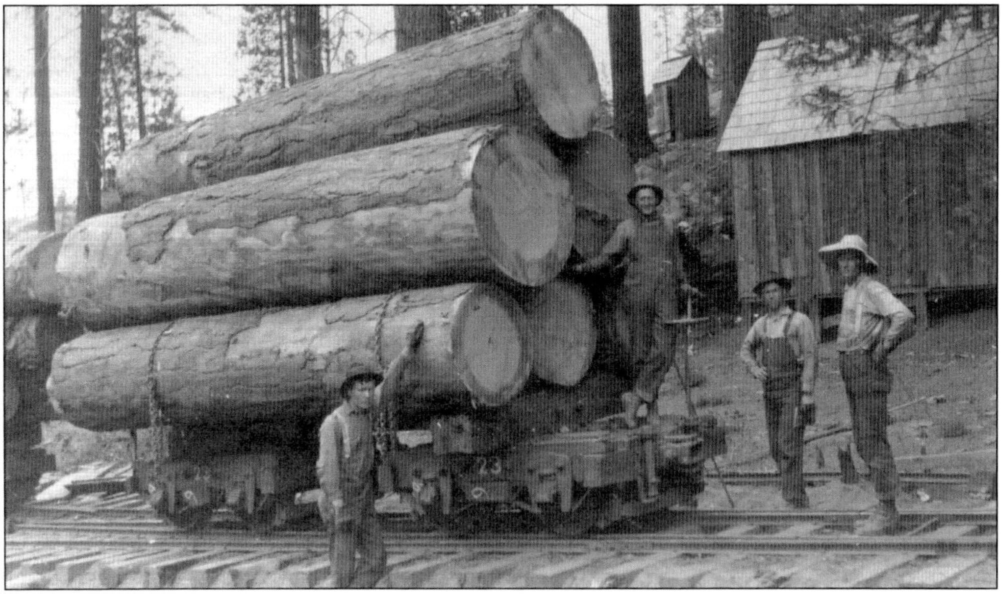

This real-photo postcard, sent from Hume in 1911, shows that these loggers could certainly load some huge logs onto the railroad flatcars that would haul them to the log dump at the millpond. Having one of the loggers stand on this flatcar clearly demonstrates how tall the load of six logs was.

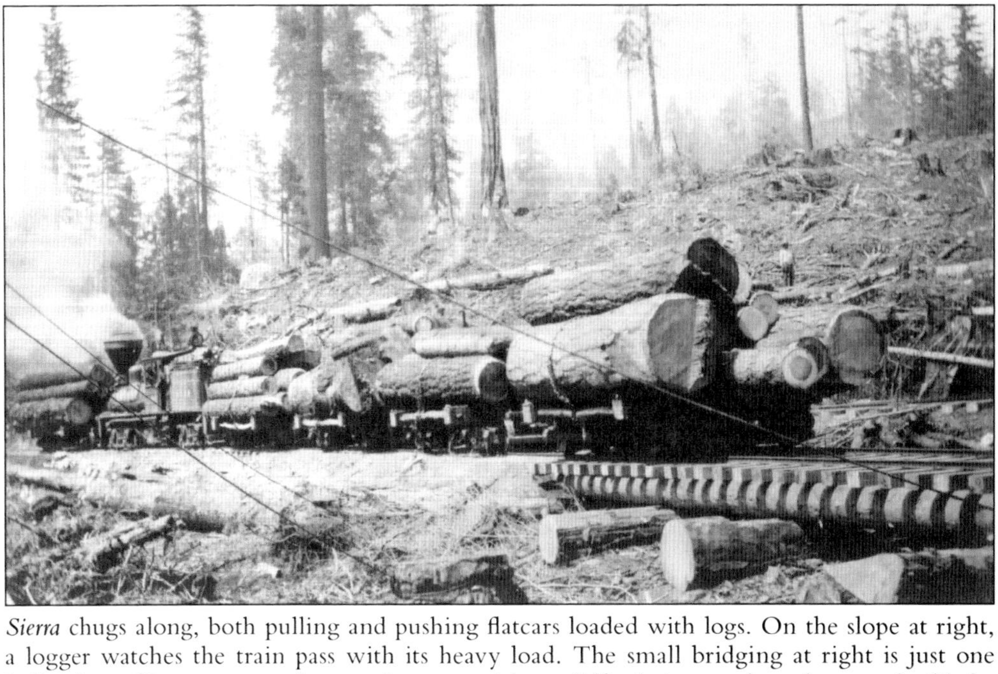

Sierra chugs along, both pulling and pushing flatcars loaded with logs. On the slope at right, a logger watches the train pass with its heavy load. The small bridging at right is just one indication of how uneven the terrain was and how difficult it must have been to build the Shaver Lake Railroad.

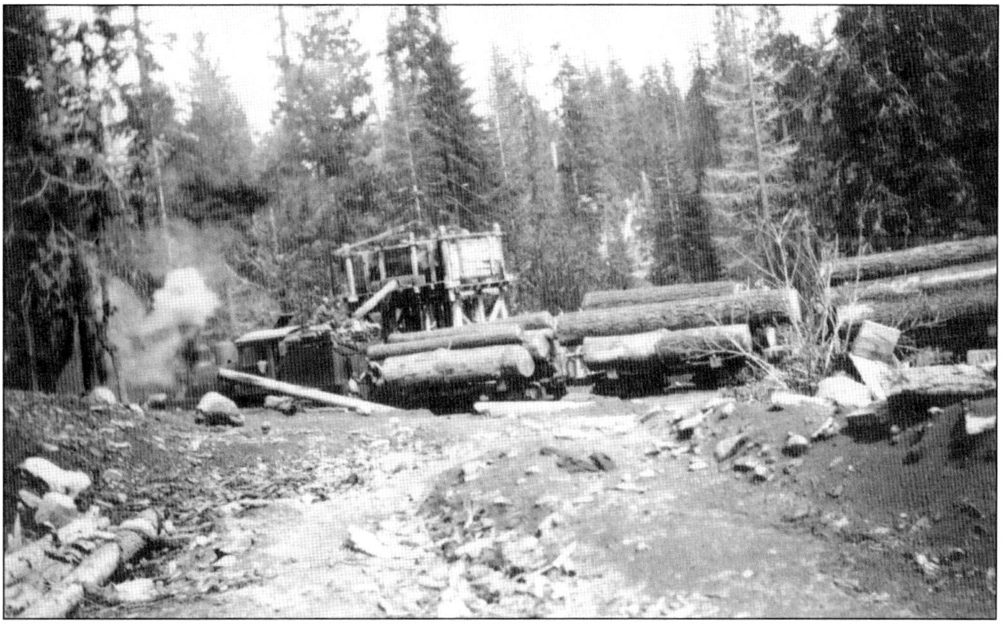

A Fresno Flume & Lumber Company train belches smoke and steam as it takes on water from the wooden tank next to the track. The photograph above may show the No. 2 Shay locomotive that the company purchased new in 1911. One of the rail crew is sitting on the tender and filling it with water before it continues to the millpond to dump the logs. The photograph below shows the number of railcars they pulled; the final car is not even visible. Photographer Manley White mailed this from Shaver in June 1913 to his sister Dora Beeson and reported, "We are all OK but to [sic] busy to write a letter."

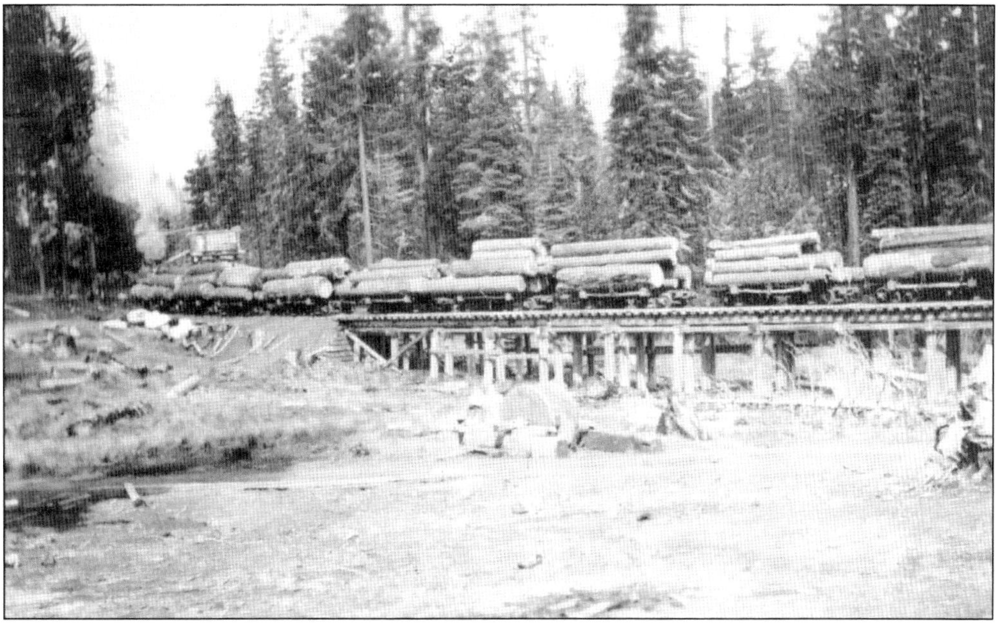

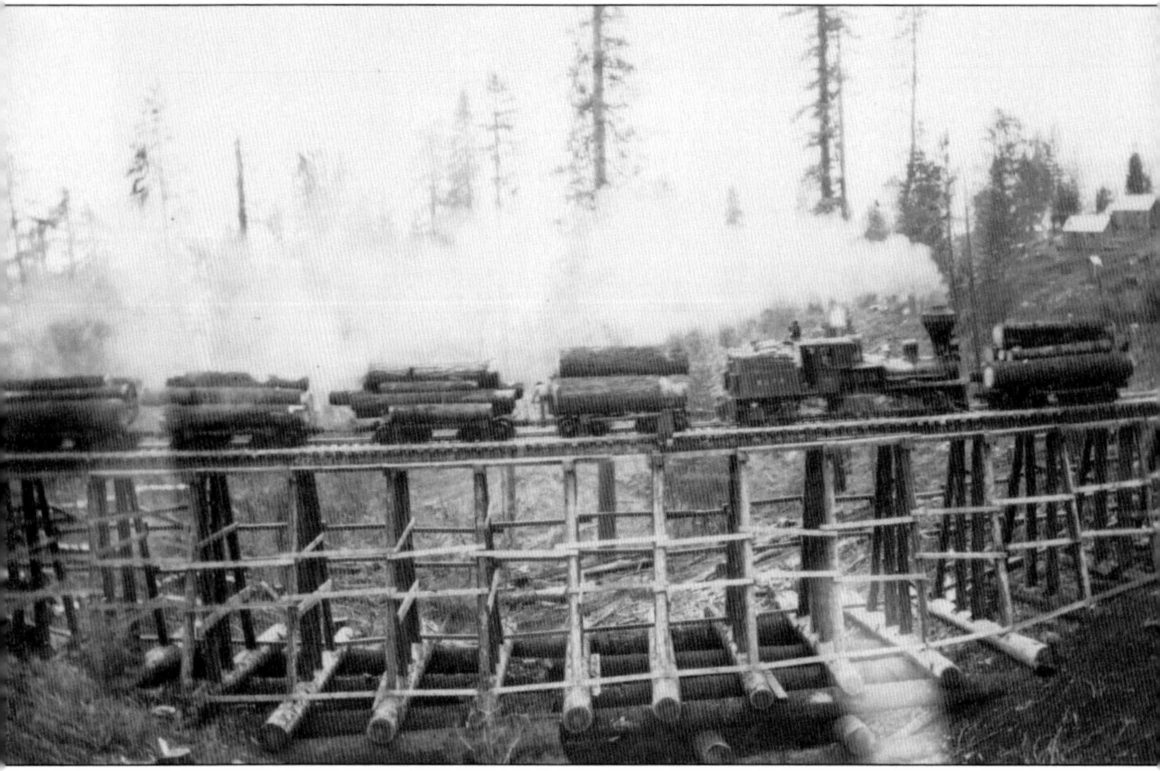

Sierra, the No. 1 locomotive of the Shaver Lake Railroad, is shown in this photograph pulling a load of logs to the millpond. Logging usually commenced near the millpond or sawmill. As years passed, the log-transport distance increased, and it became too difficult to use chutes. The use of railroads became a necessary but large investment. Just to get the locomotive into the mountains, it had to be disassembled in Clovis so that the pieces could be hauled by wagon up the steep Tollhouse road and then reassembled near Shaver Lake. A lot of lumber from the sawmill was used to build infrastructure, such as the railroad trestles and flumes that were necessary parts of the logging operation. In the upper-right corner of this photograph, two cabins and an outhouse are visible. The logging operation was a long distance from the sawmill, so housing needed to be provided for the loggers and railroad crews working in the woods.

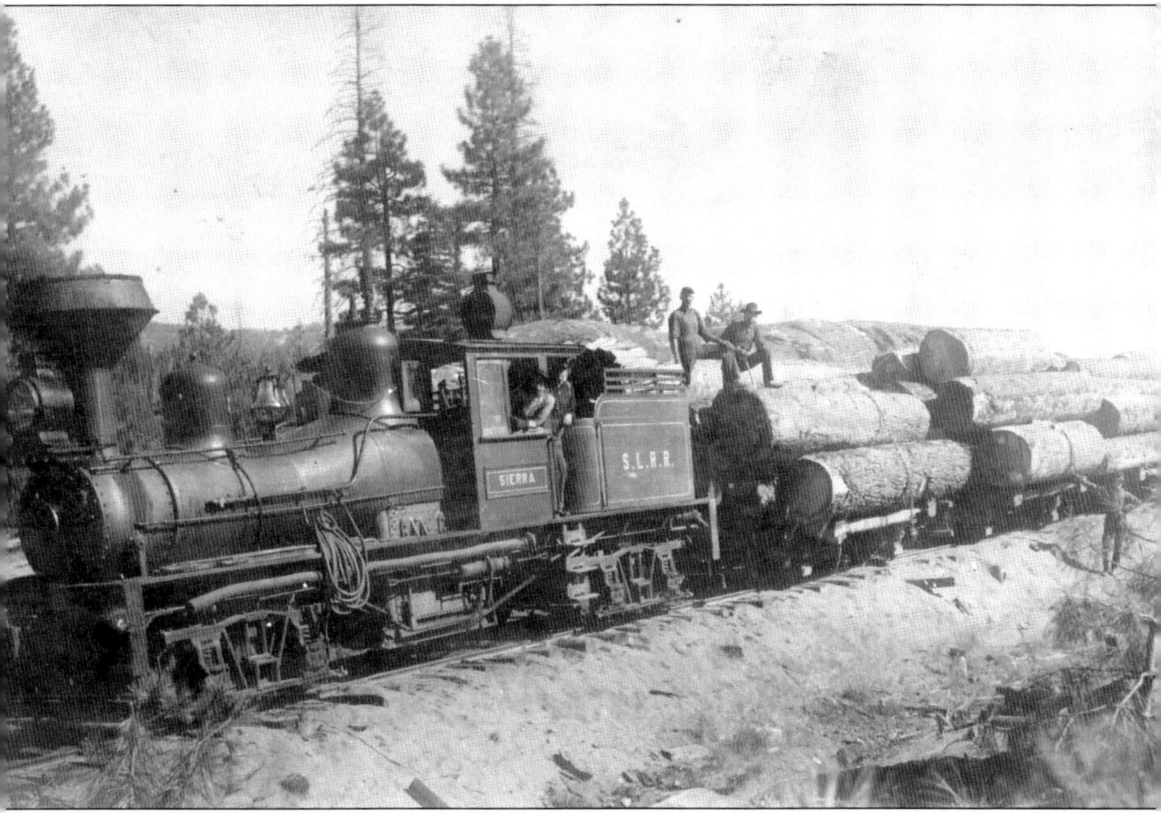

Sierra, which weighed 72,000 pounds, was built by the Lima Locomotive & Machine Works and delivered to Clovis in 1902. This was the sole locomotive on the Shaver Lake Railroad until the purchase of a second Lima Shay locomotive in 1911. Both were later sold to the Shaver Lake Lumber Company, which succeeded the Fresno Flume & Lumber Company. They were then leased to Southern California Edison from 1919 until 1926. In 1926, they were sold to the San Joaquin & Eastern, which used them for limited switching service rather than on their main line from Auberry to Cascada. Both Shay locomotives were eventually scrapped. (Fresno County Public Library.)

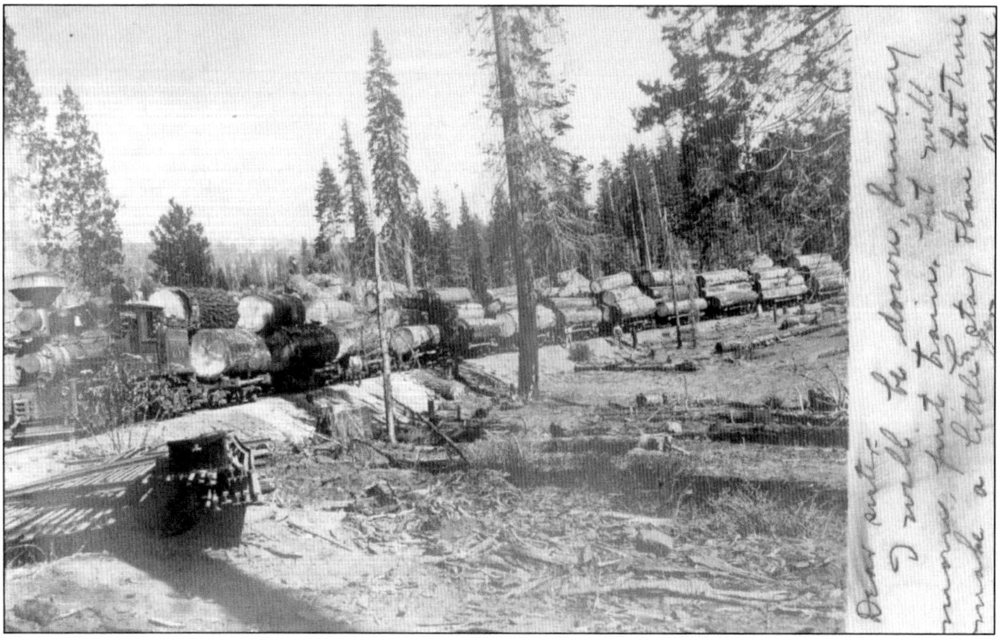

Sierra pauses for a photograph on the way to the millpond at Shaver. The large size of the logs on the railcars can be clearly seen. Moving these massive logs from the forest to the sawmill took a lot of hard work and involved a high level of danger. The locomotive engineers and the loggers always seemed ready to pose proudly at their work.

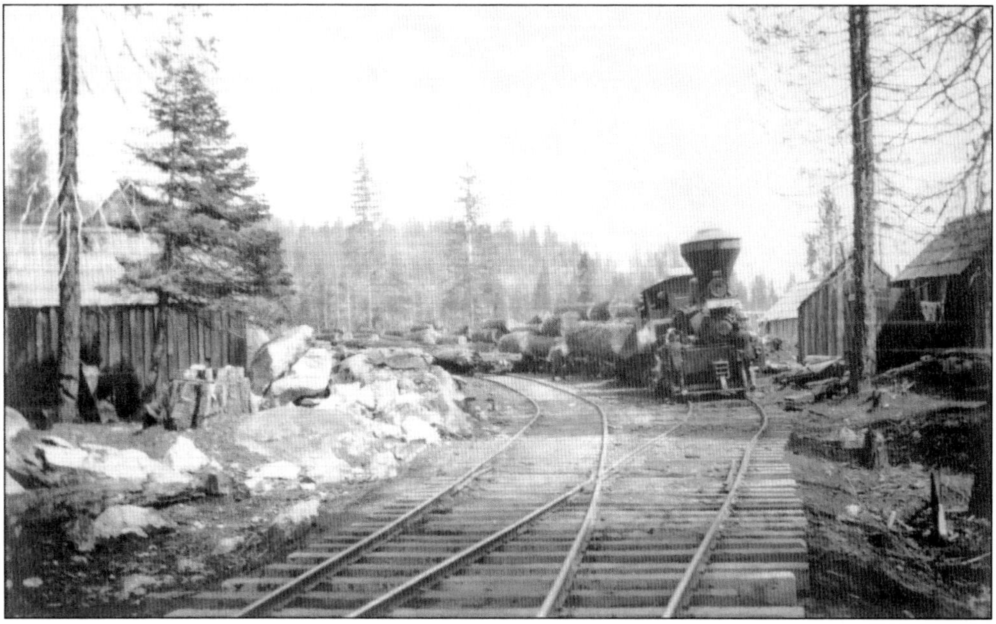

Sierra approaches a rail junction with loaded log cars in tow. The small buildings and the junction of two tracks suggest that the train was arriving at the log dump at Shaver Lake. The Fresno Flume & Lumber Company had two Shay locomotives, which enabled them to have two tracks, each going to a different logging area.

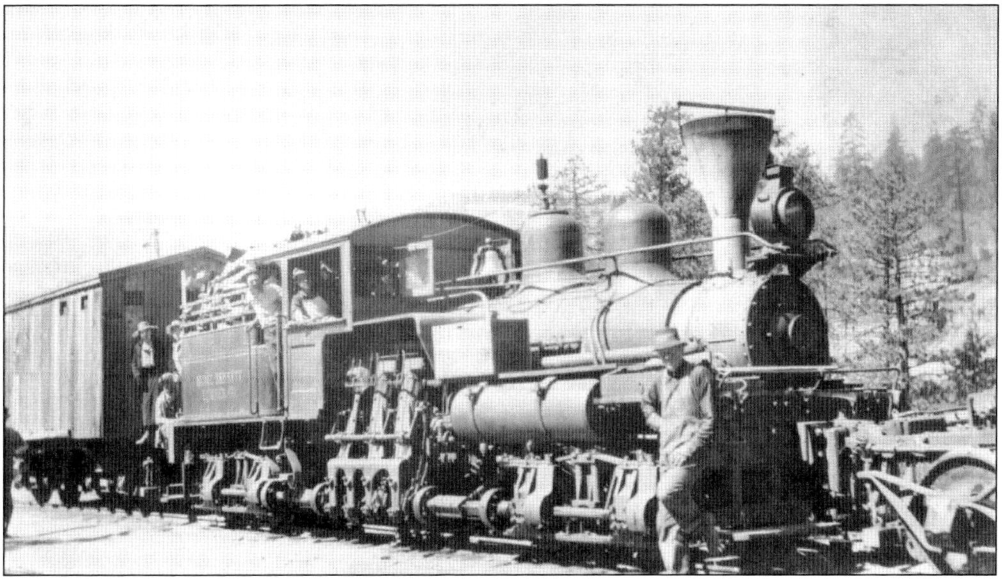

Here is an image of the Hume-Bennett Lumber Company locomotive No. 3 with what appear to be tourists behind the tender. Thomas Hume and Ira Bennett formed the lumber company and moved into the Converse Basin area in 1905. In 1908, they transferred operations to Long Meadow, dammed Tenmile and Long Meadow Creeks, and created Hume Lake. They built a new sawmill and extended the railroad and the flume.

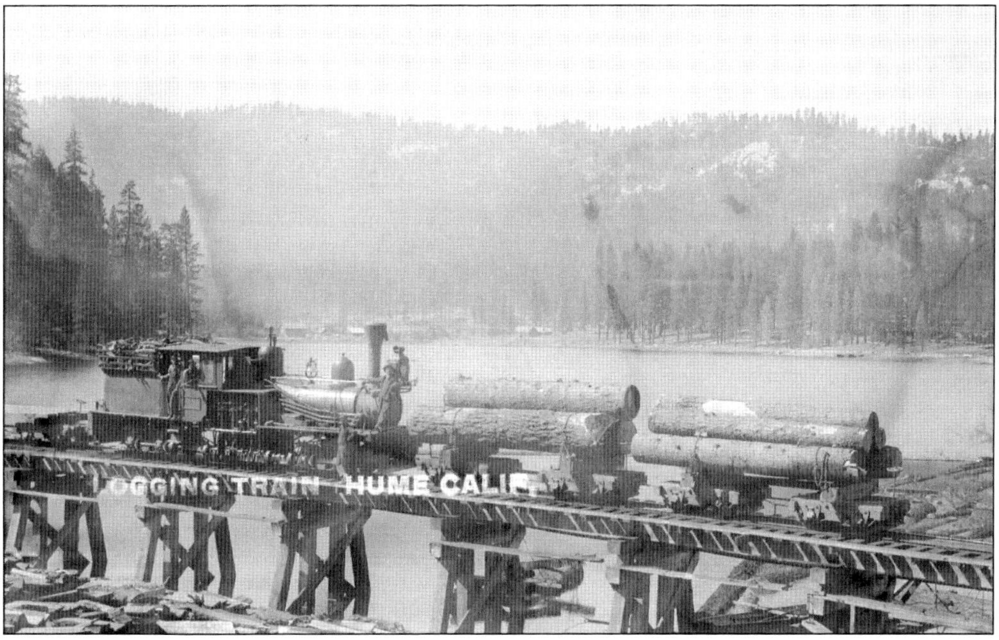

The crew poses on the Shay locomotive *Sequoia* as they prepare to dump the logs from the log-unloading trestle into Hume Lake. The Hume-Bennett Lumber Company began full operations at Hume Lake in 1910. Previously dumped logs, visible at right, float on the surface of the lake, ready for the nearby sawmill, located out of view to the right.

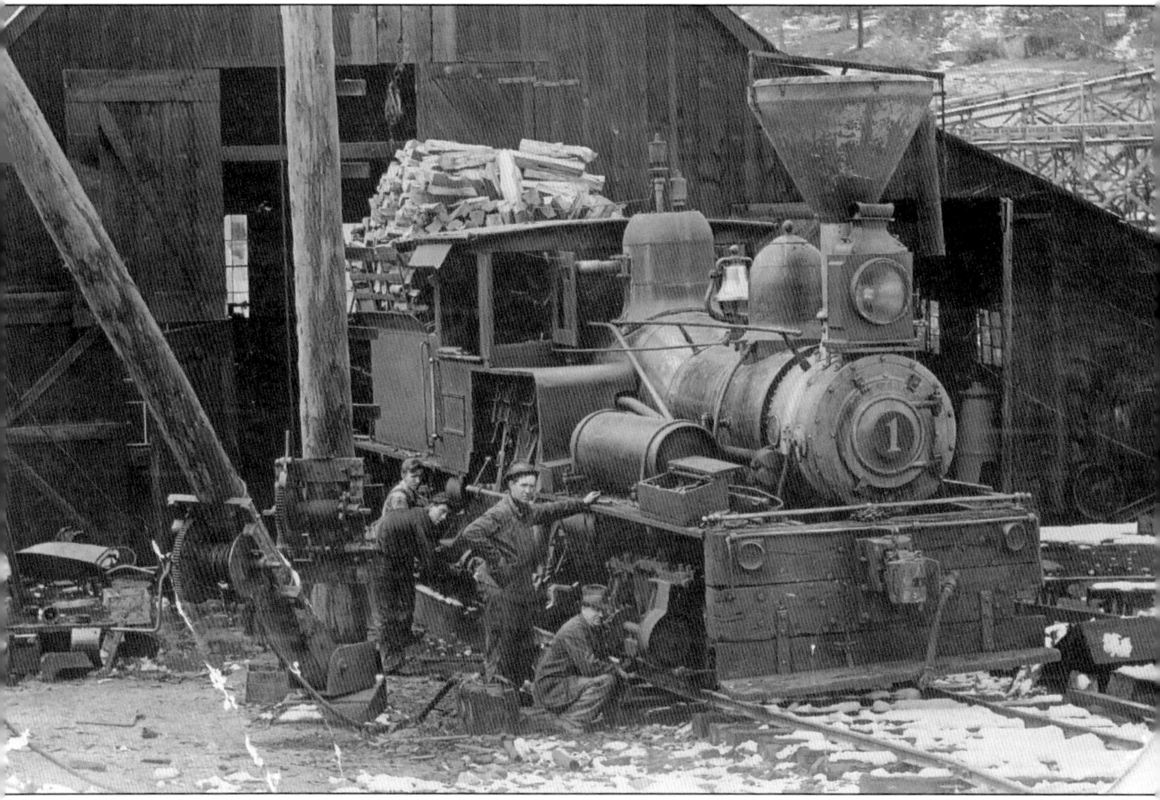

Shay locomotive No. 1, known as *Sequoia*, was built by the Lima Locomotive & Machine Works in 1891. The narrow-gauge locomotive was first used by the Kings River Lumber Company. The Hume-Bennett Lumber Company, after acquiring the Kings River Lumber Company, purchased two more standard-gauge Shay locomotives. A recession in 1913 and 1914 caused the bottom to fall out of the lumber business, and the Hume-Bennett Lumber Company, looking for a way to turn a profit, decided to resume logging the more profitable giant sequoias. To accommodate the large and heavy logs, they first needed to convert their railroad lines from narrow gauge (three feet wide) to standard gauge (four feet, eight and a half inches wide). This photograph, taken at the Hume machine shop, shows men changing the old workhorse *Sequoia* from narrow to standard gauge in 1914. (Fresno County Public Library.)

Two

SAWMILLS

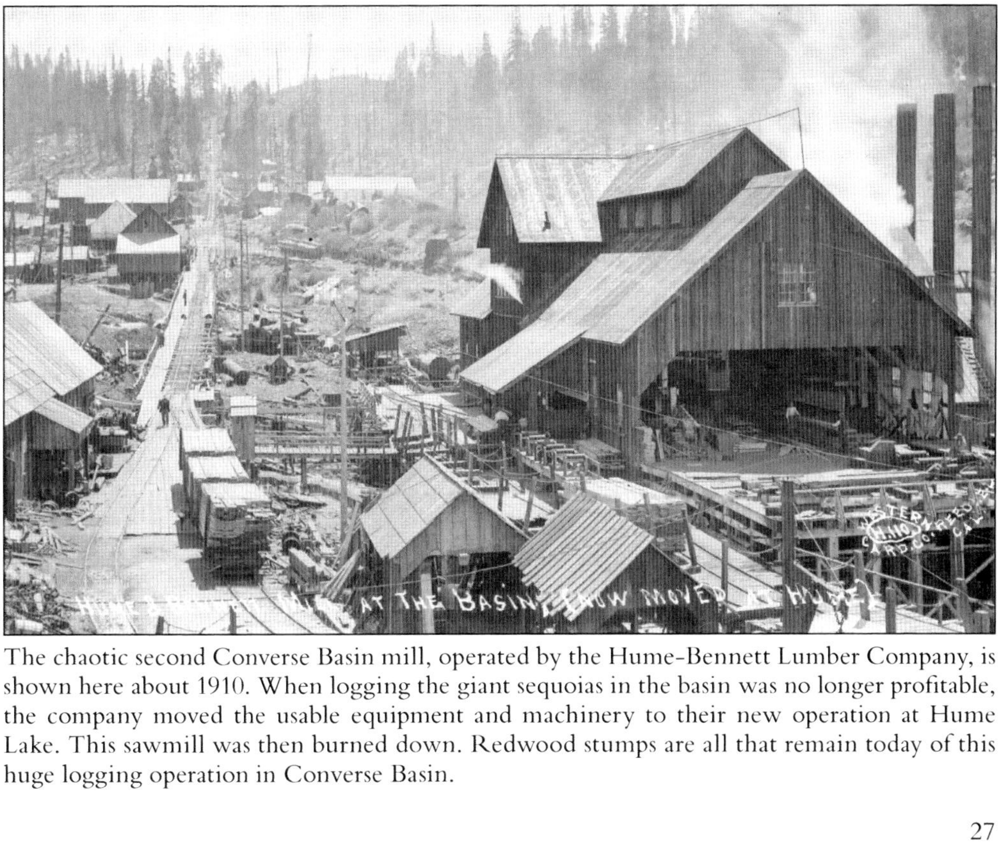

The chaotic second Converse Basin mill, operated by the Hume-Bennett Lumber Company, is shown here about 1910. When logging the giant sequoias in the basin was no longer profitable, the company moved the usable equipment and machinery to their new operation at Hume Lake. This sawmill was then burned down. Redwood stumps are all that remain today of this huge logging operation in Converse Basin.

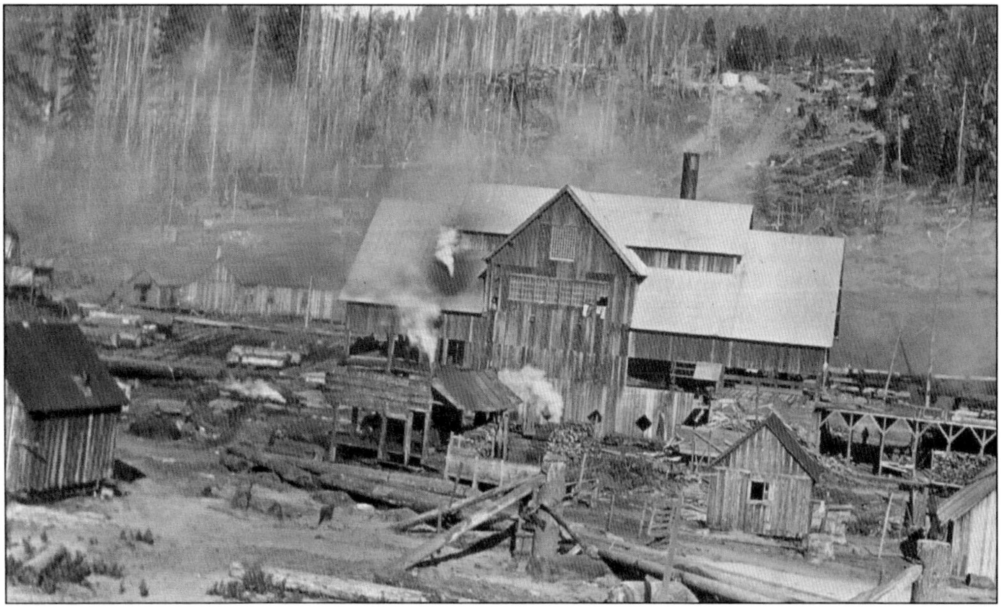

The equipment from Millwood was moved into Converse Basin in 1897. Converse Basin was named for Charles P. Converse, who unsuccessfully planned to log the giant sequoias there in the 1870s. Logging was not successful, and The Sanger Lumber Company went bankrupt. However, operations continued as the creditors tried to find a buyer. The newly created Hume-Bennett Lumber Company finally bought the logging operation in 1905.

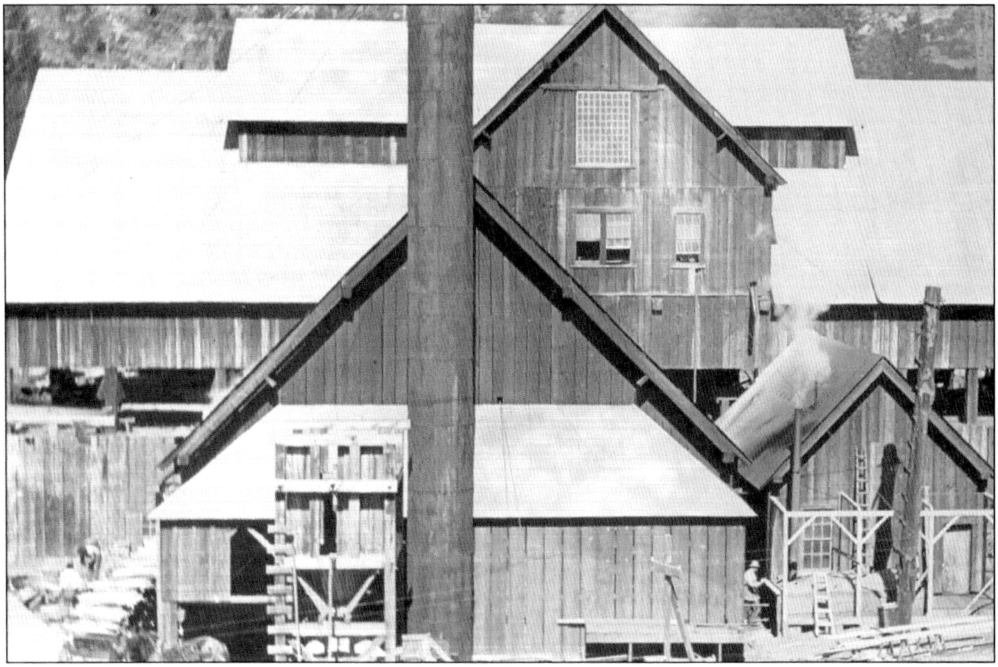

This replacement sawmill was built in Converse Basin in November 1905 following a fire that destroyed the original; it began operating in July 1906. The boiler house for this sawmill is in the nearest building with a lone smokestack. The Hume-Bennett Lumber Company continued logging in Converse Basin for two seasons as it prepared to move farther into the mountains.

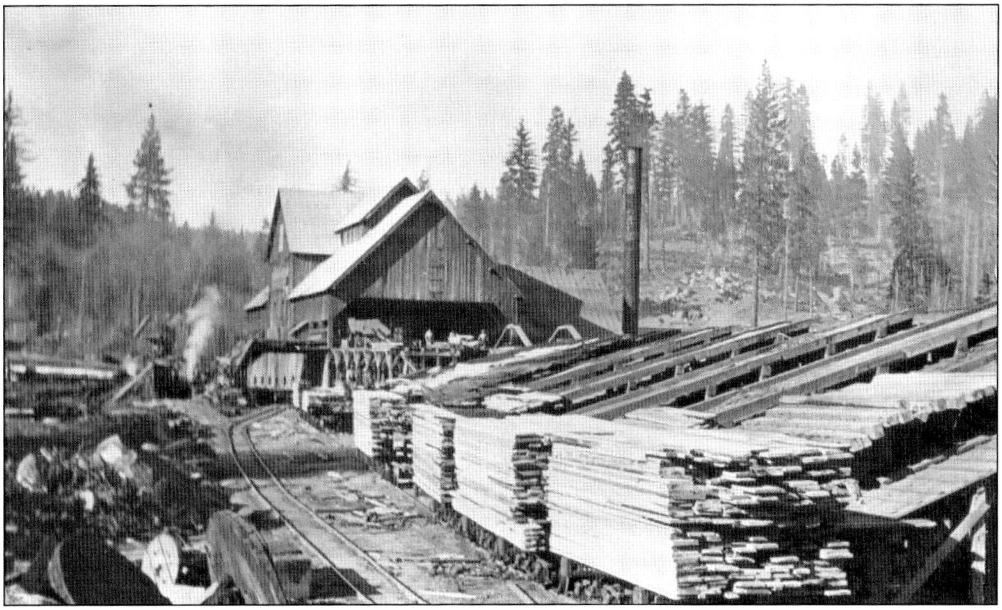

The second sawmill in Converse Basin was a large investment, but it was not used for long. Tramcars hauled the lumber by incline over Hoist Ridge and down to the railroad, which took it to the start of the flume at Millwood. By 1909, this operation had been moved four miles east to the newly created Hume Lake. This mill was then burned to the ground.

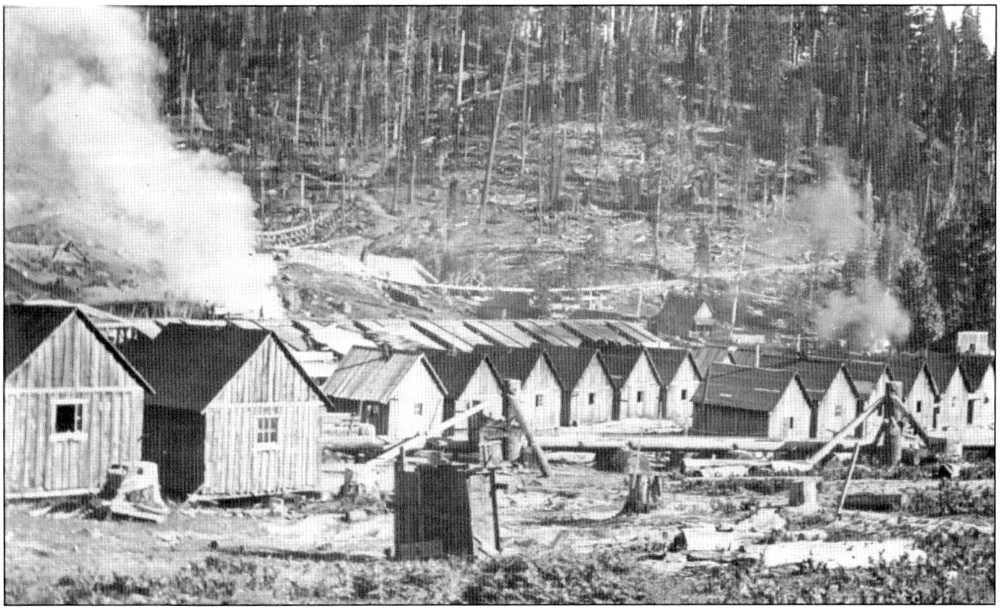

This is one of five lumber camps in the large Converse Basin. The basin was about four miles long, so it made operational sense to disperse the loggers. Felling a giant sequoia that could be about 25 feet thick and weigh several tons took many days. After it fell, the logs still had to be moved to the mill.

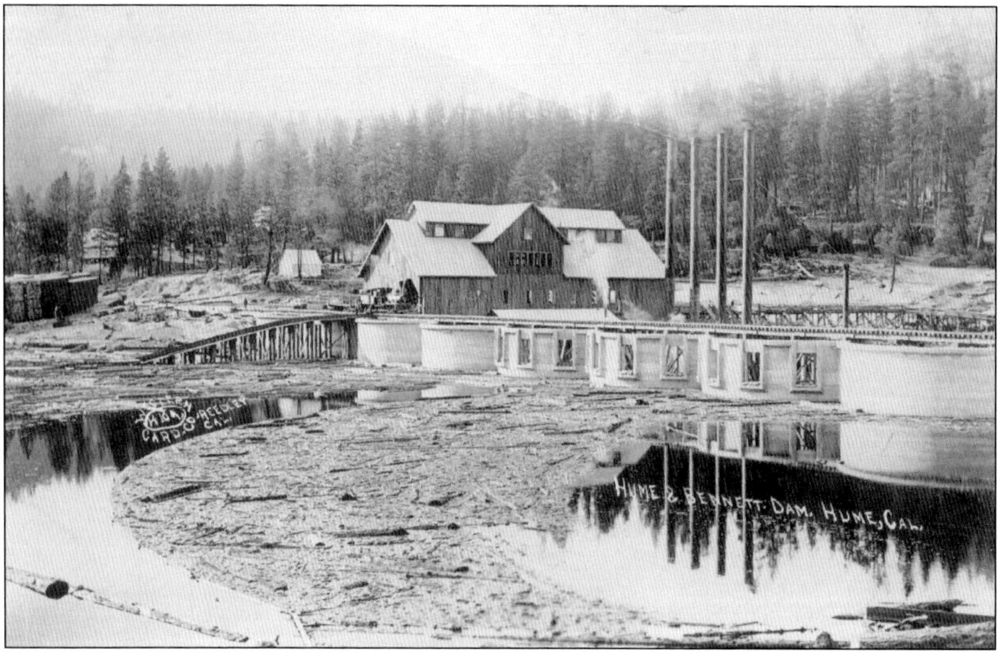

The Hume-Bennett Lumber Company began operations at Hume Lake in the summer of 1909 and reached full production during the summer of 1910. The dam, designed by John Eastwood, was the first multiple-arch, reinforced concrete dam built in the United States. It was completed in November 1908, and the lake was filled in June 1909.

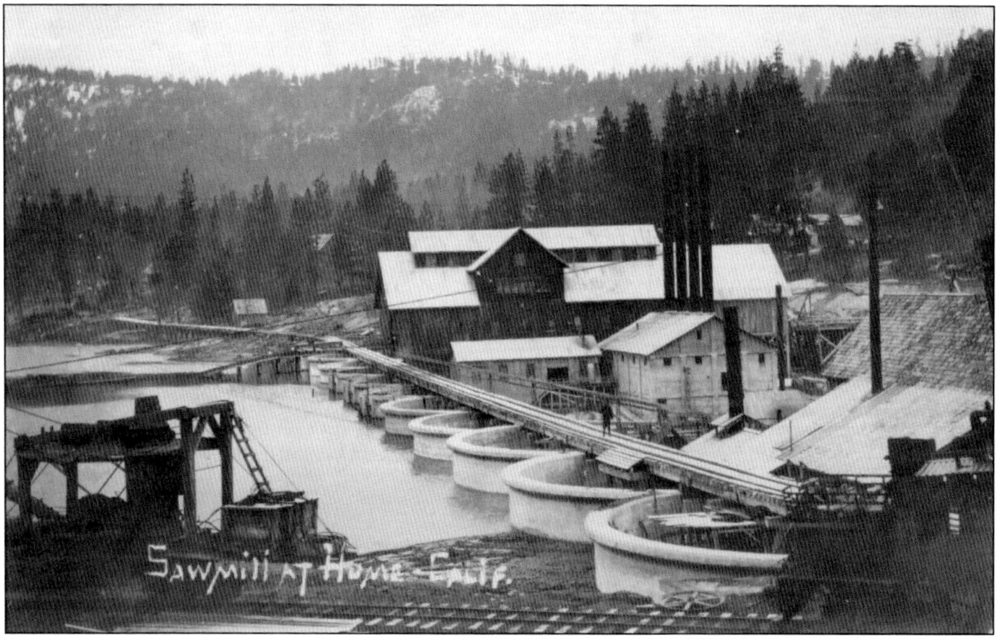

The Hume Lake operation was large and complex. The log pickup is the incline visible to the left of the sawmill. The logging railroad tracks, in the foreground, went into the woods, and the log dump was a short distance to the left of where this photograph was taken. The roof of the machine shop and foundry is visible to the right.

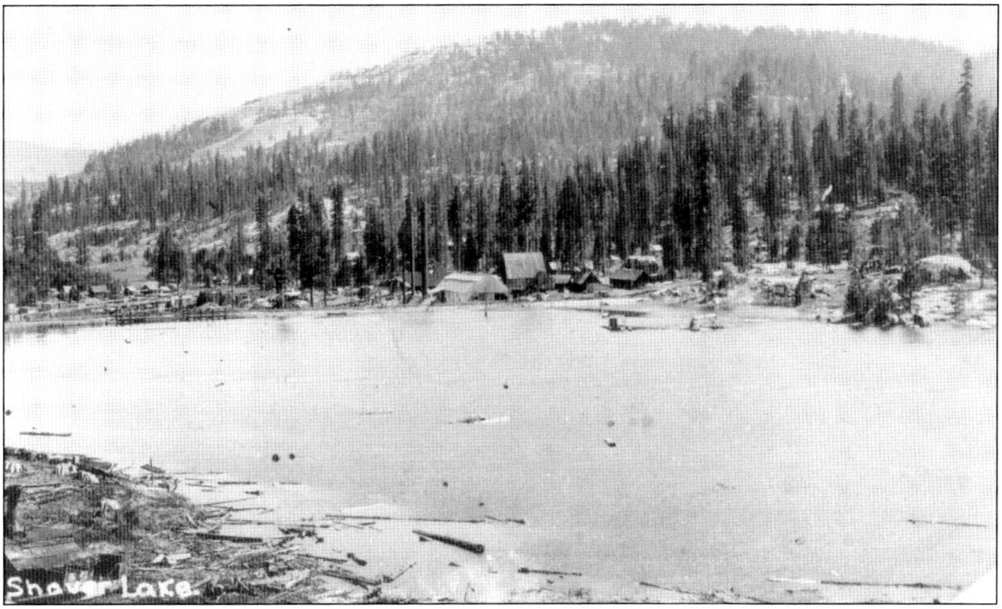

The Fresno Flume & Irrigation Company, incorporated in 1891, built a rock-fill dam on Stevenson Creek in 1893. The result was Shaver Lake, a millpond for the sawmill (the largest building visible just beyond the dam). They also built a 42-mile-long flume to carry lumber to Clovis using water from the lake. This was one of the largest lumbering operations in Fresno County.

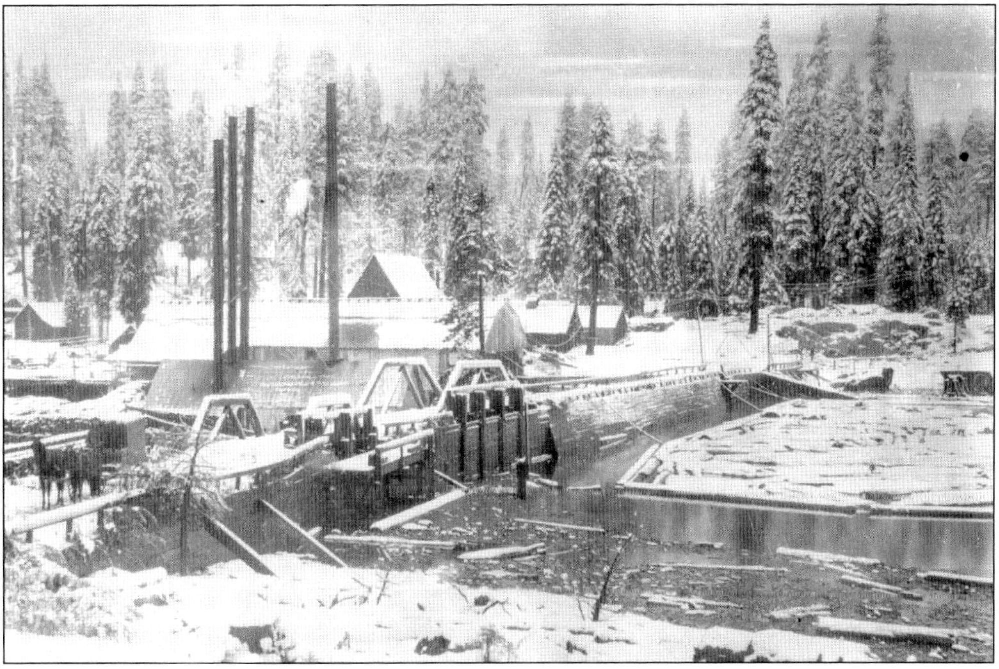

Snowfall has covered the mountains in this chilling winter view of the Shaver sawmill. The top of the dam was wide enough for wagons to cross. The lake level appears lower than usual, and the water is frozen. Clearly, with the available equipment and methods, it was impossible to log in the Sierra Nevada during winter.

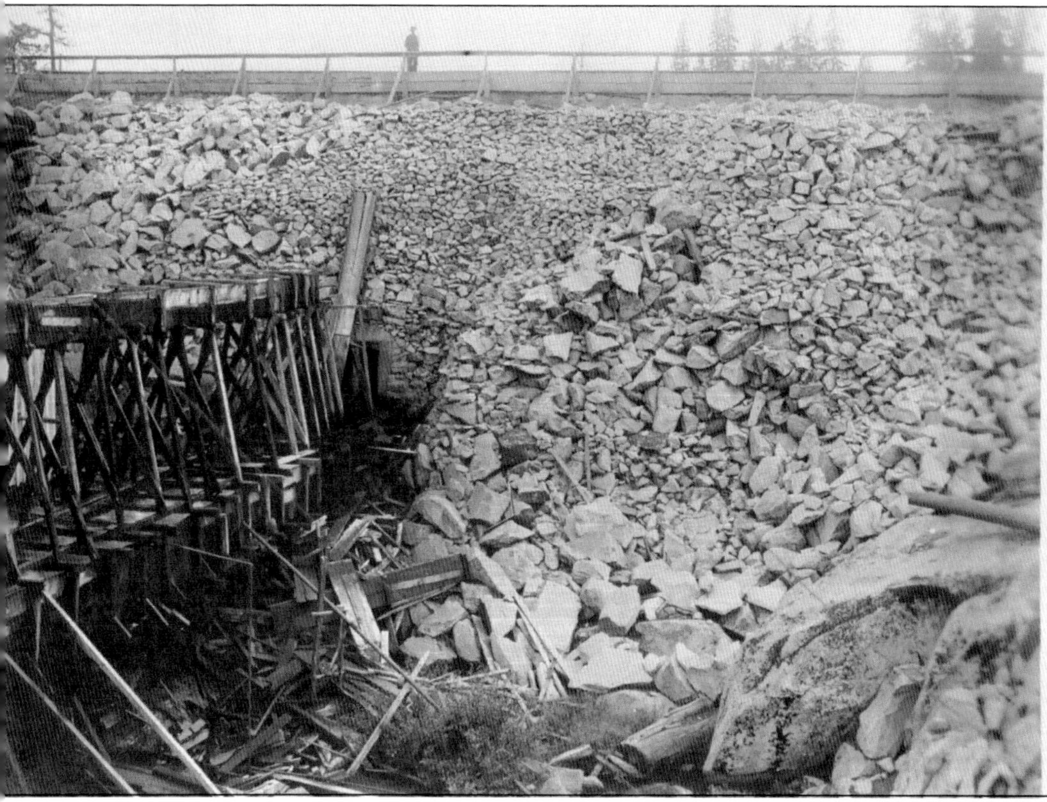

Seen here, the original Shaver dam was a small rock-fill dam that was 40 feet high and about 300 feet long. It was built across Stevenson Creek and created Shaver Lake, which had a capacity of 5,000 acre-feet. The lake was a millpond used to float logs to the sawmill. Southern California Edison built a much larger hydroelectric dam, just downstream, between 1926 and 1927 as part of their Big Creek Hydroelectric Project. This postcard was sent by the photographer, Manley White, to his cousin in San Francisco.

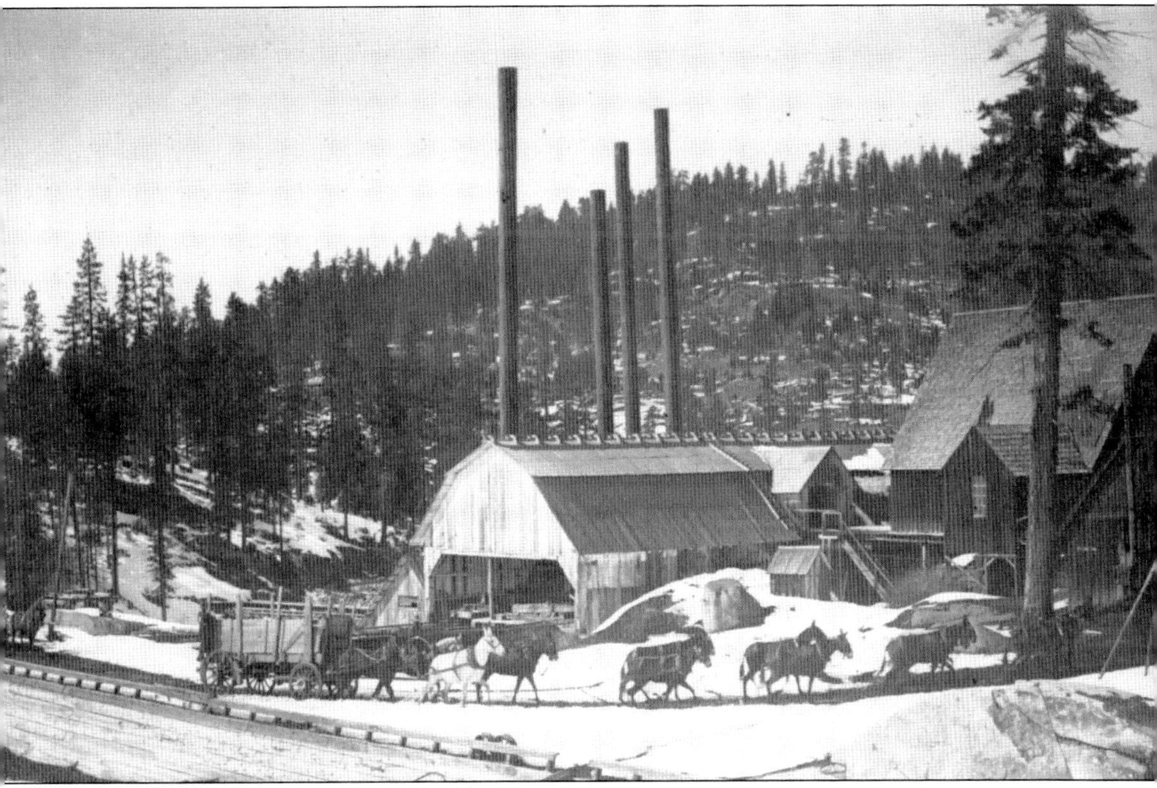

A large team of mules pulls a freight wagon over the rock-fill dam that created Shaver Lake. The sawmill, built in 1893, looms in the background. Its gaping front was where the logs first entered and began the process of being cut into boards. High-quality lumber was hauled out of the mountains in freight wagons to avoid the risk of damage, but most of the lumber was sent by flume to reduce transportation costs and therefore increase profits. The mill ceased operation in 1914, and the Shaver properties were sold to Southern California Edison in 1919. The current Shaver dam was built downstream from the abandoned sawmill, thus flooding the entire site seen in this photograph.

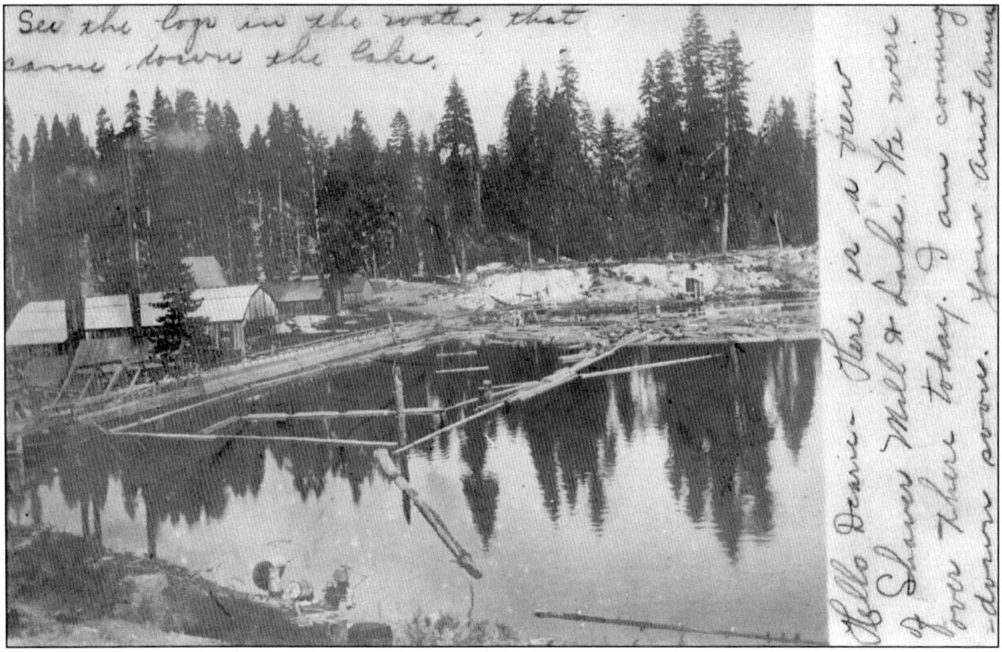

Smoke comes out of the smokestacks of the Shaver sawmill in this view looking north. The logs are gathered on the millpond near the log pickup. This is where they would be floated onto a loading car and moved on tracks to the mill, just below the dam.

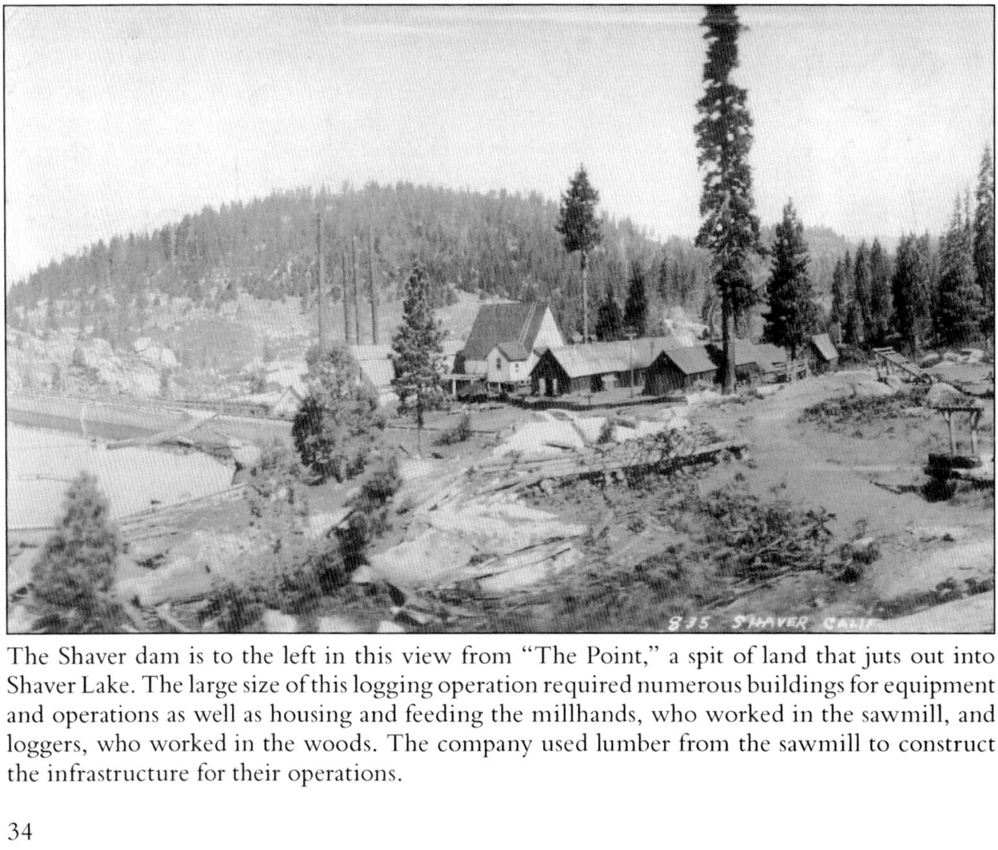

The Shaver dam is to the left in this view from "The Point," a spit of land that juts out into Shaver Lake. The large size of this logging operation required numerous buildings for equipment and operations as well as housing and feeding the millhands, who worked in the sawmill, and loggers, who worked in the woods. The company used lumber from the sawmill to construct the infrastructure for their operations.

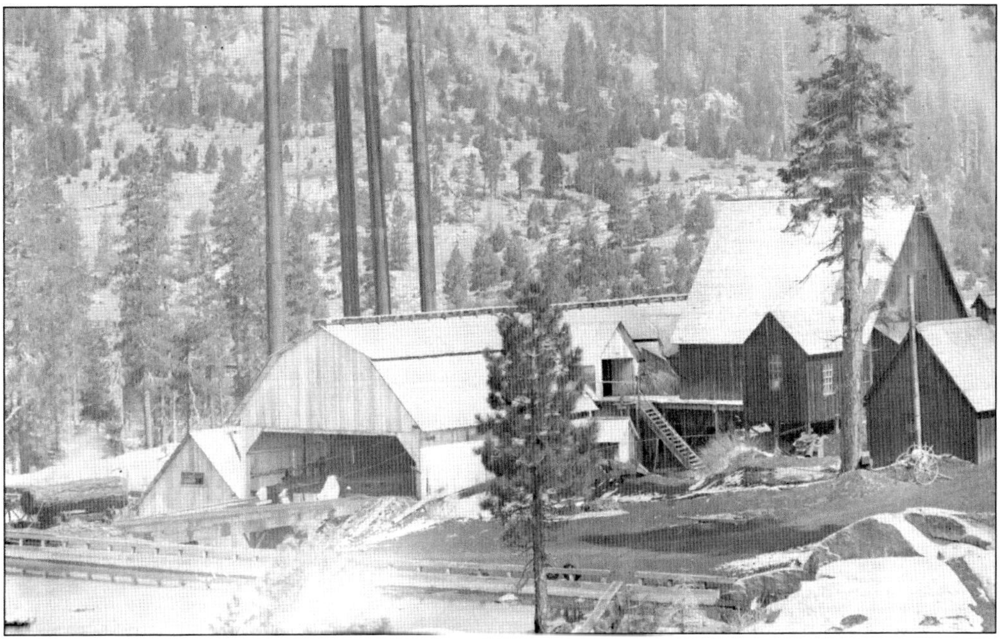

The Shaver sawmill, built in 1893, was just below the dam visible at lower left. The sawmill, with a capacity of 90,000 board feet per day, originally used a double circular saw, but it was replaced in 1901 with a band saw. The smokestacks rise up from the five boilers that provided steam for both the large engine that powered the sawmill and for the kiln.

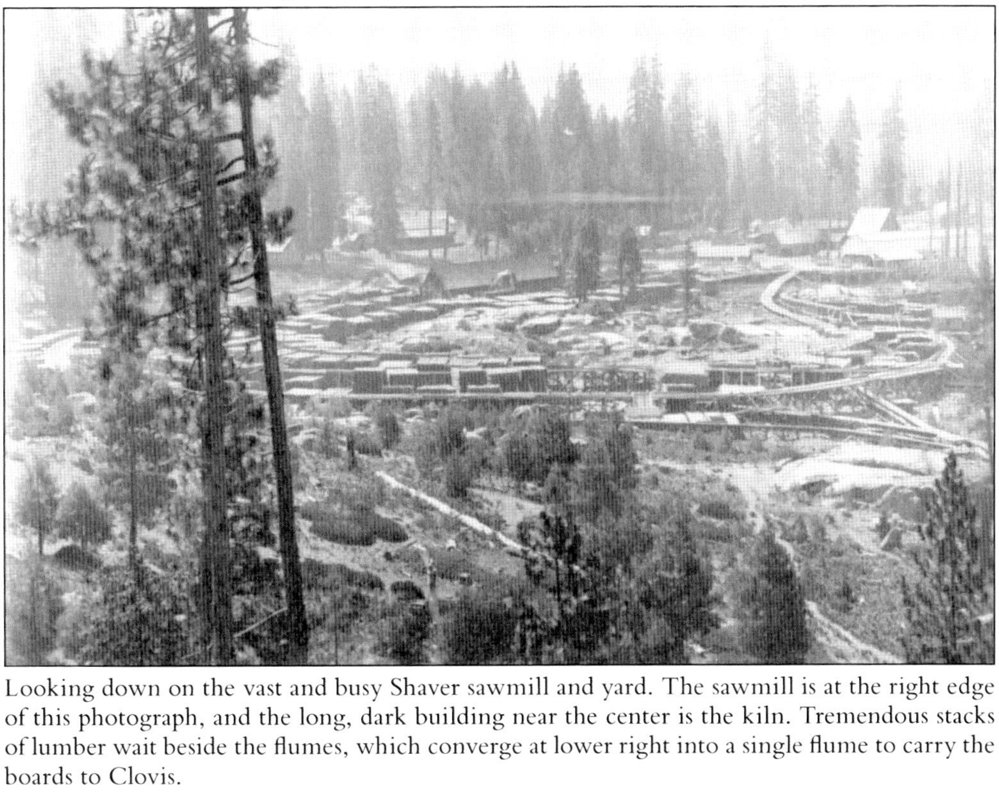

Looking down on the vast and busy Shaver sawmill and yard. The sawmill is at the right edge of this photograph, and the long, dark building near the center is the kiln. Tremendous stacks of lumber wait beside the flumes, which converge at lower right into a single flume to carry the boards to Clovis.

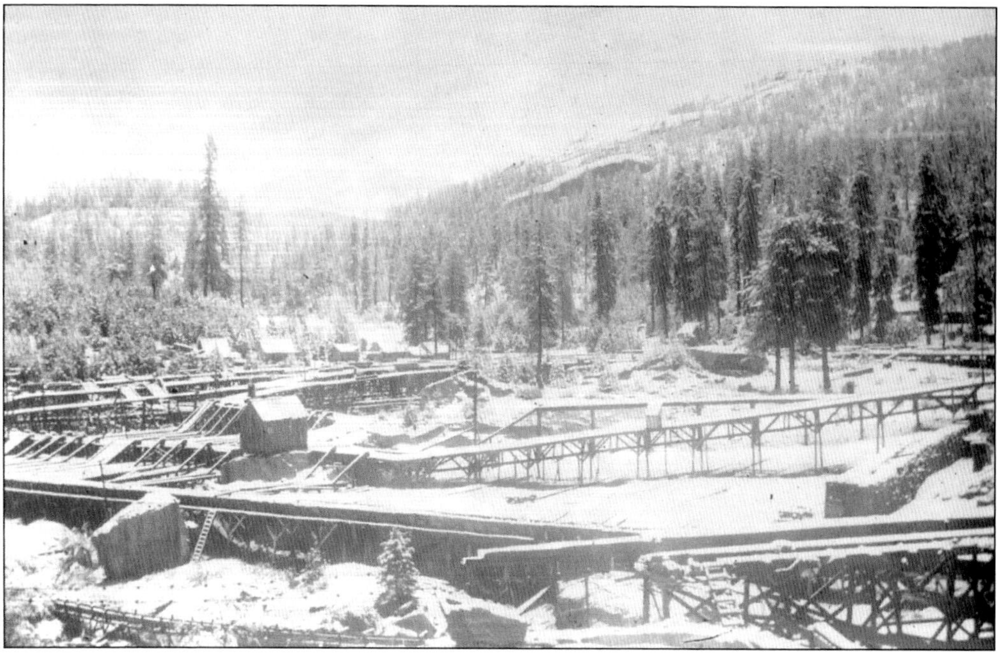

Snow has blanketed the lumberyard at Shaver. Because the Sierra sawmills, such as Shaver, did not operate in winter, there is no lumber drying in the yard and awaiting the ride on the flume. This quiet winter scene is in stark contrast to the cacophony of the sawmill and yard operations in summer.

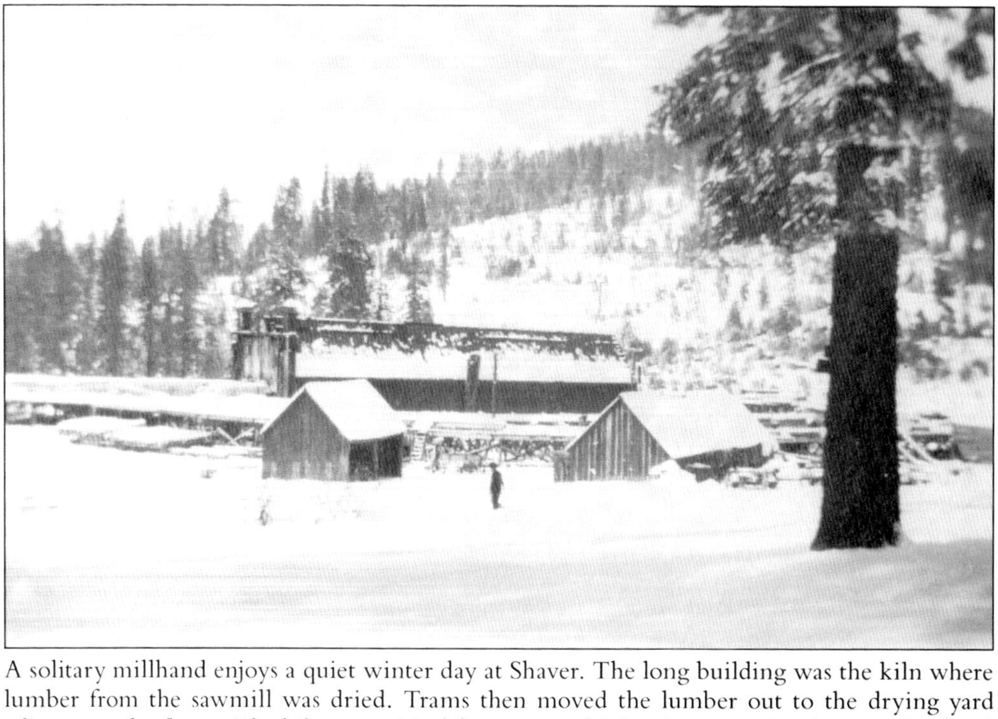

A solitary millhand enjoys a quiet winter day at Shaver. The long building was the kiln where lumber from the sawmill was dried. Trams then moved the lumber out to the drying yard adjacent to the flume. The kiln was critical for a successful fluming operation because the dried boards were lighter and could float down the flume.

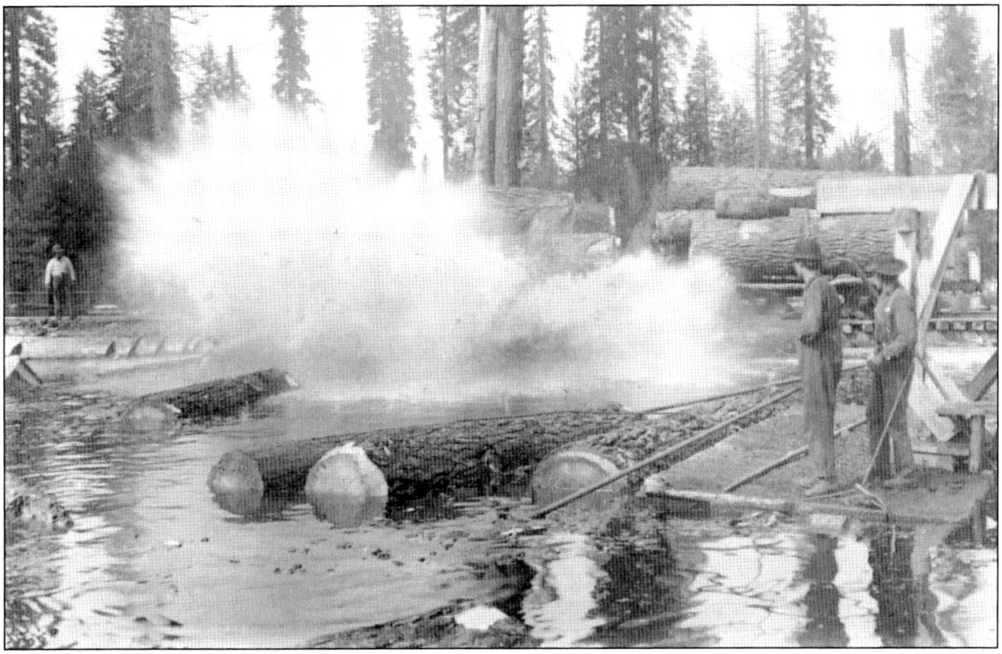

Men at Shaver Lake, which was built as a millpond, watch logs being dumped from the railroad flatcars in the background. The log dumps were often at the far end of the millpond, opposite the sawmill. The men are standing on a "mallard," a device used to raise sunken logs, called "sinkers," from the lake.

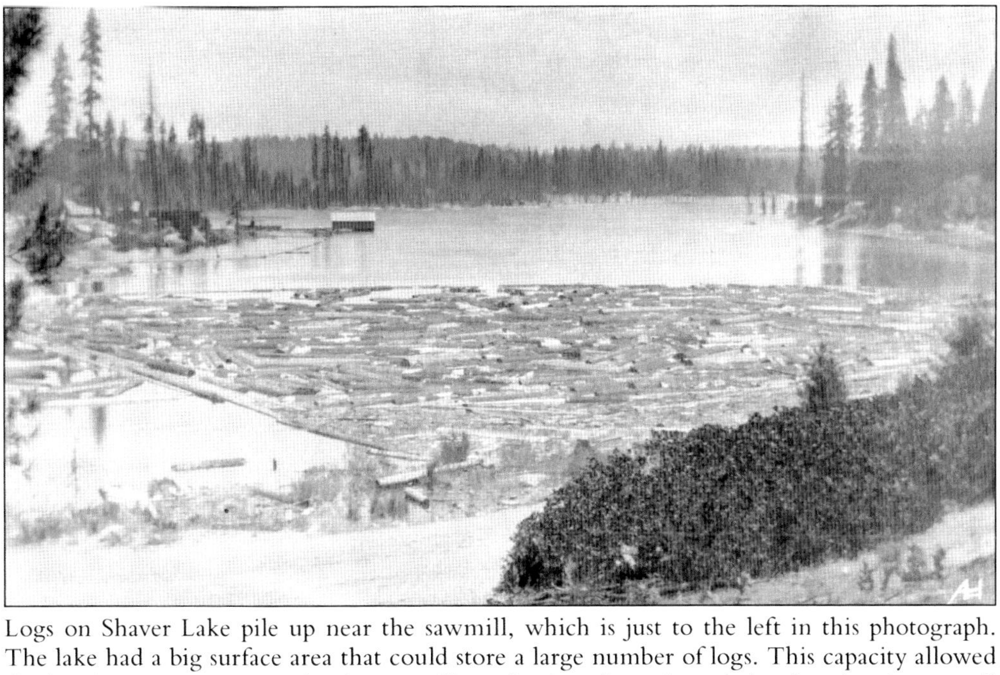

Logs on Shaver Lake pile up near the sawmill, which is just to the left in this photograph. The lake had a big surface area that could store a large number of logs. This capacity allowed the logging company to maintain sawmill production through periods when logging or rail deliveries might be interrupted by weather or equipment failure.

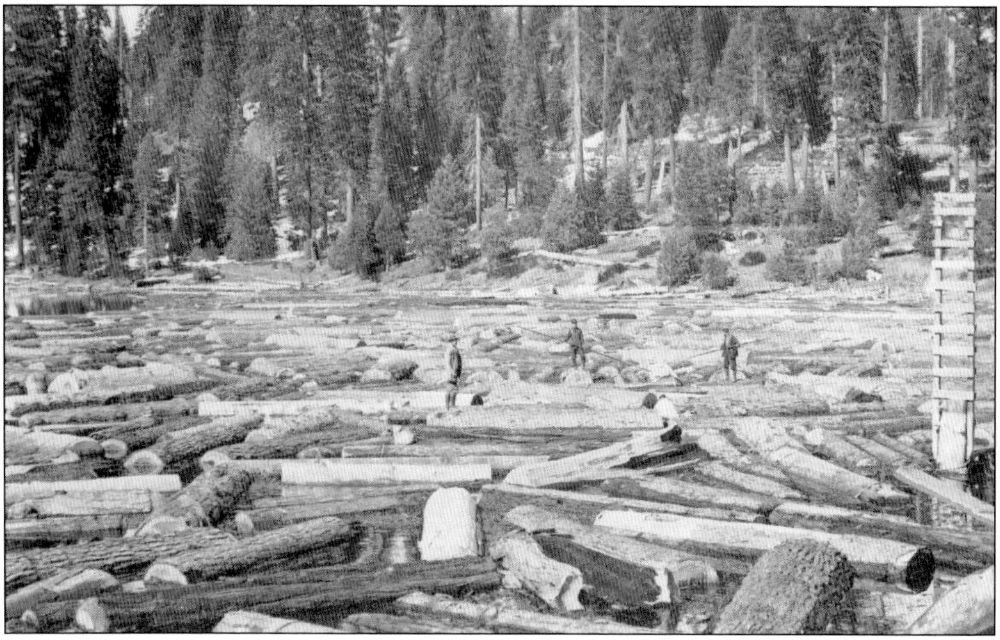

Near the sawmill, Shaver Lake is completely covered with logs in this photograph by Manley White. Two of the three men out on the logs have peaveys, tools used to roll and handle logs in water. The peavey was named for Joseph Peavey of Stillwater, Maine, who invented it in 1858. This was yet another dangerous job in a logging operation.

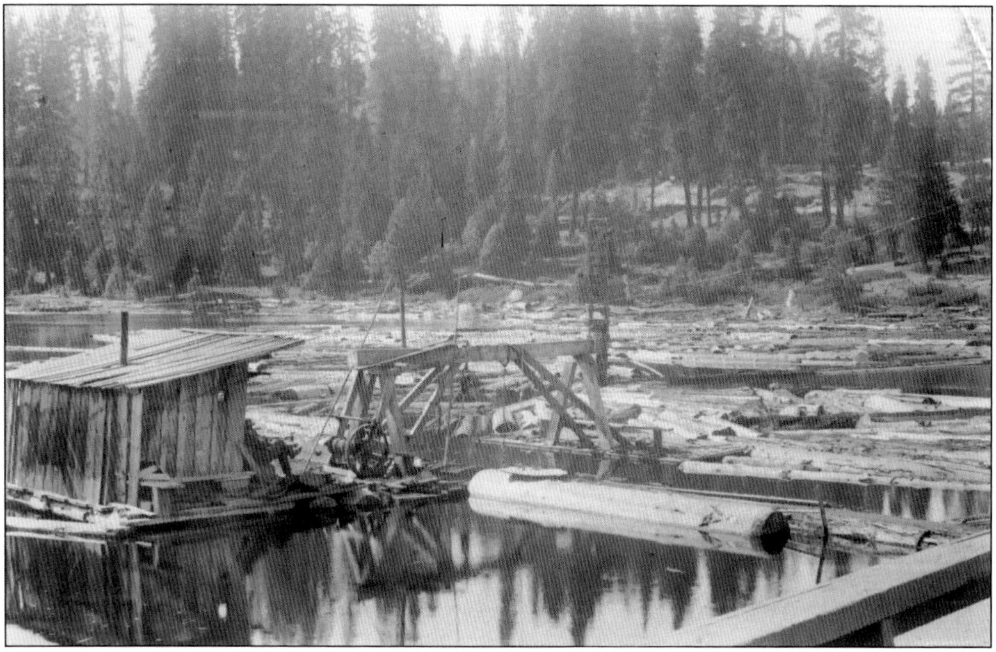

These logs floating in Shaver Lake are waiting to be cut into boards in the nearby sawmill. A relaxed man leans against the floating hut next to a mallard. The cost of cutting sugar pines and white pines in the forest, getting them to the railroad, and hauling them to the lake was too great to waste any logs that sank, so sunken logs were retrieved with the mallard.

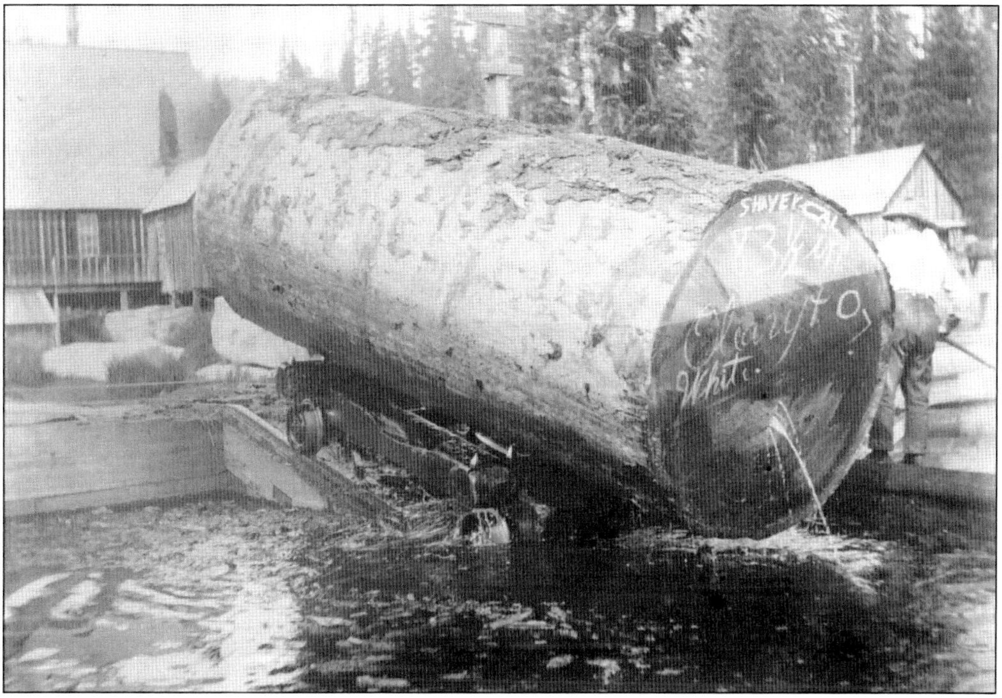

Logs floating in the lake were positioned over a small, submerged tramcar that was then pulled by a cable to the sawmill. Logs were often marked on the end with their estimated board footage. This log's markings read, "Shaver, Cal" and include its diameter.

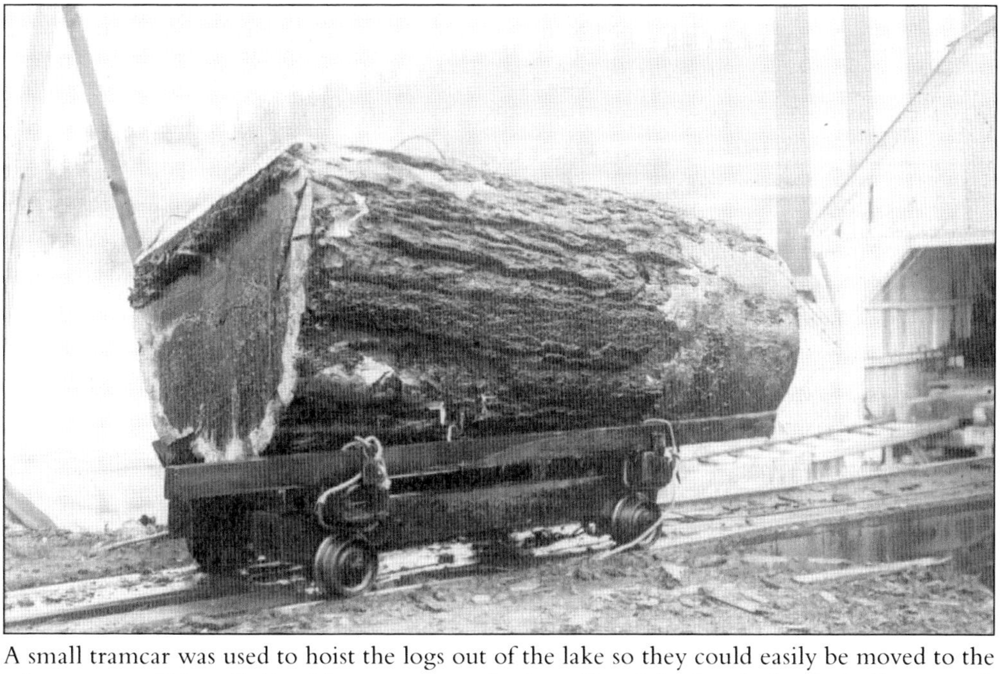

A small tramcar was used to hoist the logs out of the lake so they could easily be moved to the adjacent sawmill by rail. For this system to work, the mill and the dam had to be built near each other. Tramcars were also used to move boards from the Shaver sawmill through the kiln and on to the flumes.

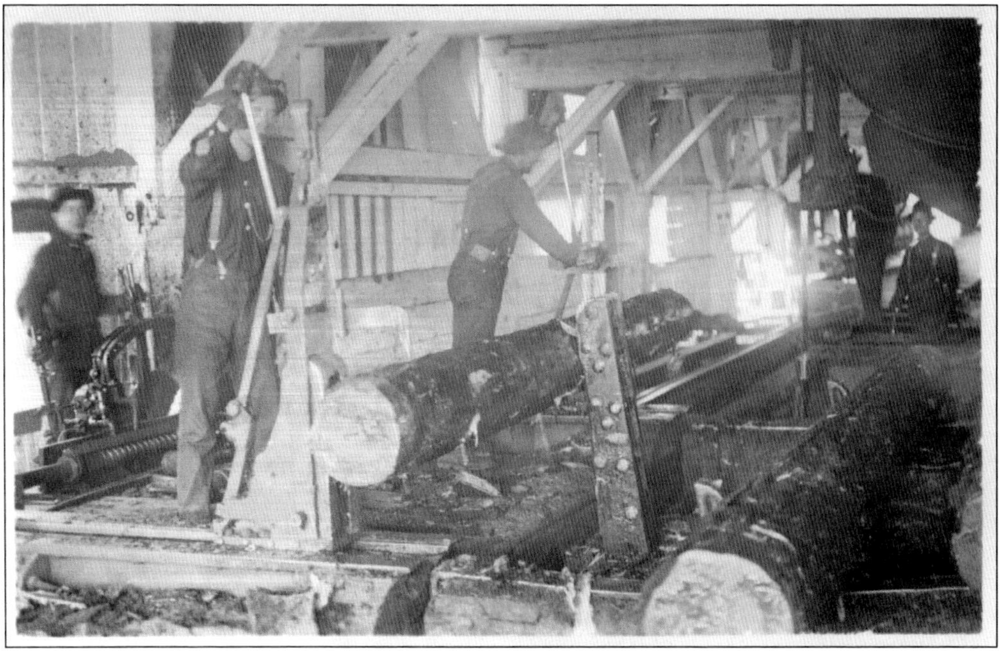

These millhands are hard at work in the Shaver sawmill. The log is on the carriage ready to be moved through the saw. The man against wall was the "setter" who controlled the thickness of the boards. The two "doggers" at right set the "dogs" into the wood to hold the log in place while it was sawed.

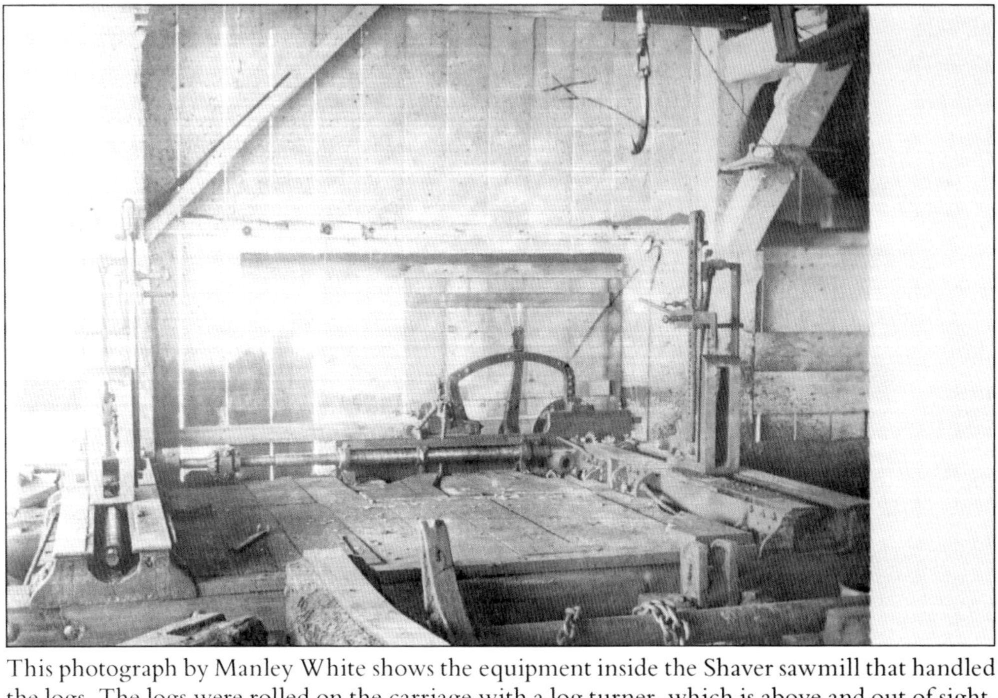

This photograph by Manley White shows the equipment inside the Shaver sawmill that handled the logs. The logs were rolled on the carriage with a log turner, which is above and out of sight. The lever against the wall, marked "3" by White, controlled the thickness of the cut. The hook hanging above, marked "4," was used to lift the heavy logs.

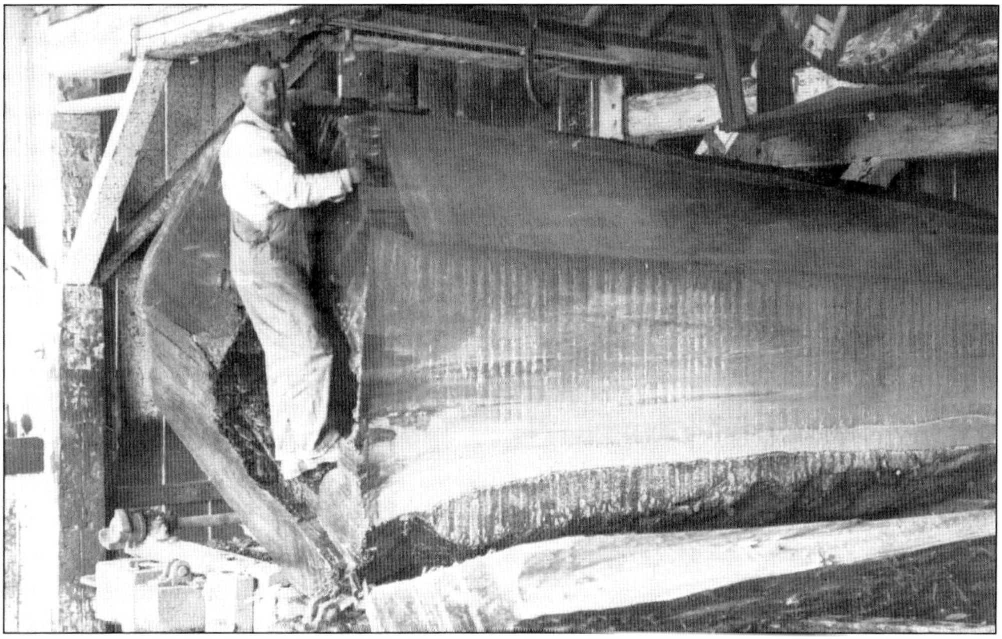

A millhand poses next to a sugar pine log that is being run through the sawmill at Shaver. The head saw cut logs into cants (unfinished logs) and flitches (unfinished planks). The piece of this log that has already been cut off can be seen in the foreground. Handling such massive logs must have been challenging for the millhands.

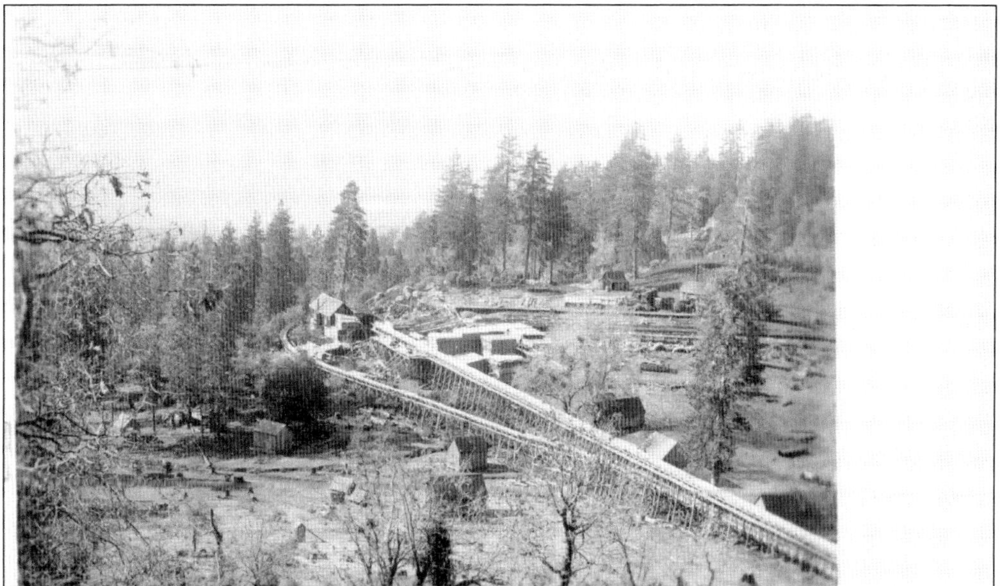

Manley White wrote on the back of this postcard, "Saddle on flume where the flume starts down the steep grade about 12 miles [from the Shaver sawmill.]" This location is near what is now Pine Ridge Elementary School, and the yard was for lumber from other sawmills on Pine Ridge that contracted to use the flume after completion of the regular daily run of lumber from the Shaver sawmill.

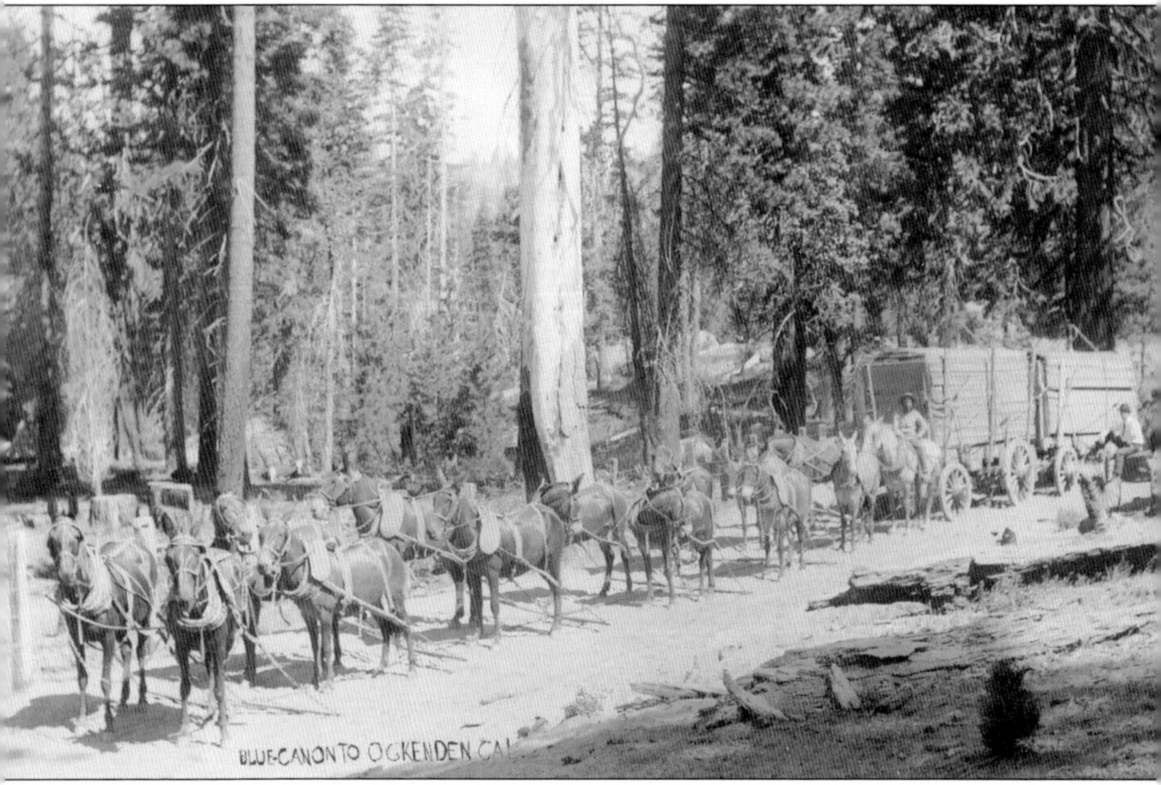

These 14 mules, pulling wagons of lumber, pause for a photograph between Blue Canyon and Ockenden, south of Shaver Lake. The Sierra Nevada was dotted with small sawmills at the end of the 19th century. Only large sawmills could afford flumes to transport their lumber; the remainder used teams of mules or oxen. However, even the large sawmills moved their highest-grade lumber by freight wagon to minimize loss or damage to their most valuable product.

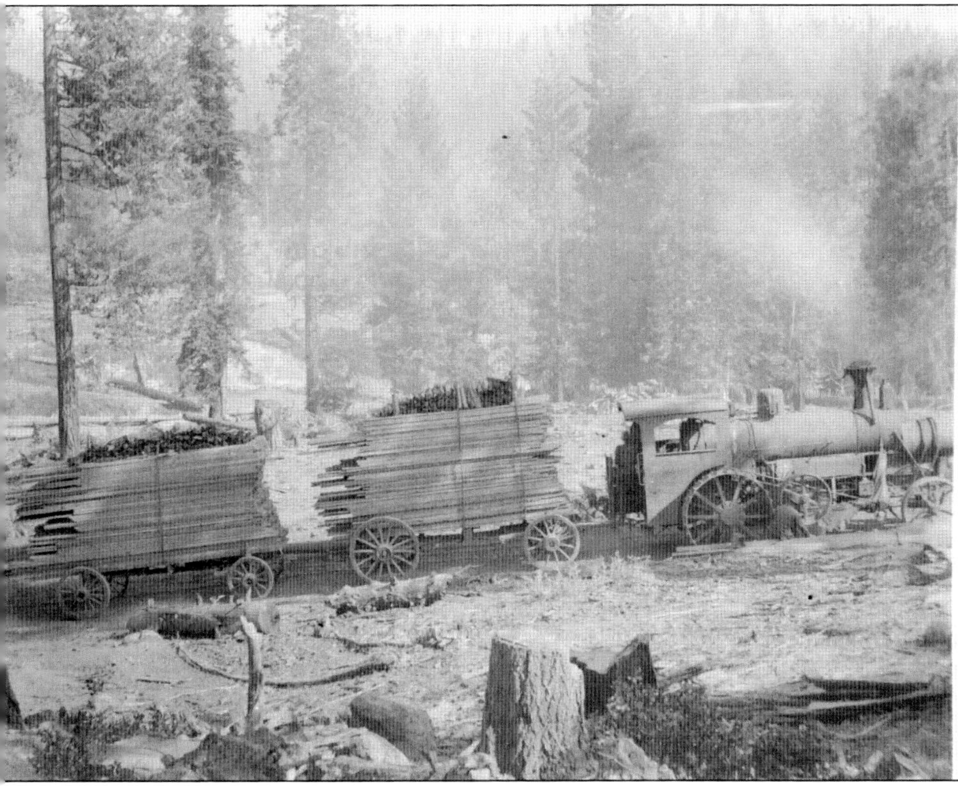

An Avery steam traction engine pulls a large load of high-grade lumber from the Shaver sawmill. Sometimes called road locomotives, traction engines were used around the world to move heavy loads by road rather than rail. Two brothers, Robert and Cyrus Avery, operated their equipment company in Peoria, Illinois, at the turn of the 20th century. The photographer, Manley White, mailed this rare postcard in 1908.

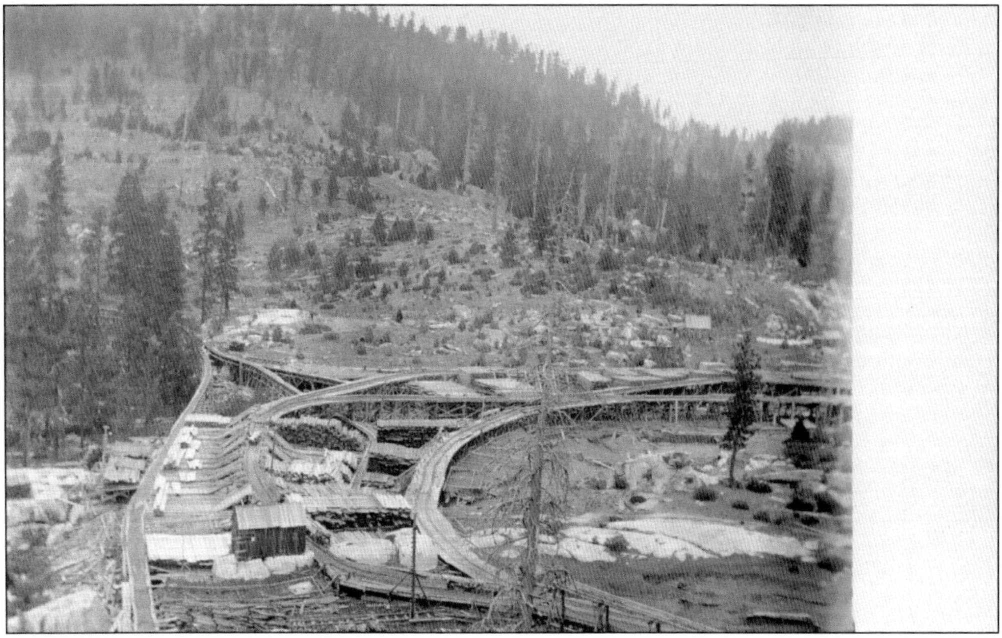

The maze of raised tram tracks and flumes in the yard at the Shaver sawmill is shown in this photograph by Manley White. From this high vantage point, the stacks of drying lumber can be seen. Dried boards were eventually moved from the stacks into the various feeder flumes that converge into a single flume in the distance. The photograph on the opposite page shows the remainder of the yard.

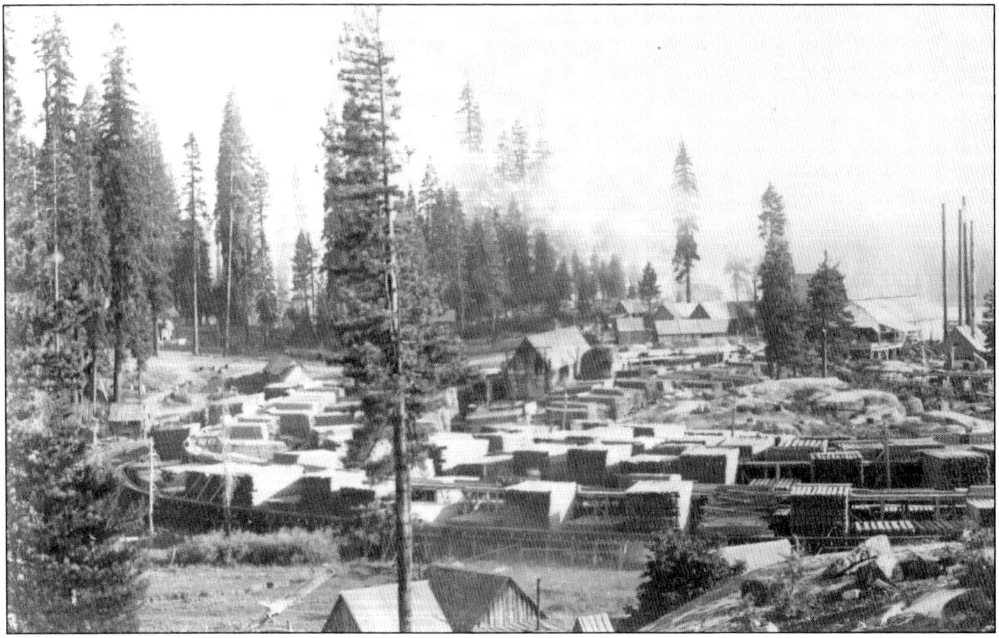

Tall stacks of drying boards crowd the yard adjacent to the Shaver sawmill, which is visible at the right in this photograph by Manley White. The elevated tramway was used to carry the dried lumber from the kiln. The stacks of lumber flank the various feeder flumes, which converge to the left out of the picture.

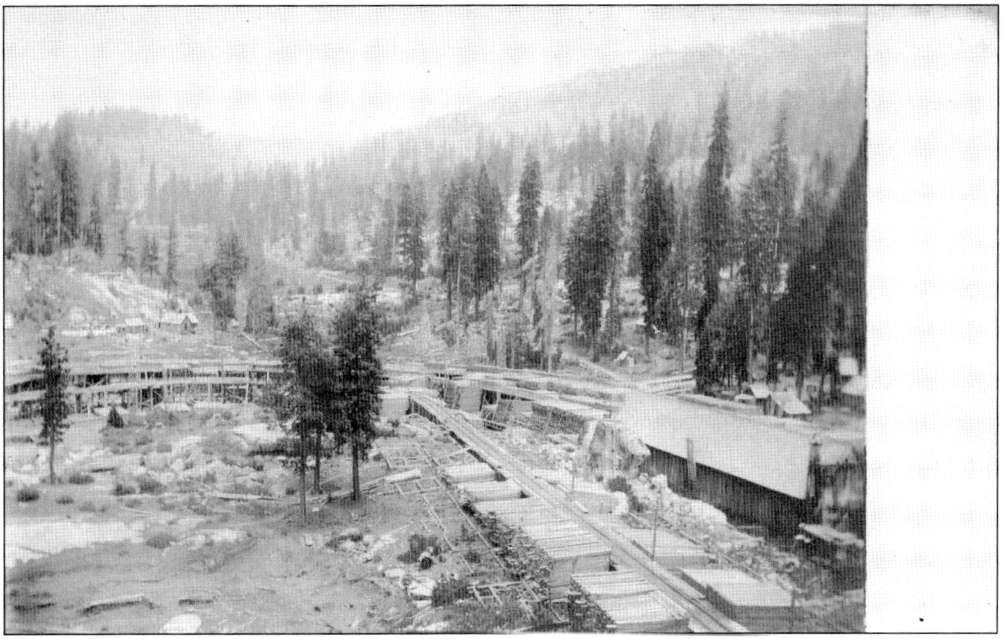

Lumber from the sawmill first went to the kiln, the long building at right. Once dried, it was moved by tramcar out into the yard, where it was off-loaded and stacked for further drying. The lighter, dried boards were eventually moved from the stacks into the various feeder flumes to begin their trip to Clovis.

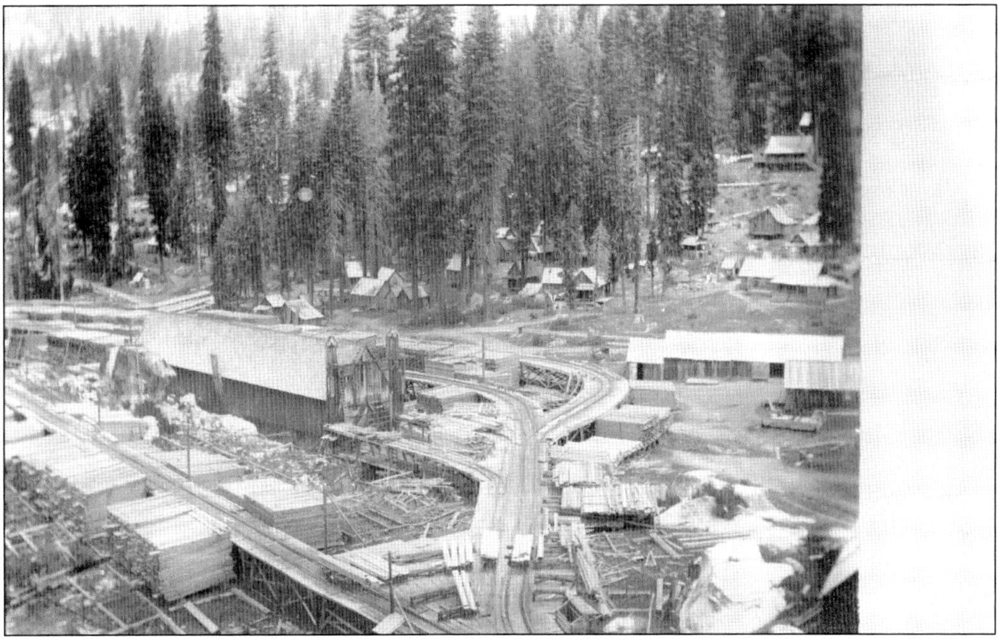

A portion of the large sawmill complex at Shaver Lake is seen here with a large number of cabins scattered on the hillside beyond. The sawmill operated from 1893 to 1914. In 1914, a snowstorm destroyed sections of the flume, and World War I began. Logging operations at Shaver ceased almost overnight. In 1919, Southern California Edison purchased the property, razed the buildings, and built a new, large dam for hydroelectric generation.

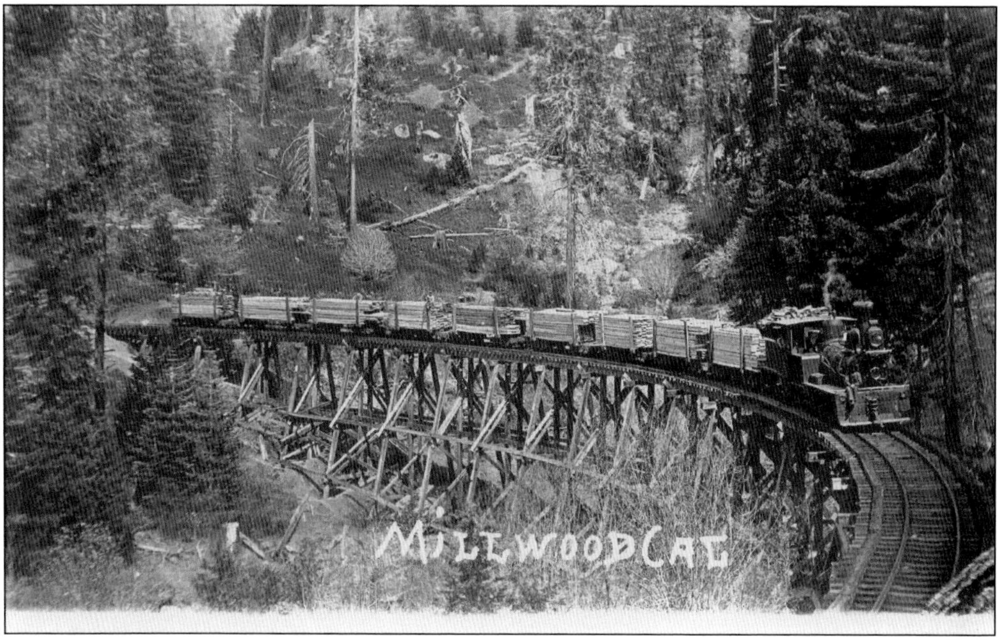

A load of lumber is pulled across one of 23 trestles on the Sequoia Railroad. This Shay locomotive, *Sequoia*, was purchased new by the Kings River Lumber Company. It was later used by The Sanger Lumber Company at Millwood. The Hume-Bennett Lumber Company moved *Sequoia* to their new sawmill at Hume Lake, where it continued service. The locomotive was scrapped after logging ceased in 1926.

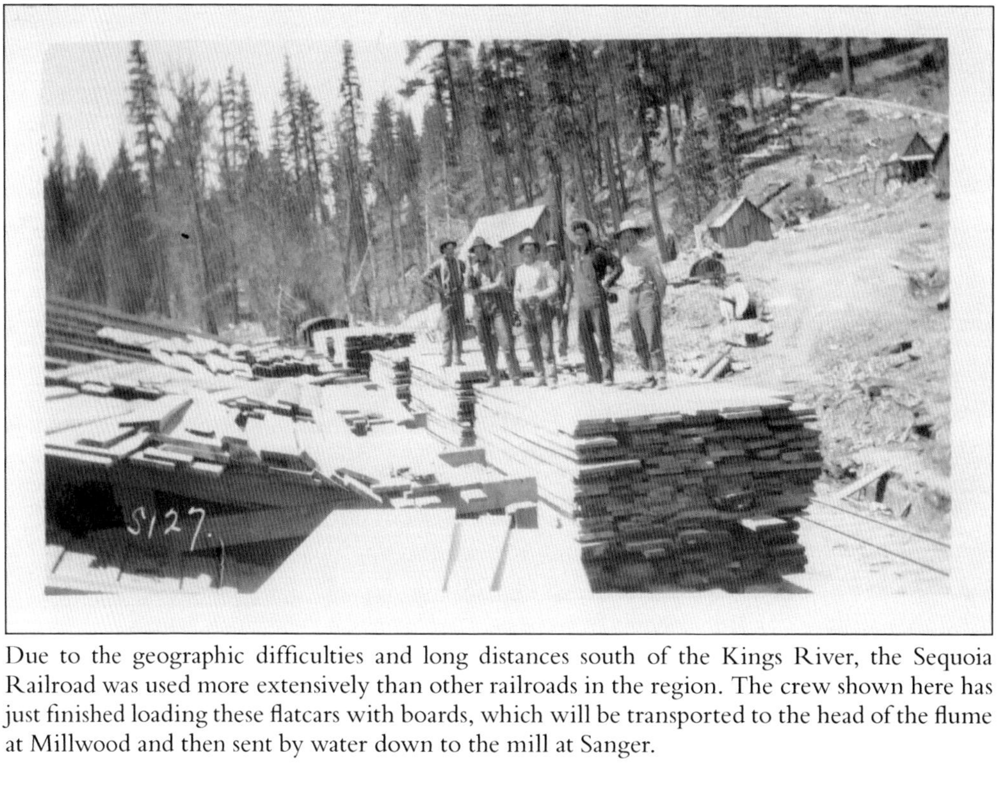

Due to the geographic difficulties and long distances south of the Kings River, the Sequoia Railroad was used more extensively than other railroads in the region. The crew shown here has just finished loading these flatcars with boards, which will be transported to the head of the flume at Millwood and then sent by water down to the mill at Sanger.

Three

FLUMES

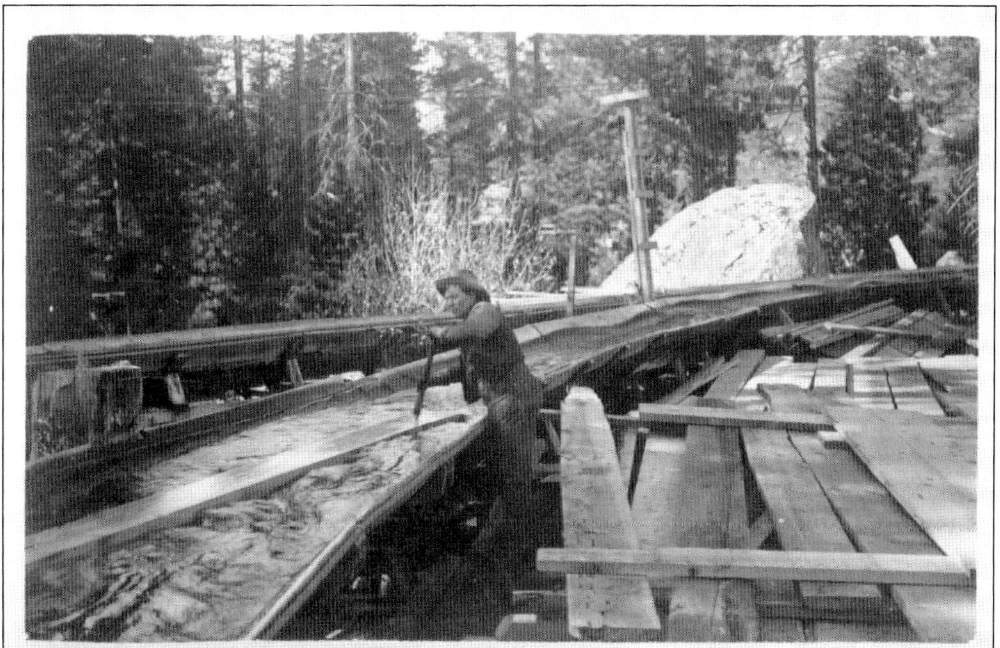

A lumber herder loads boards into the Pine Ridge flume in 1909. The boards from the Shaver drying yard are being placed in the flume, which is running full with water from the millpond. The herder is using a special flume tool called a "picaroon" to handle the boards. The pole in the background has telephone wires that connect the flume houses for communication by the flume tenders.

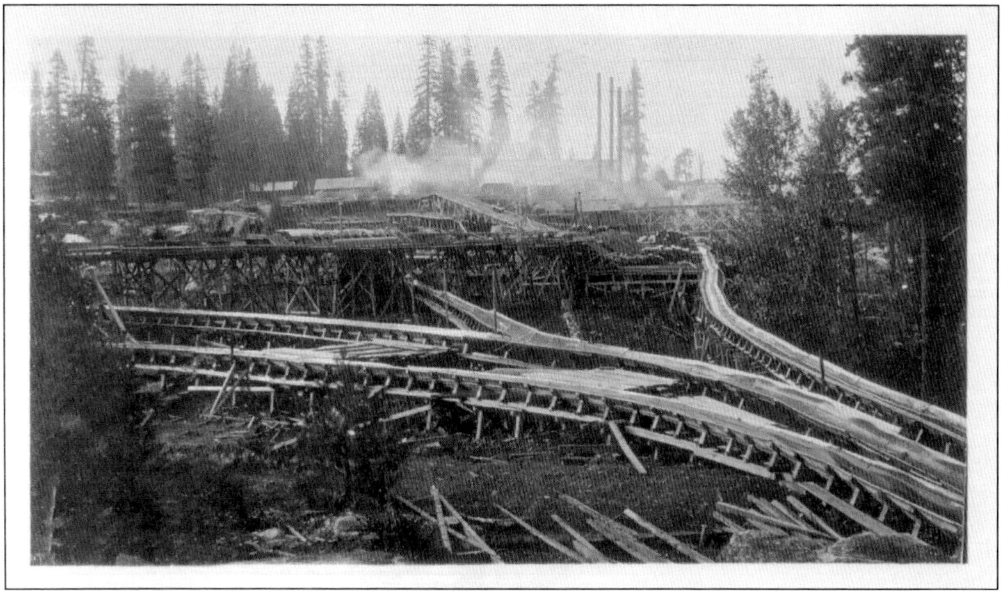

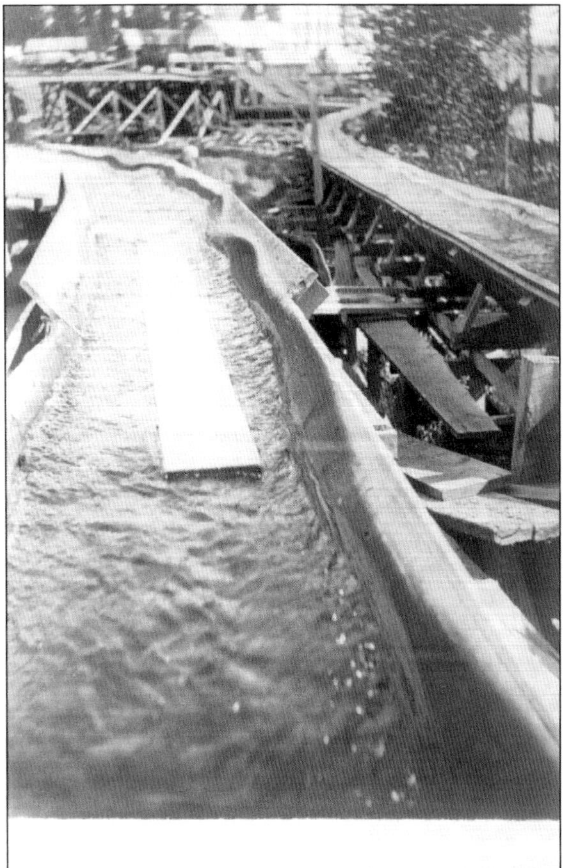

The Shaver sawmill and vast drying yard are visible in this photograph of several flumes coming out of the yard. The flumes eventually converge into one flume to the right; this was the beginning of the 42-mile-long flume that ended at the planing mill in Clovis. It took about six hours for the lumber to float that distance, dropping over 5,000 feet in elevation.

Manley White took this intriguing photograph of flumes leaving the drying yard at the Shaver sawmill, which is visible in the background. The V shape of the flumes kept boards moving better than squared "box" flumes. However, flume tenders were still needed to keep the boards moving down the mountain to Clovis.

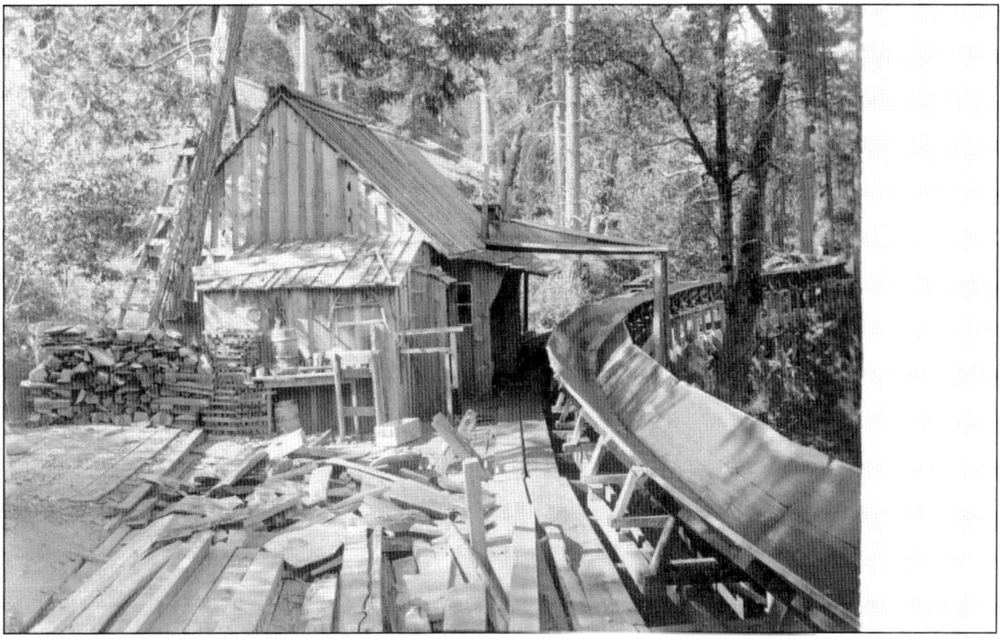

Flume houses, such as this one, were located several miles apart along the flume that is visible at right. They provided rustic homes for the flume tenders, who maintained the flume and kept the boards moving. The flume house had a telephone that allowed the tender to report any problems or damage. Photographer Manley White spent two winters (and played a lot of solitaire) in this cabin.

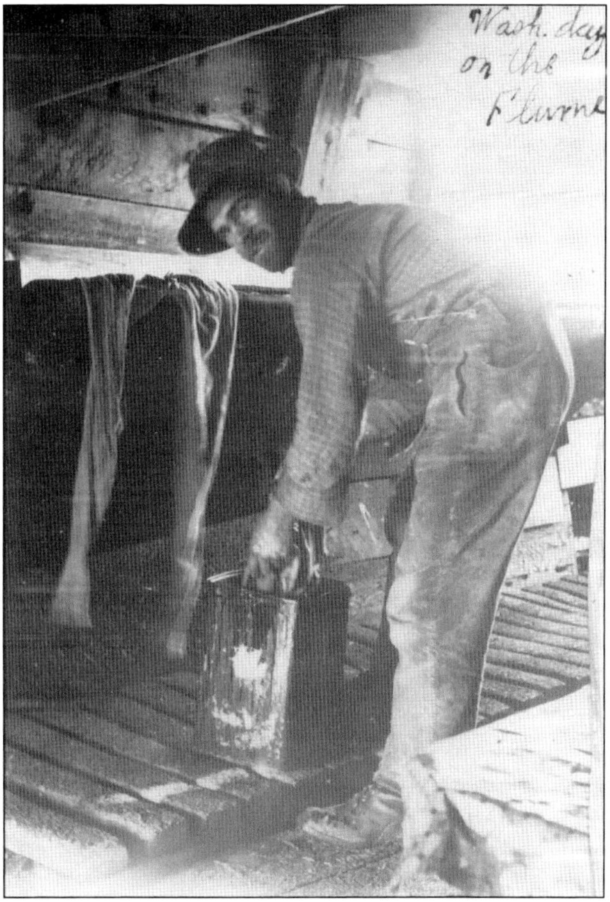

A flume tender cleans his long johns on wash day. The tenders lived very isolated lives with little outside contact except for the telephones that connected the flume houses. The pay was $1.50 per day. There was some use of flume boats, built specially for the V-shaped flume, to carry supplies and, occasionally, daring people. (Central Sierra Historical Society.)

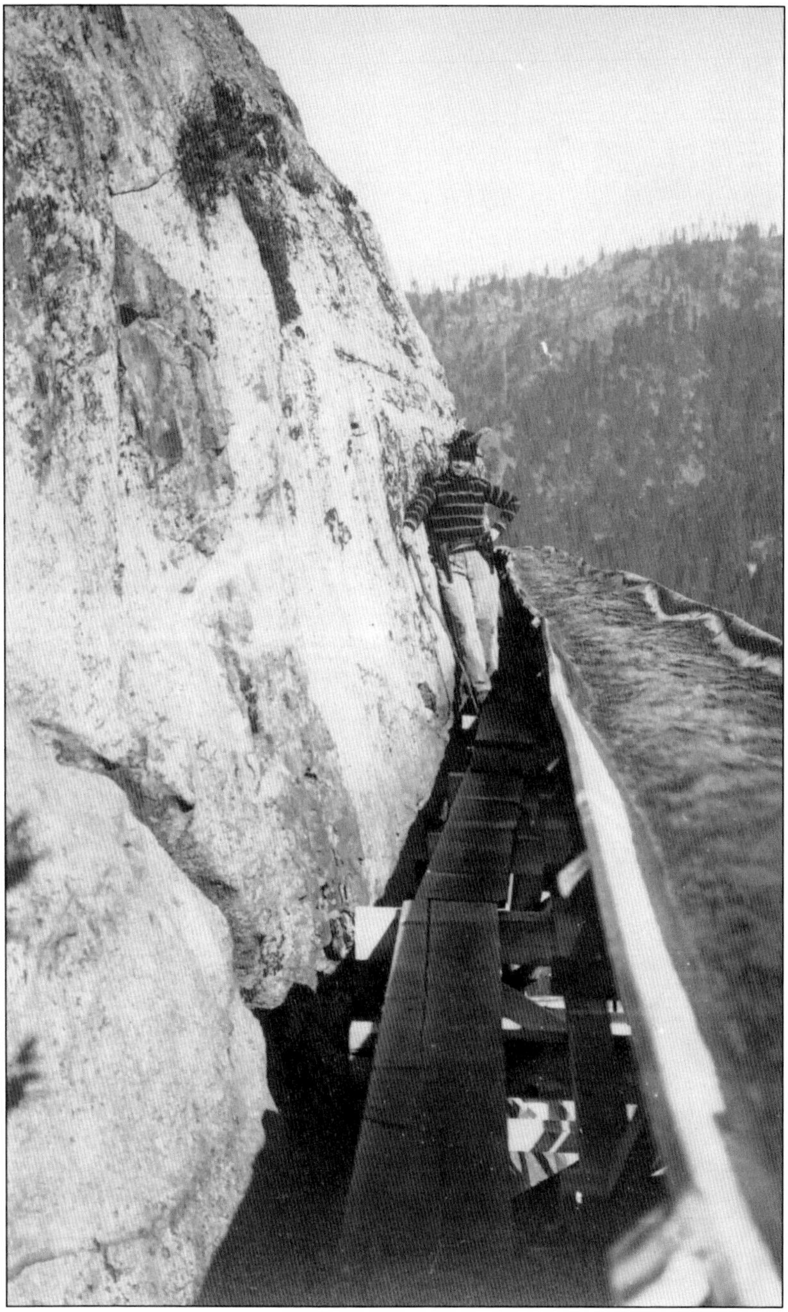

A dandy, looking rather relaxed and jaunty with a feather in his hat and two pistols on his belt, leans against a nearly vertical granite rock face beside the Pine Ridge flume. This was the beat of the flume tenders, sometimes called herders, who used the narrow catwalk to patrol an assigned section of the flume that was usually several miles in length. They had to separate lumber and prevent it from getting jammed up, in addition to repairing leaks in, or damage to, the flume. It was dangerous and lonely work in all types of weather, but the views were often spectacular. However, one did have to watch one's step, since the catwalk was sometimes on the outside of the flume.

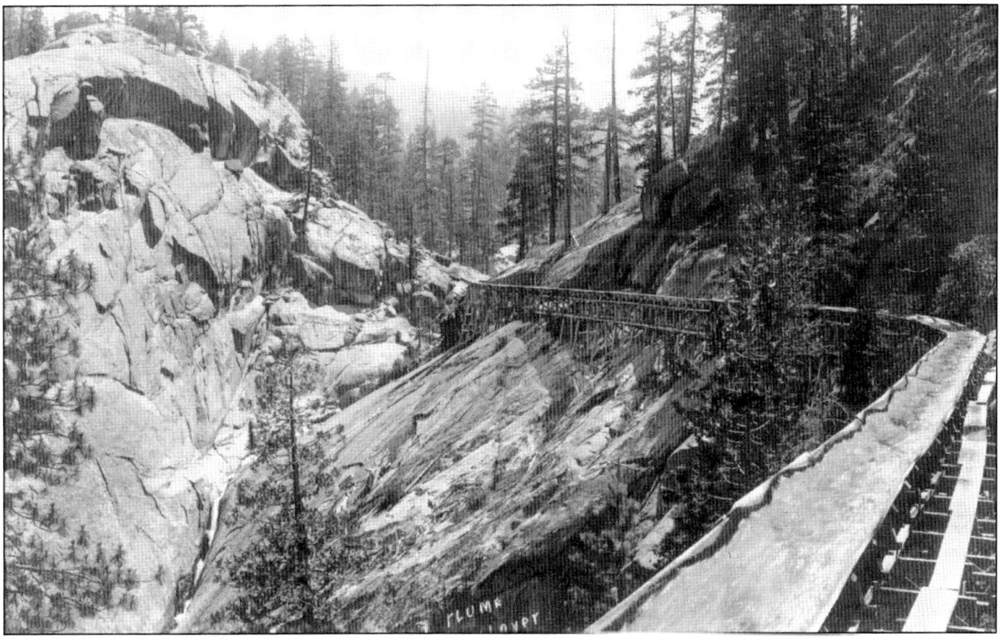

The Pine Ridge flume flows passed Shaver Rock as it traverses the head of Devil's Canyon. The flume was well surveyed to maintain the flow of water necessary to move the boards. Although no boards are visible in the flume, it is full of water from Shaver Lake. The walkway, visible to the right, was used by the flume tenders on their patrols.

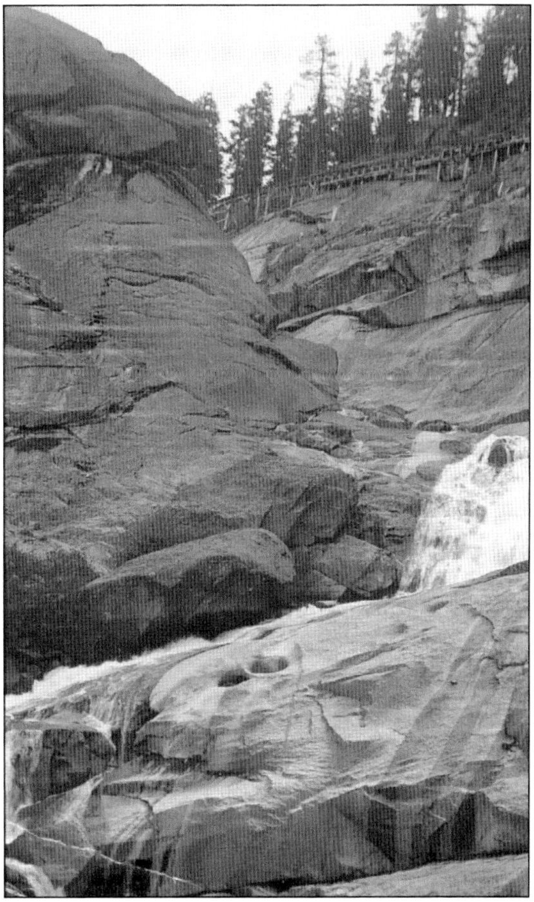

Manley White was looking up Devil's Canyon when he took this photograph. Stevenson Creek, which was dammed to create Shaver Lake, is seen here cascading down Devil's Canyon below the dam. The creek makes a drop of over 2,600 feet from Shaver Lake to the San Joaquin River. This is a dramatic view looking up at the flume high on the granite face.

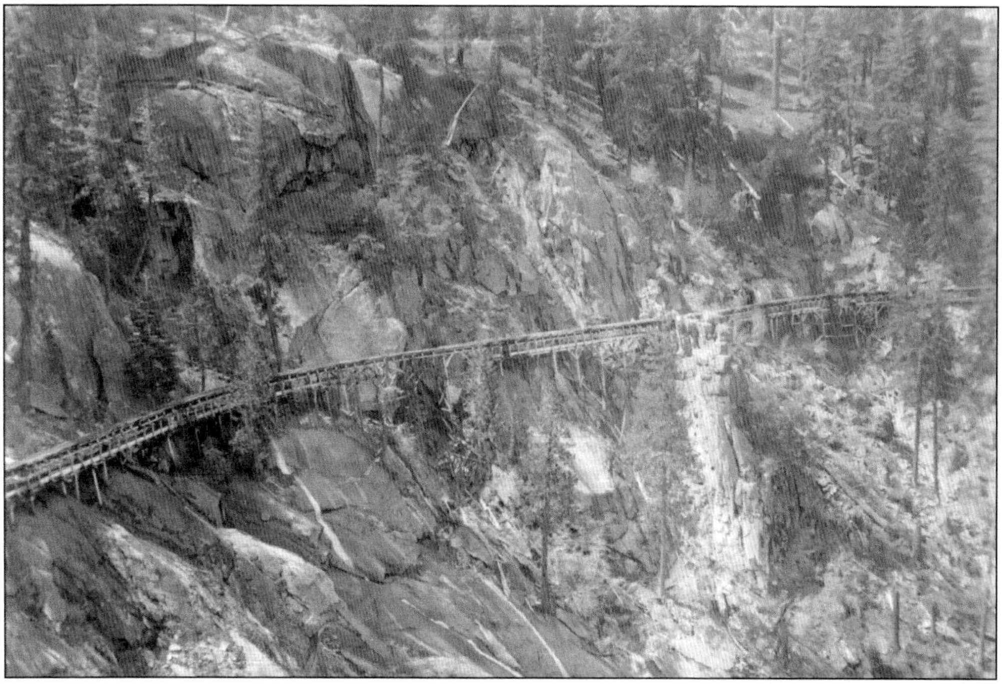

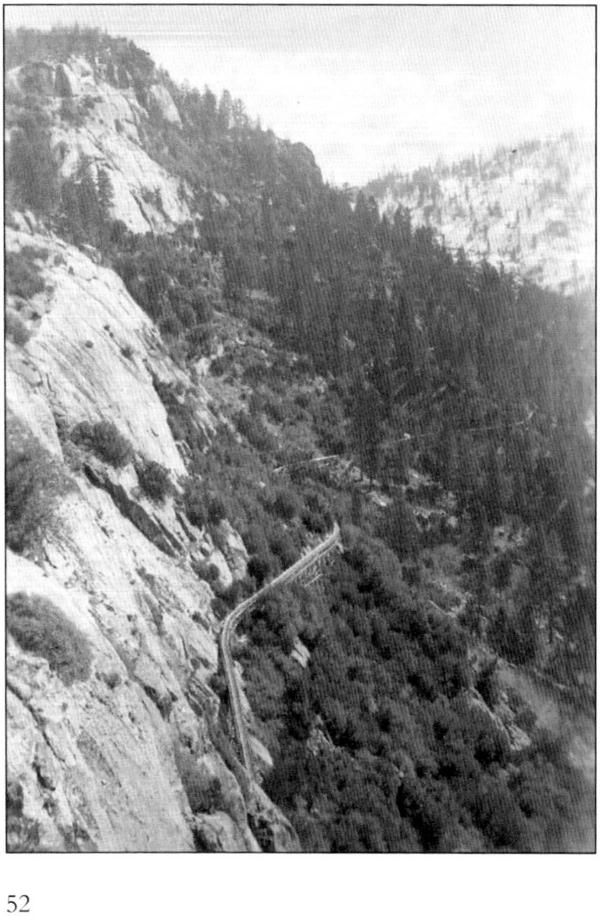

Building a flume across a granite rock face, as seen here, required lowering men by ropes to cut the rock and set the footings. Construction must have been very slow during 1893 and 1894. These sections were easily damaged during winter by ice and avalanches. Manley White wrote on the back of this postcard, "Flume in Devil's Canyon where foreman's wife fell off of flume."

A long stretch of the Pine Ridge flume comes out of the forest near Shaver Lake and traverses this rocky slope known as Flume Peak. Manley White must have done some serious hiking to get his camera to the vantage point for this unusual view looking down on the flume.

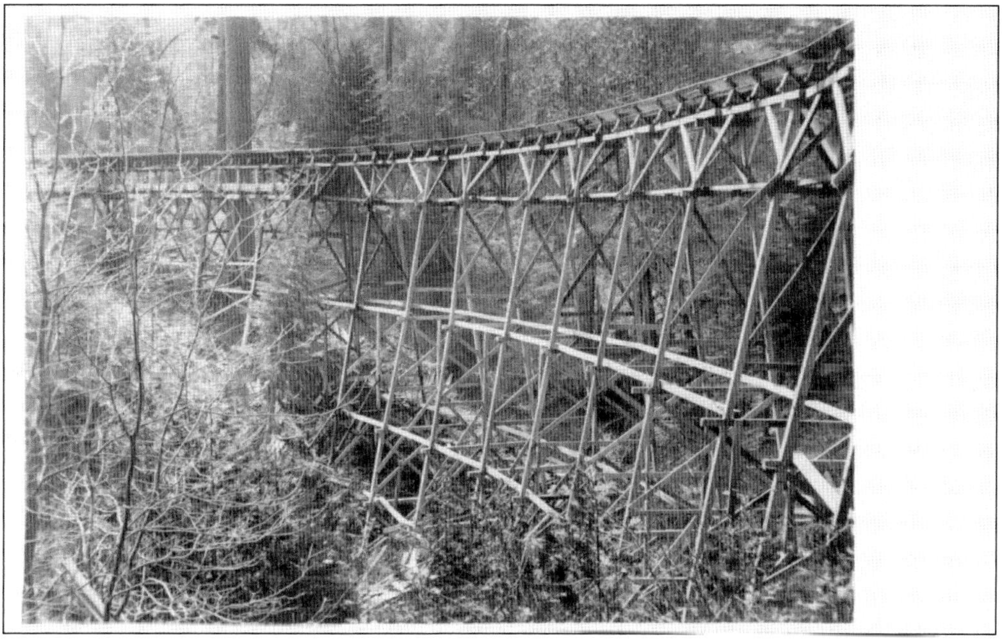

The flume construction methods are clearly visible on this short, curved section of flume below Shaver Lake. The numerous creeks and snowmelt drainages in the Sierra Nevada required many trestles such as this. Forest fires presented a significant threat to the wooden flumes, occasionally destroying or damaging sections of flumes in the mountains.

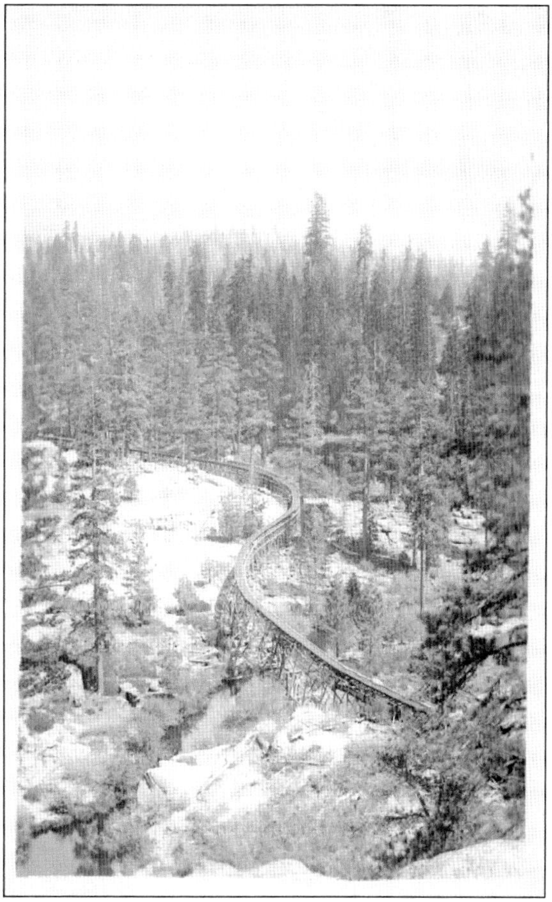

Even in relatively level areas like this stretch between Shaver Lake and Pine Ridge, flume construction was a challenge. This curving section, built completely on trestles, was required to get around granite outcrops and maintain the slope necessary for the flow of water. Manley White sent this postcard from Fresno in January 1910, to report that he had been taking photographs in Fresno and "made good wages—but that's all."

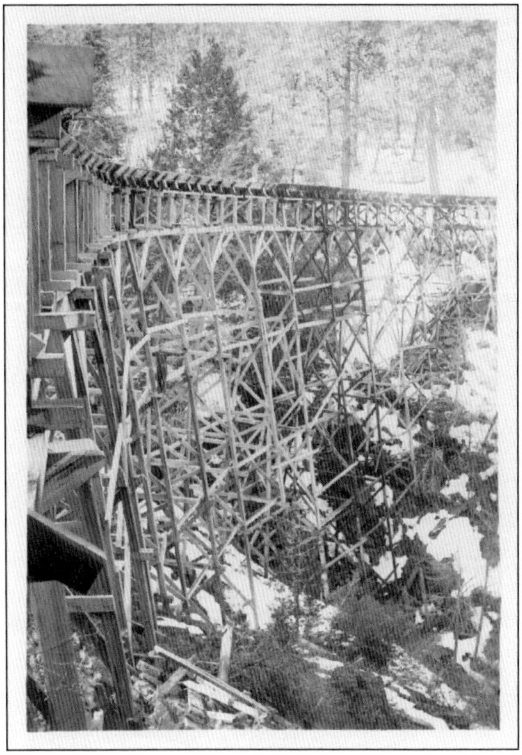

The Pine Ridge flume was perhaps at its tallest where it crossed Musick Creek between Shaver Lake and Pine Ridge. A man, visible at left center, provides a very good perspective on the height of the flume trestle—about 90 feet at this point. It is easy to see why the construction of the entire flume required about nine million board feet of knot-free lumber.

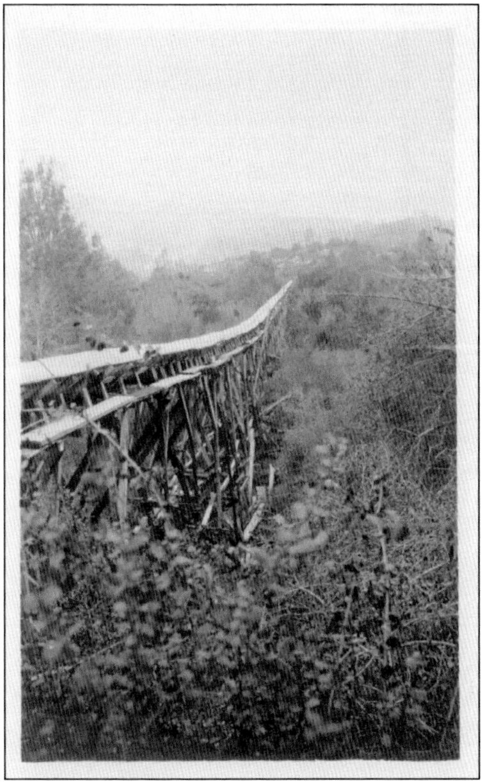

A less dramatic section of the flume comes straight down through the Sierra Nevada foothills. The flume still required high trestles, as shown here, to maintain the slope necessary to keep the water flowing and the boards moving. To the right of the flume is the precarious catwalk.

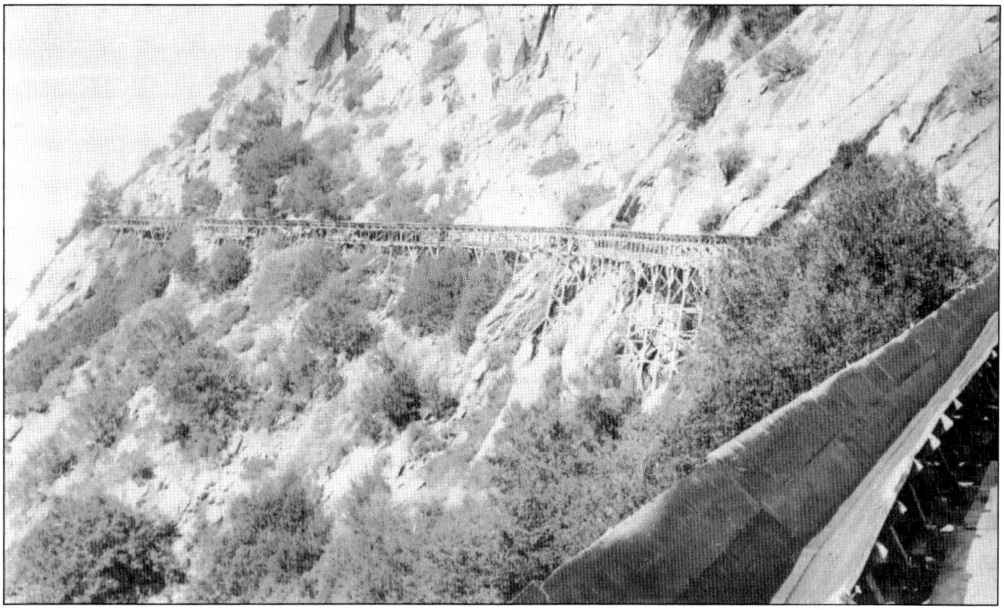

Manley White used the catwalk, visible at lower right, to get a good vantage point for a dramatic photograph of the Pine Ridge flume, possibly at Rocky Point. There is no water in the flume, indicating that this photograph may have been taken in winter. The chaparral suggests this section of the flume was a little lower in the mountains and would have received much less snowfall.

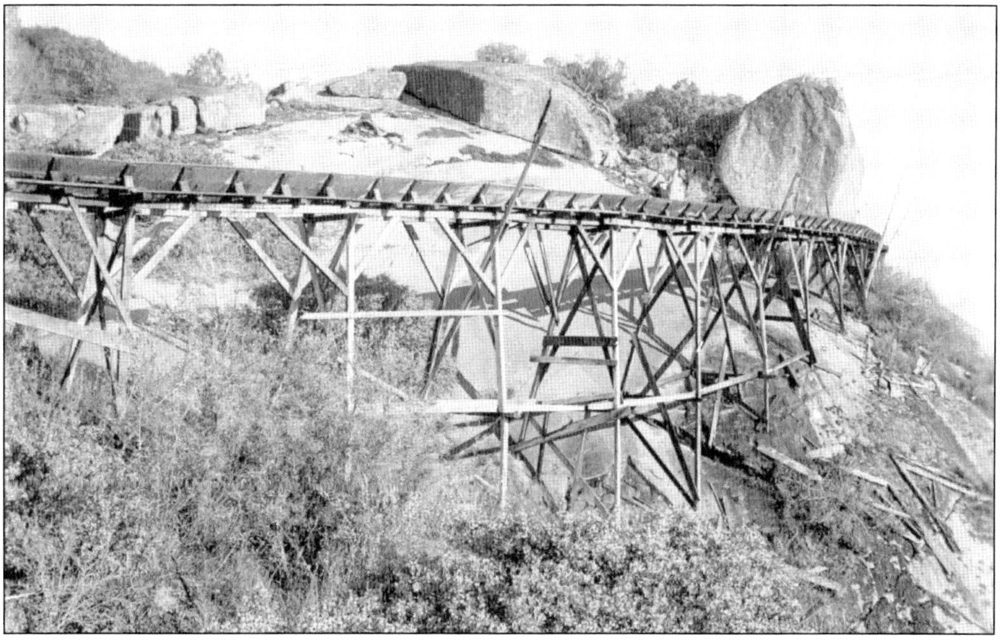

The flume bends around a rock outcrop about four miles below "the Saddle," the current site of the Pine Ridge Elementary School. This middle section of the flume is actually where the water traveled the fastest, about 15 miles per hour. The telephone line, used for communication between the flume houses, can be seen supported on poles extending up from the right side of the flume.

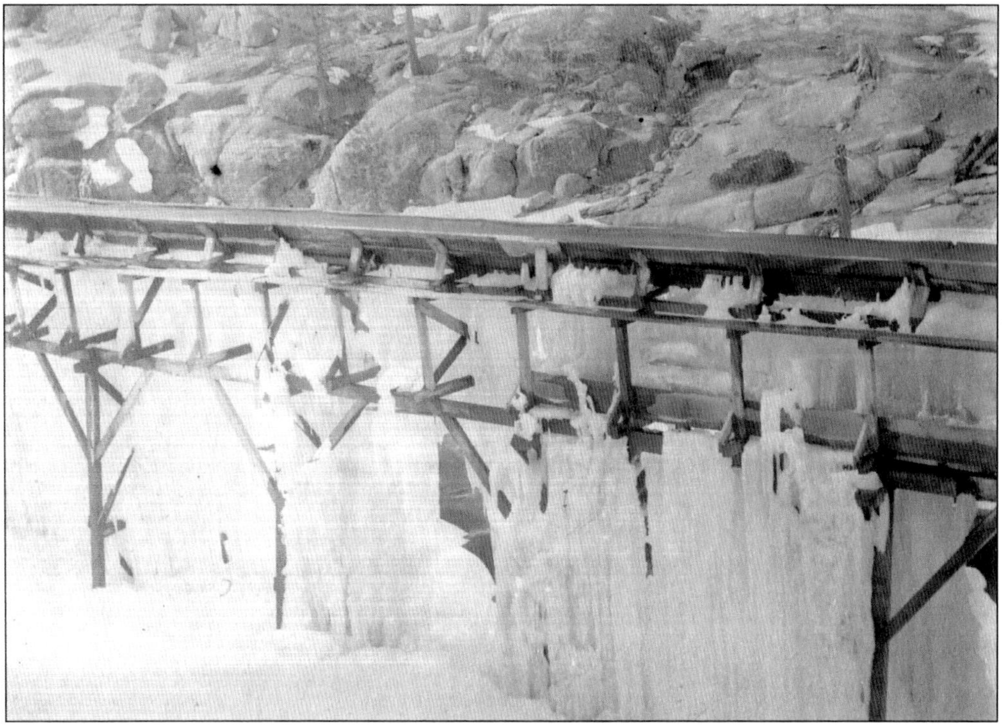

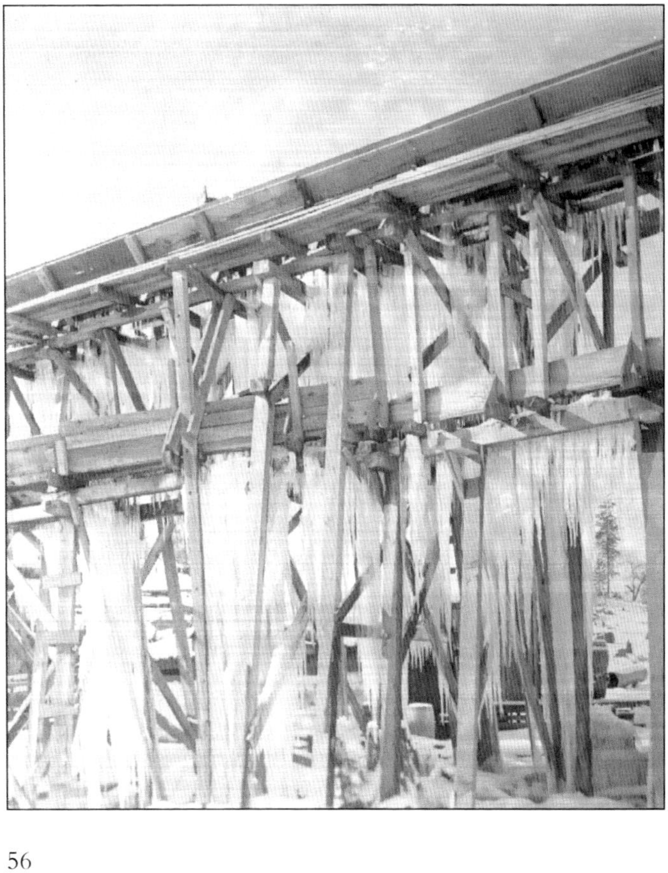

With long, cold winters, the Sierra Nevada was not friendly to wooden flumes. Most sawmills did not operate in winter, so the flumes were not used. But ice could still cause problems. It is possible these photographs were taken in fall, while the flume was still in use, and that the frozen water was caused by a drop in temperature. The weight of this much ice could easily cause the flume to collapse. Even without water flowing in the flume, snow could pile up, and the resulting weight could cause damage. That is what happened to the 20-year-old Shaver flume in 1914. The damage from the snow and the beginning of World War I combined to end the operation of the Shaver sawmill.

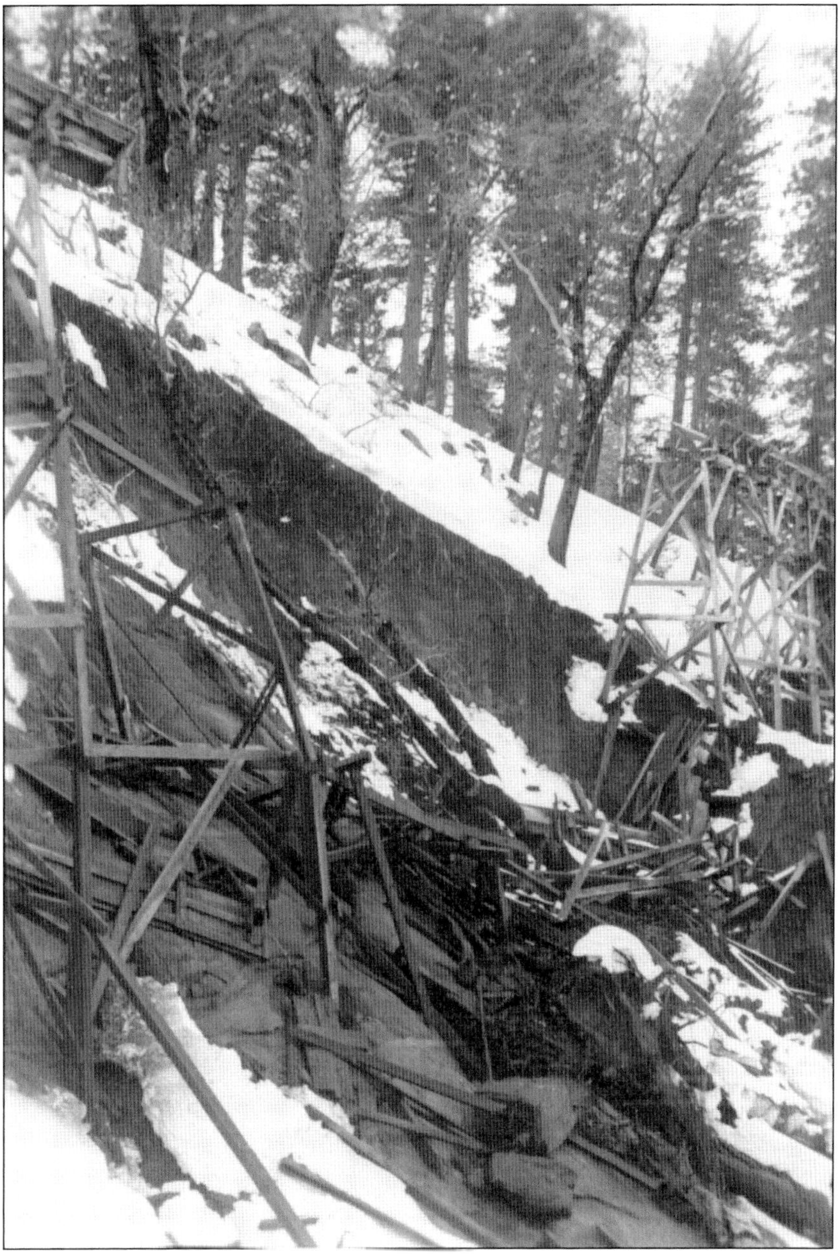

A variety of natural forces caused serious disruptions to lumbering operations in the Sierra Nevada. These could affect logging operations, railroads, and the transportation of lumber, especially by flume. In this case, a landslide on a steep hill has destroyed a section of the Pine Ridge flume. It probably took several days to rebuild this section and get water and boards flowing down the flume once again. Other threats to the wooden flumes included forest fires, ice, and snow. The flume cost $200,000 in 1893 and 1894 and required nine million board feet of lumber to construct. At maximum use, it carried about 200,000 board feet of lumber in a day. This was more efficient that hauling the lumber in wagons down the tollhouse grade. After operations ceased at the Shaver sawmill in 1914, the flume was eventually sold for $20,000 to be used as scrap lumber.

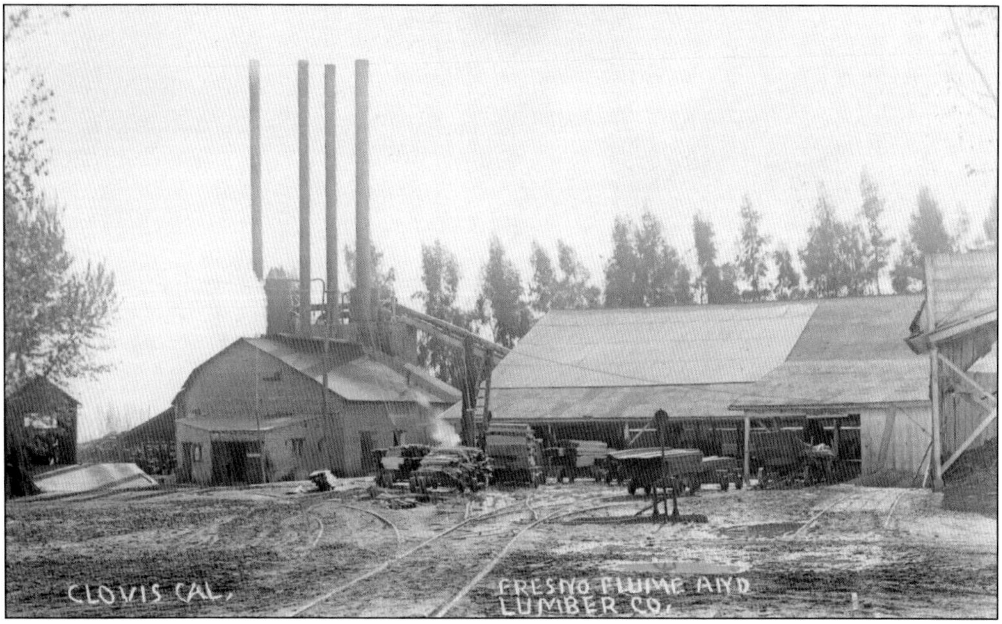

Rough-cut lumber from the Shaver sawmill reached Clovis via the 42-mile-long flume. The Clovis facility, shown in these two real-photo postcards, was east of the Clovis railroad station. The mill began operations in 1894 with about 140 employees. Covering about 40 acres, it included a planing mill, box factory, and drying yards. The facility burned in 1898 but was quickly rebuilt. In the yard, boards from the flume were sorted and stacked to dry. Finished lumber was easily transported to the San Joaquin Valley Railroad (later Southern Pacific Railroad), just south of the Clovis station, for shipment. The mill burned again in 1914. Later, Clark Intermediate School and the Clovis Rodeo Grounds were built on the site of the mill. (John Reynolds Collection.)

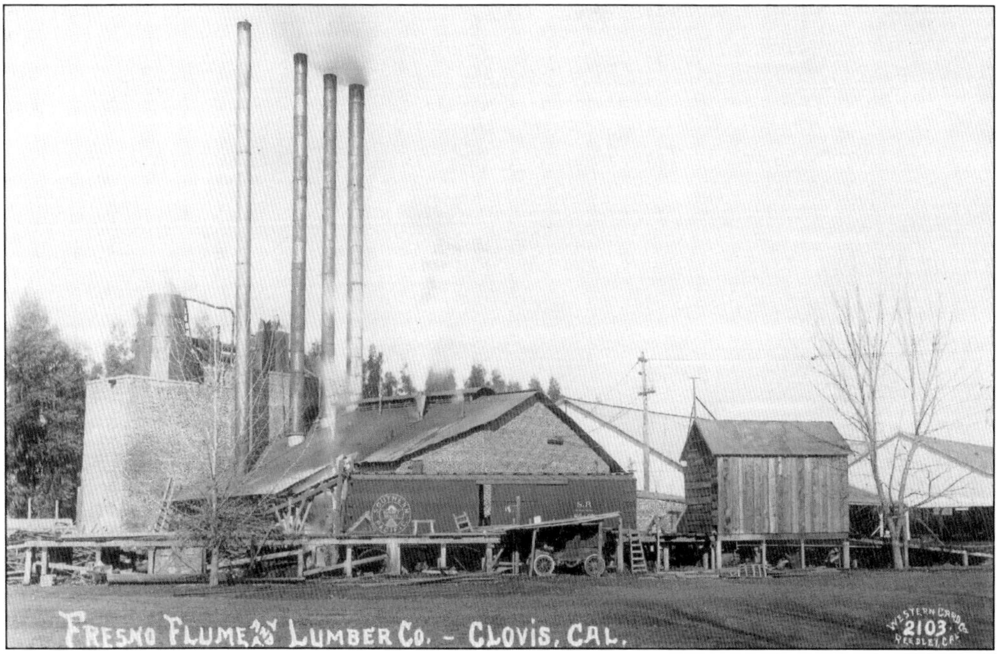

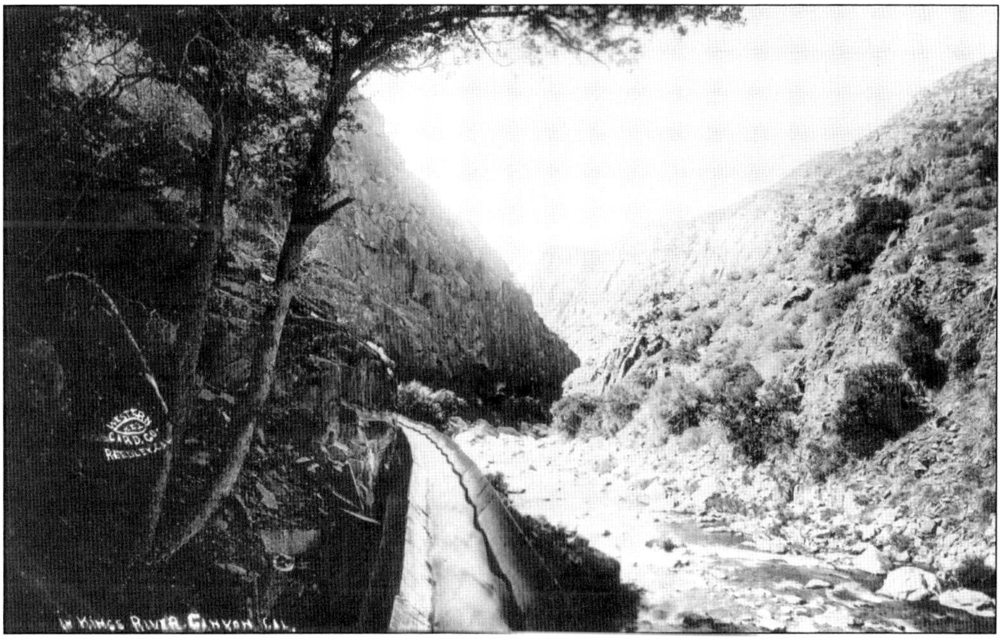

This photograph of the Hume-Bennett Lumber Company flume shows the ruggedness of the Kings River canyon. The original flume from Millwood required nine million board feet of knot-free lumber and cost about $300,000 to construct in 1890. Maintaining a grade that would keep the water flowing fast enough to move the boards was a challenge in the rugged Sierra Nevada.

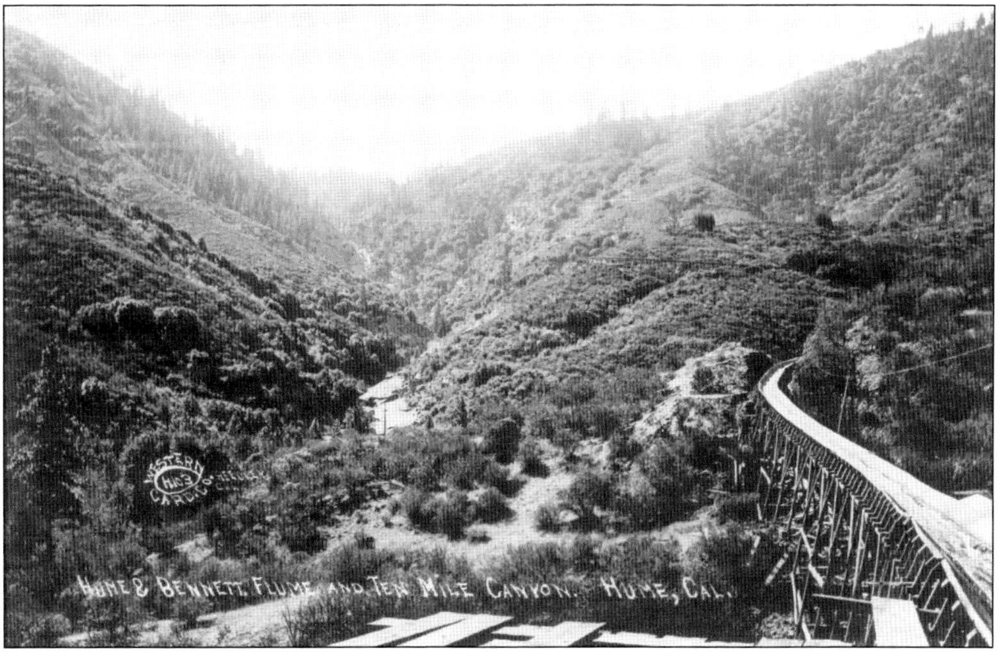

The relocation of the sawmill to Hume Lake in 1908 required a 17-mile flume extension along Tenmile Creek. The flume extension joined the original flume from Millwood near the Kings River. The new flume was about 59 miles long, making it one of the longest in the world.

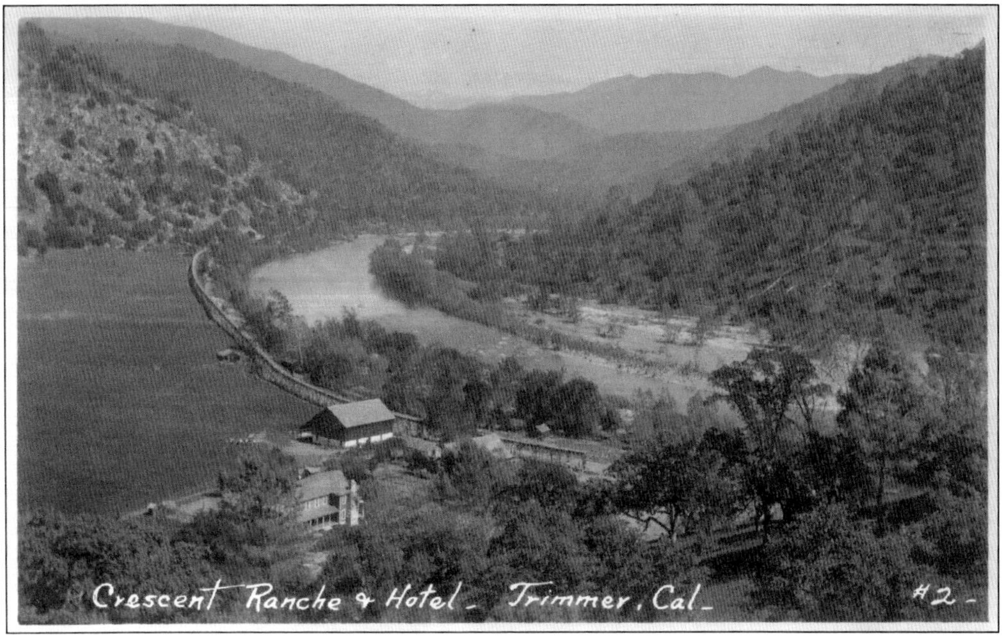

The flume from Millwood, and later Hume Lake, crossed the Kings River upstream from Trimmer. The sawmills were on the south side of the river, and Sanger, the terminus of the flume, was on the north side. Although not completely out of the foothills, the flume reached a more level stretch at this bucolic ranch and hotel.

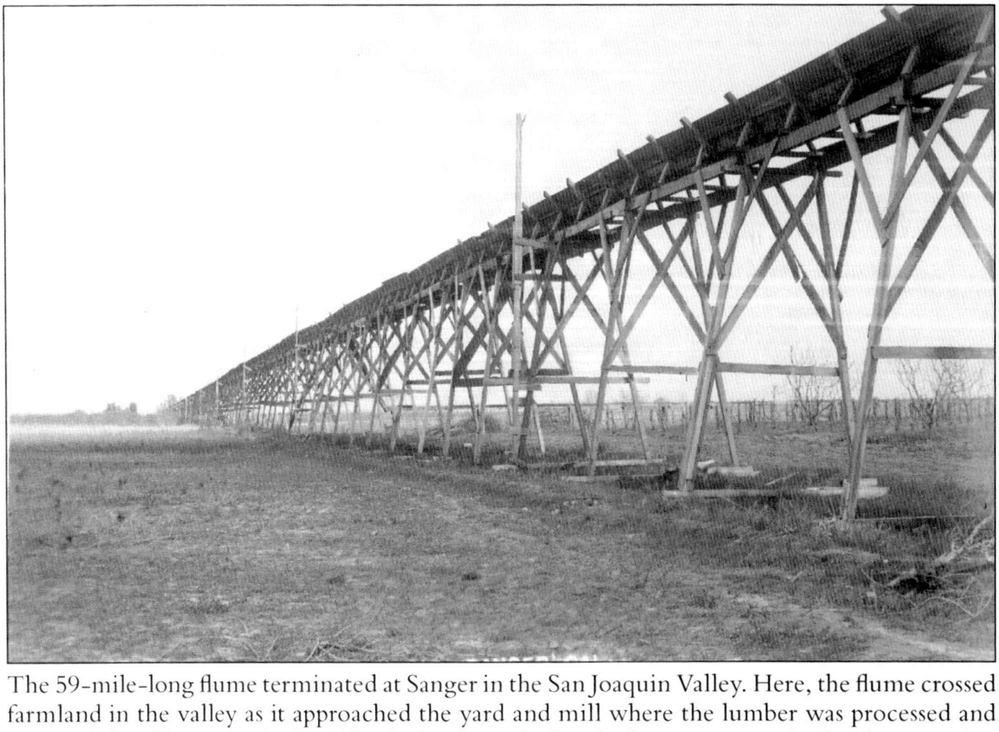

The 59-mile-long flume terminated at Sanger in the San Joaquin Valley. Here, the flume crossed farmland in the valley as it approached the yard and mill where the lumber was processed and prepared for shipment. On level land, the flume had to be larger to contain the slow-moving water and the cargo of lumber.

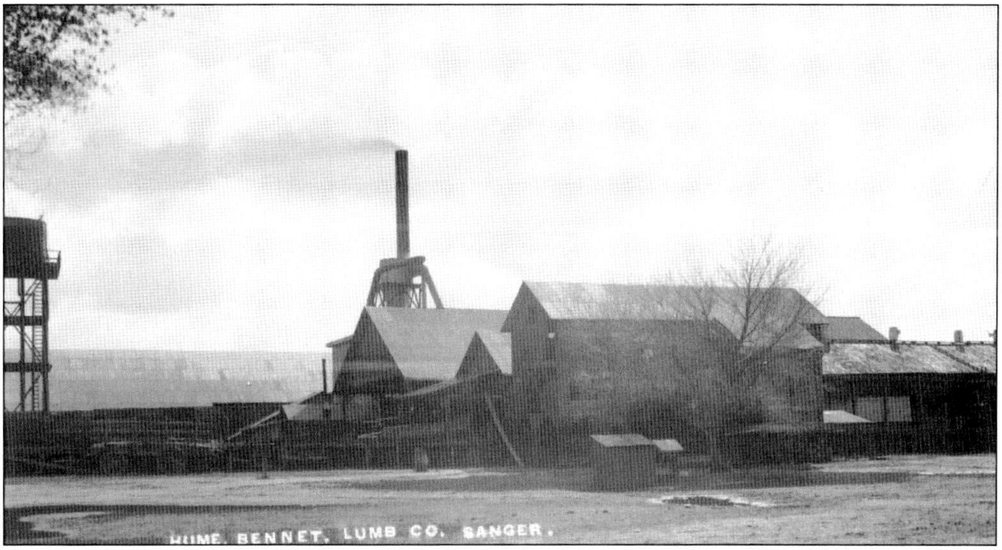

Sanger, 15 miles east of Fresno, was located on a branch of the Southern Pacific Railroad, which allowed ready shipment of finished lumber. In 1889, the town donated 65 acres to the lumber company to induce them to build their facility at the terminus of the flume. Constructed in 1890, the facility included a box factory, planing mill, engine house, and drying yard.

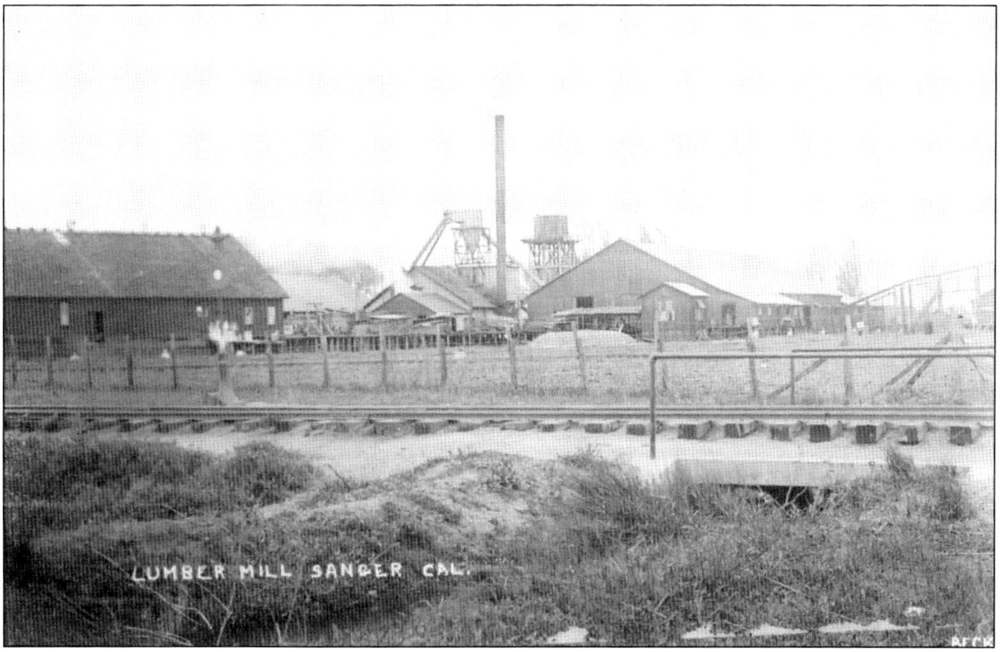

When the lumber arrived at the mill, "dumpers" manually lifted the wet boards out and put them on a skidway that sloped down to a platform. Lumber was sorted in the yard, with knotted boards going to the box factory and better lumber going to the planing mill. A tramway with small cars was used to move lumber to the mill. (Fresno County Public Library.)

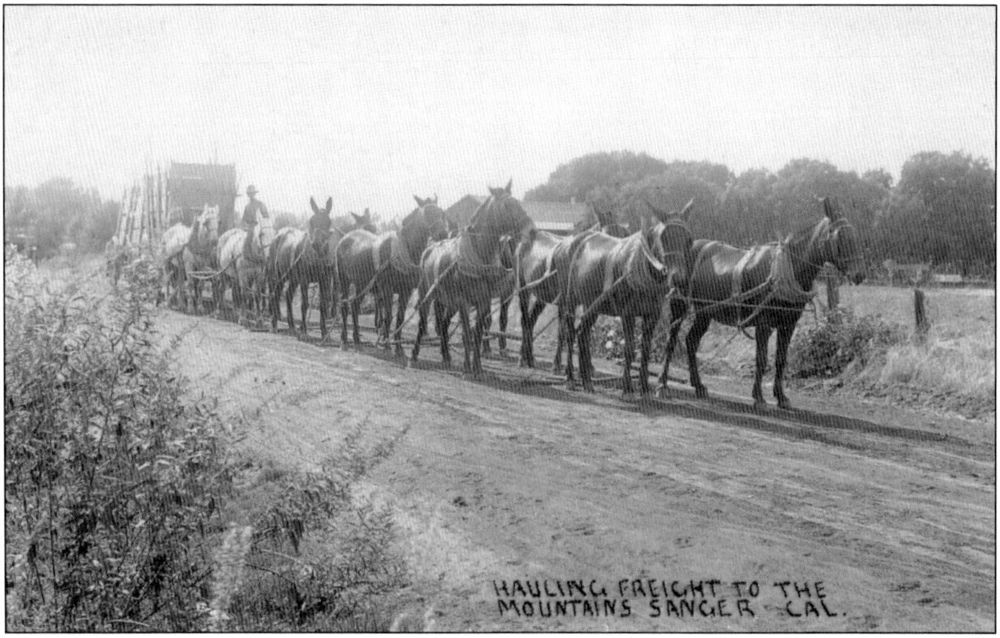

A large team of mules and horses has it easy on this flat road in the San Joaquin Valley. Soon, the road would ascend into the Sierra foothills and mountains. With hundreds of loggers and millhands working in the mountains, a lot of supplies, including food, needed to be freighted in. The freight wagons would bring higher-grade lumber down to Sanger on the return trip.

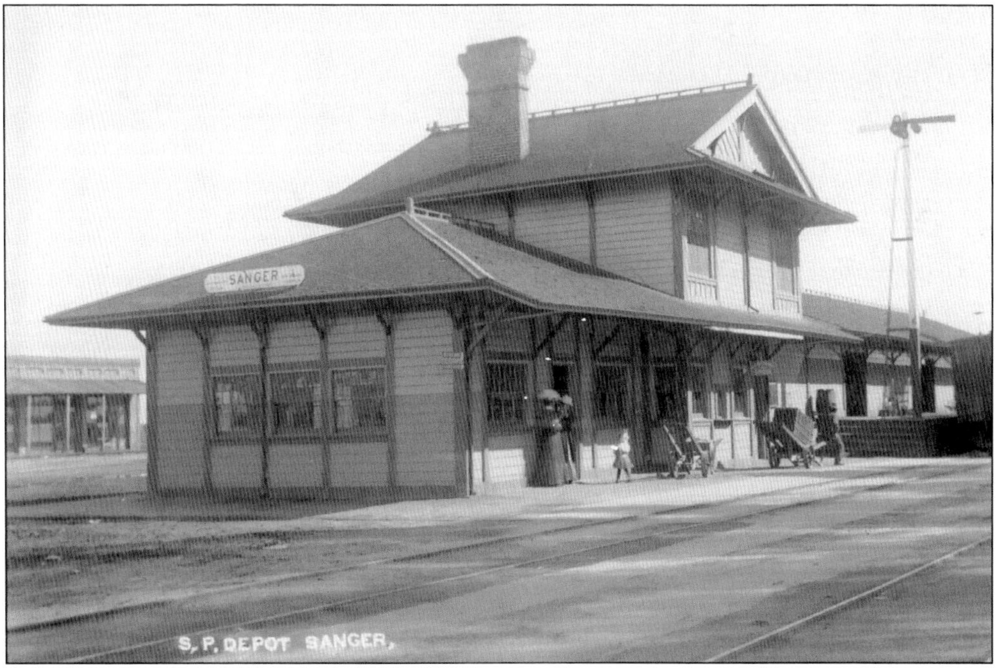

Sanger, located about 13 miles east of Fresno, was established on the Porterville branch of the Southern Pacific Railroad. The depot was built in 1887, and the branchline was completed in 1888. Southern Pacific switch lines ran into the drying yard at the mill, so milled and dried lumber could be easily shipped up and down the West Coast as well as overseas.

Four

Hydroelectricity

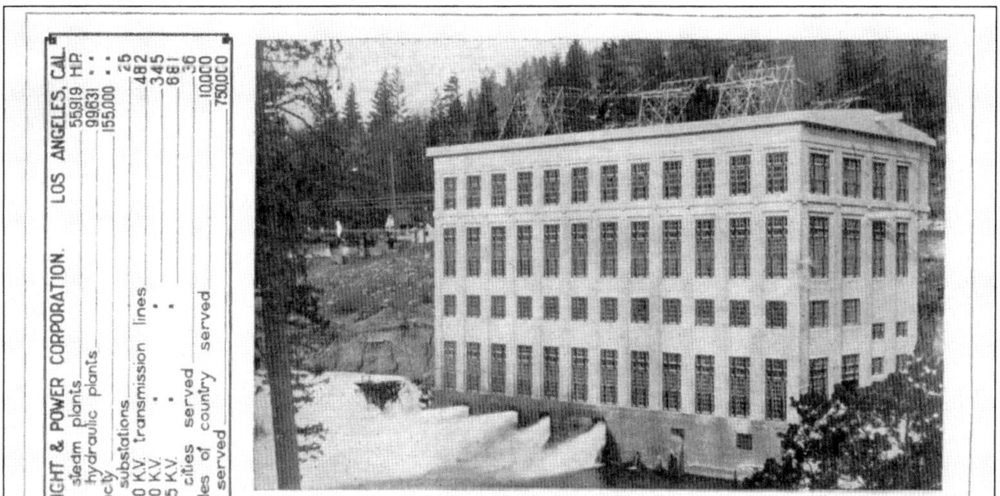

The Sierra Nevada has a steep western slope where snowmelt is harnessed to generate electricity. The Pacific Light & Power Company needed power for the Los Angeles area, and they found it on the San Joaquin River in eastern Fresno County. The Big Creek Hydroelectric Project was a massive project centered at Cascada, renamed Big Creek in 1926. Construction of Powerhouse No. 1 began in 1912.

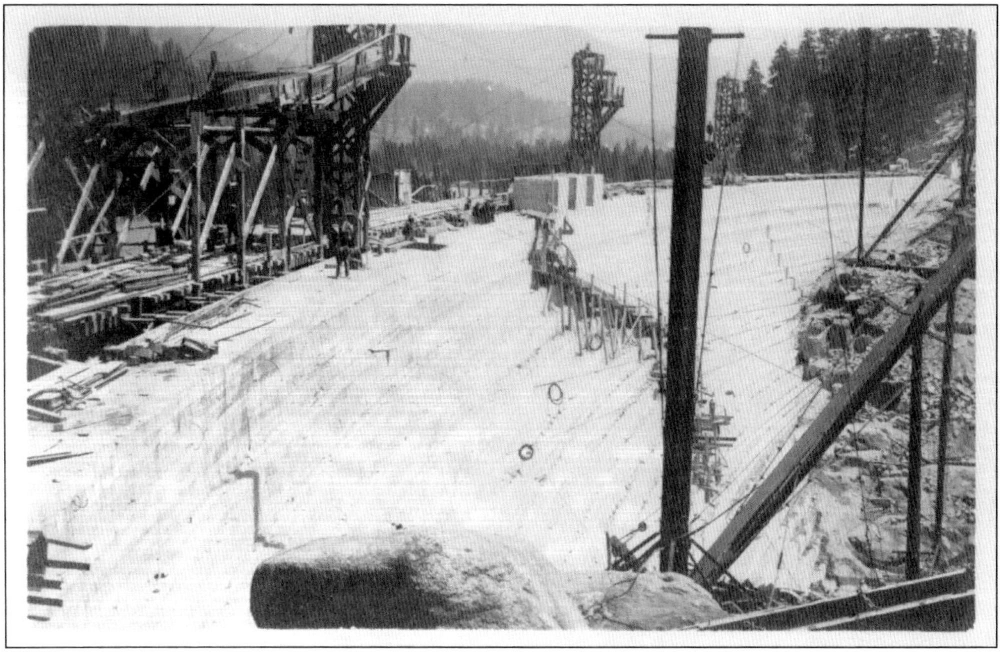

Huntington Lake Dam No. 1 was nearing completion when this photograph was taken just before June 1913. Built across Big Creek, this dam was one of three constructed to create Huntington Lake. The lake, part of the vast hydroelectric project of the Pacific Light & Power Company, quickly became a popular recreation destination in the central Sierra Nevada.

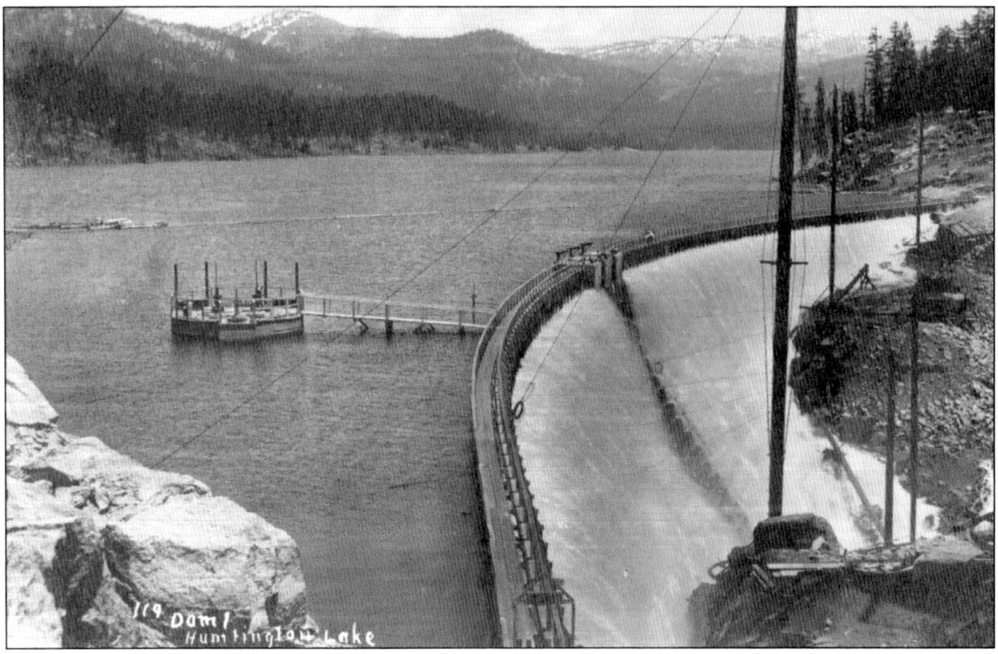

This early photograph by A.C. Mudge shows Dam No. 1 and Huntington Lake. This dam is the easternmost of the three that created Huntington Lake. The intake tower at left housed the controls for the nine-foot tunnel gate through which water flowed to Powerhouse No. 1. To increase electricity production, the dam was raised 35 feet in 1917.

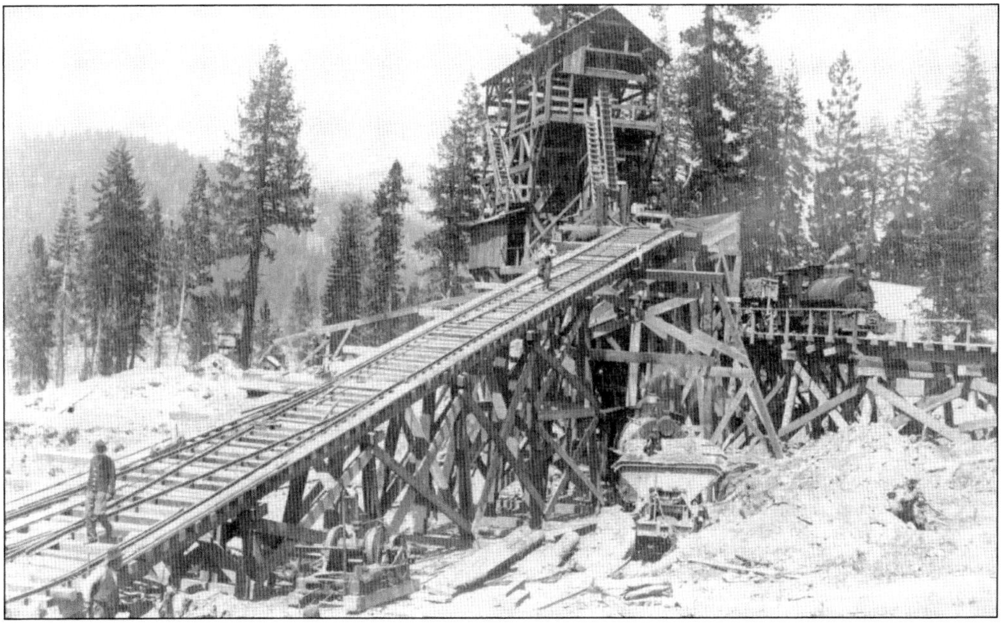

Building the initial three dams to create Huntington Lake took a lot of material. This rock crusher was built in the basin that was eventually filled to create the lake. A construction railroad was built to haul the crushed rock in work cars, seen at bottom, to the construction sites. Locomotive 5, at middle right, was acquired by construction contractor Stone & Webster. (Fresno County Public Library.)

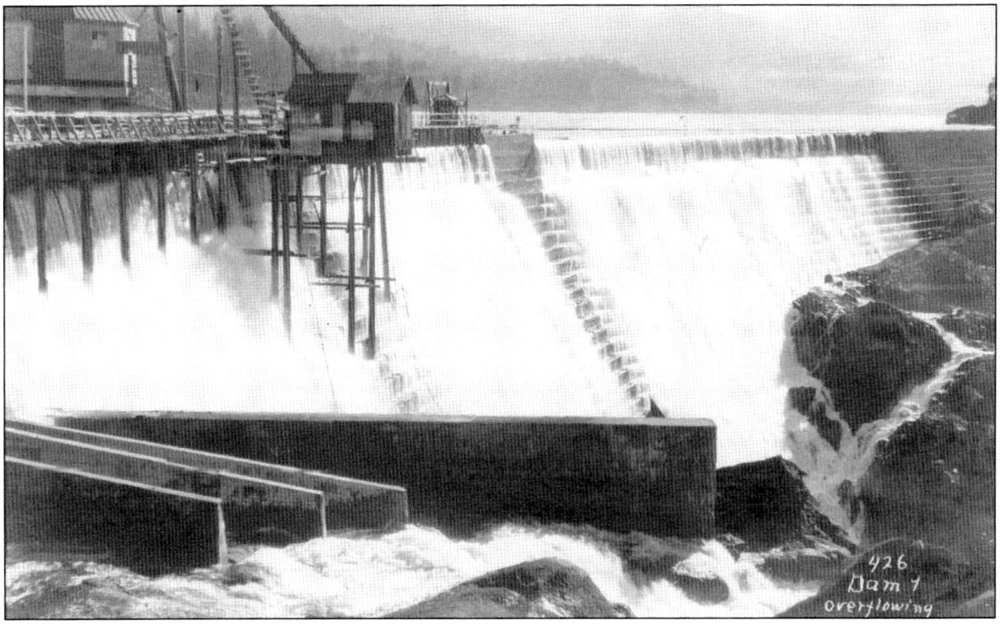

Dam No. 1 at Huntington Lake, completed in 1913, was raised 35 feet in 1917. Raising the level of Huntington Lake increased the storage capacity to about 89,000 acre-feet. The intake tower at top left was also raised and enclosed to protect the machinery that operated the gate that controlled water flow to the powerhouse. This unusual photograph shows the dam overflowing. (Fresno County Public Library.)

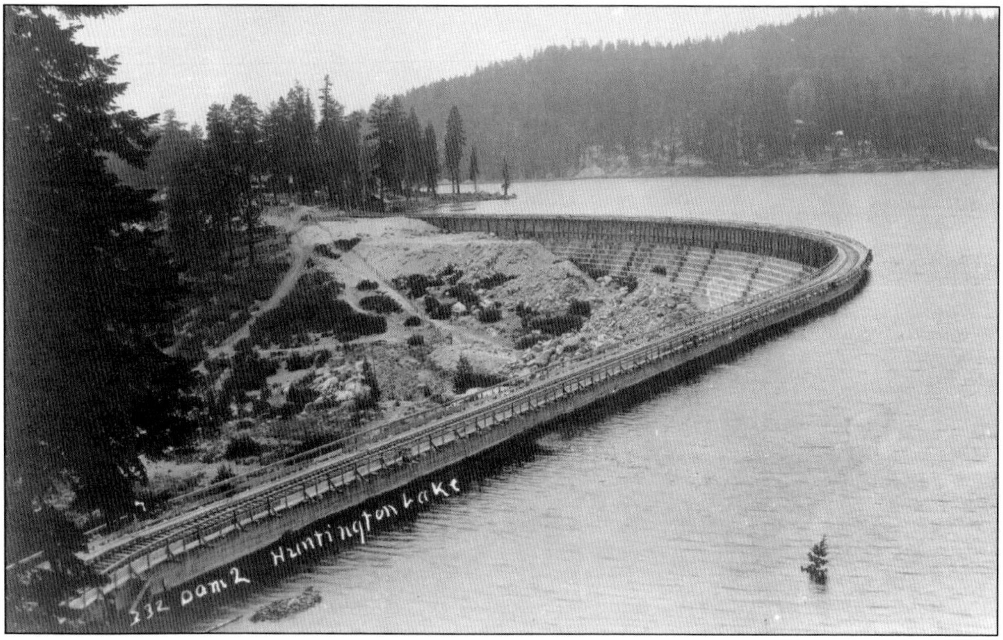

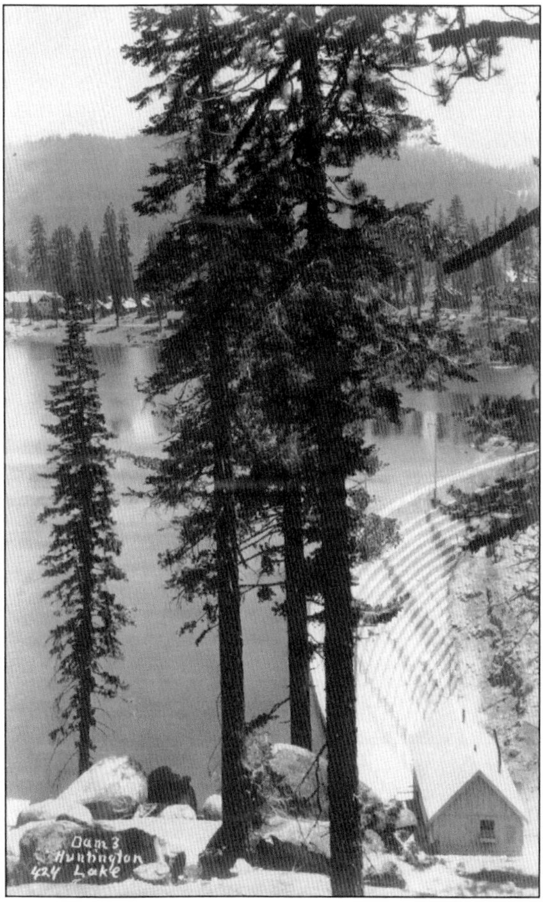

Dam No. 2 was the middle of the three dams that created Huntington Lake. It was built by the Pacific Light & Power Company and was completed early in 1913. This dam was also raised in 1917. This real-photo postcard was made by A.C. Mudge, the principal photographer of Huntington Lake, where he had his studio.

Dam No. 3 was the westernmost and smallest of the three dams that created Huntington Lake. Construction on the dams started with clearing and excavation in 1912. This was the first phase of the Big Creek Hydroelectric Project. The lake needed to be full when Powerhouse No. 1 was completed so electricity could be transmitted to Los Angeles. The dams were completed by December 1913.

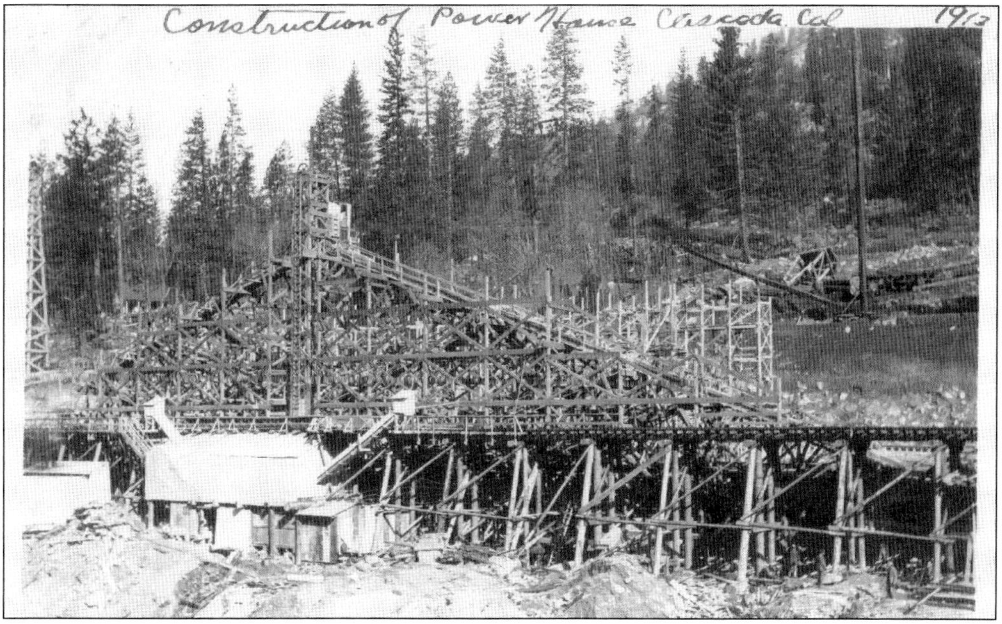

The Big Creek Hydroelectric Project marked the transition from the construction of isolated power plants serving local markets to the construction of large integrated systems connected to distant markets via high-voltage transmission. The project was among the world's largest hydroelectric systems at the time of its construction. Pacific Light & Power's contract with the Boston-based Stone & Webster Construction Company covered the construction of the 56-mile San Joaquin & Eastern Railroad, three dams to create Huntington Lake, Powerhouses Nos. 1 and 2, and the 240-mile transmission line to Los Angeles. At the end of 1912, excavation for the foundations of Powerhouse No. 1 was under way. In March 1913, the foundation was poured. The powerhouse structure was built in just three months, with the roof finished on July 18, 1913.

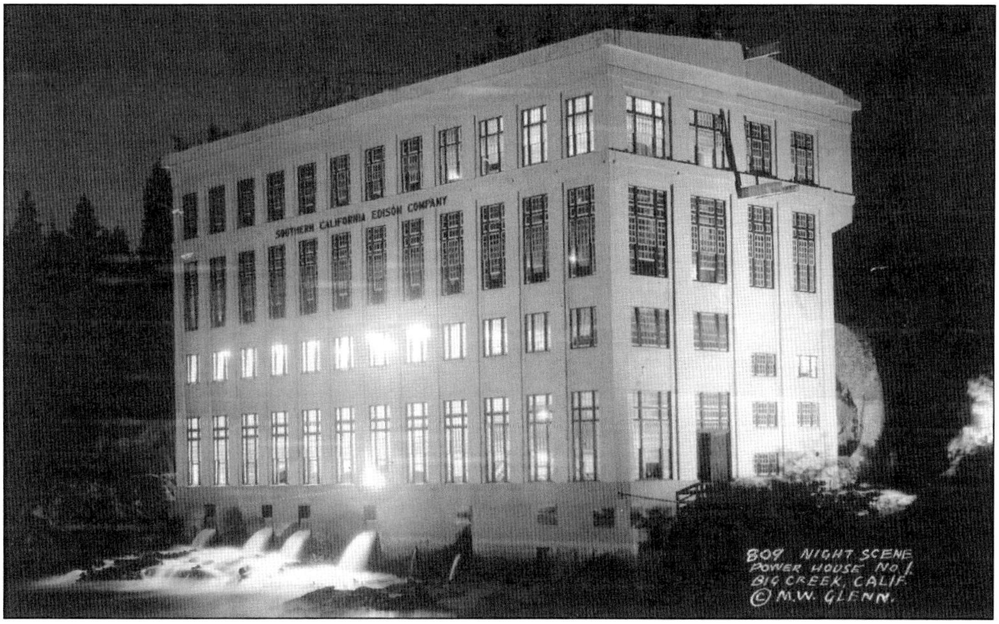

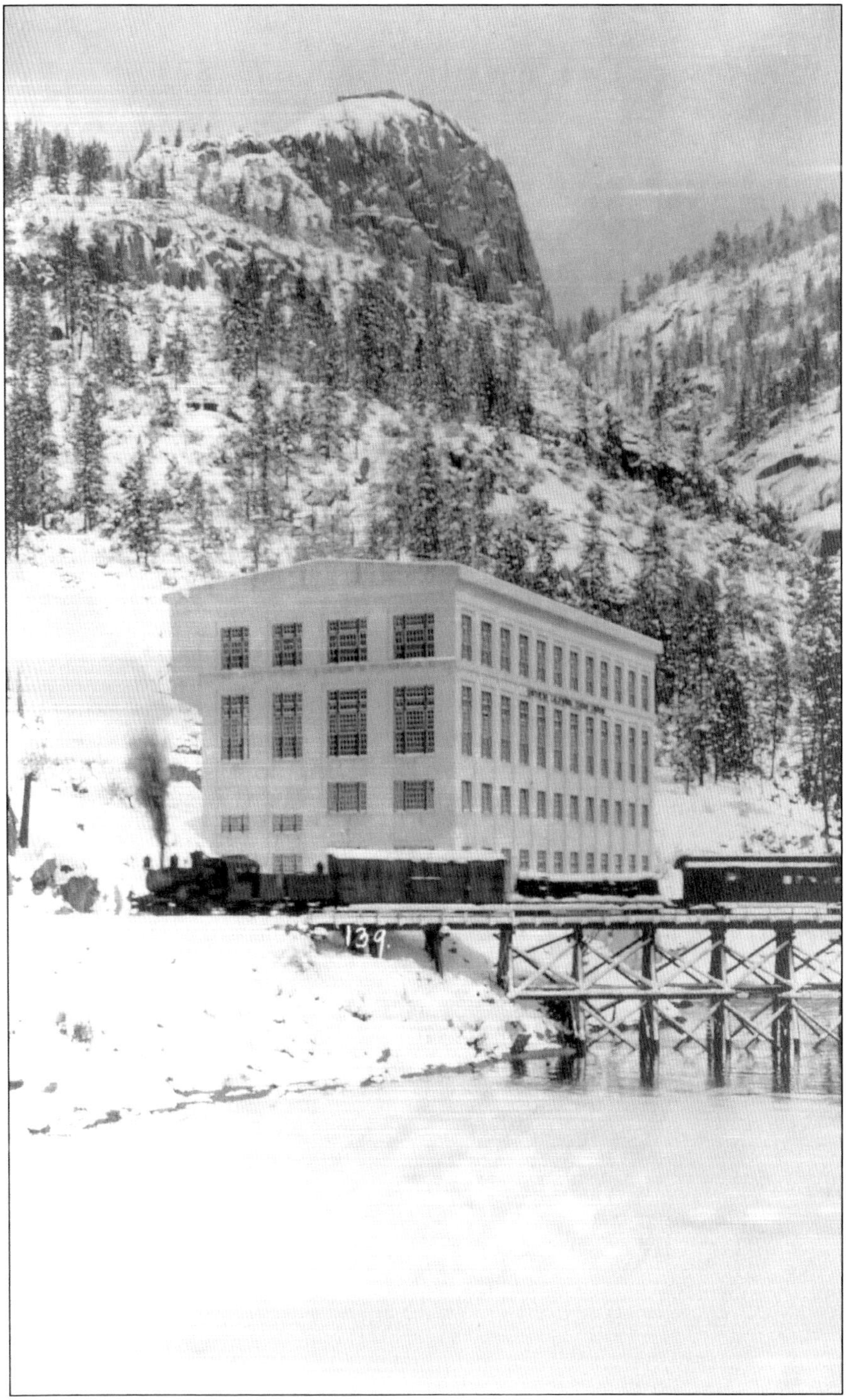

A mixed train steams across the San Joaquin & Eastern Railroad bridge over Big Creek in 1920 on its way to Cascada. The massive Powerhouse No. 1 was built between 1912 and 1913 on Big Creek below Huntington Lake. Snow-covered Kerckhoff Dome, at 6,321 feet, towers in the background.

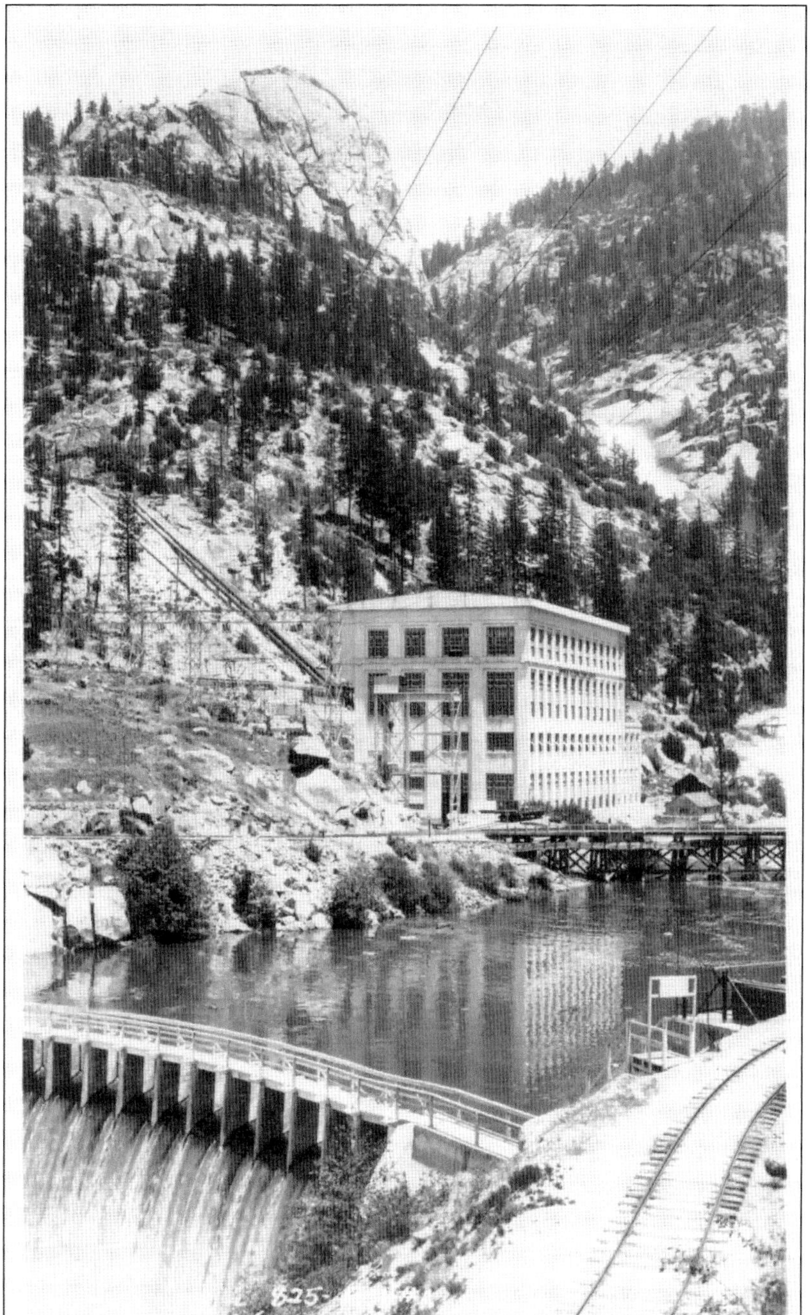

This powerhouse was part of the initial work of the Pacific Light & Power Company. A penstock, visible to the left of the powerhouse, carried water from Huntington Lake down the 2,100-foot drop to the powerhouse. The water in the foreground, impounded behind Dam No. 4, has already generated power and will pass through a four-mile-long tunnel to Powerhouse No. 2 to generate even more power. The Big Creek Hydroelectric Project was a massive and expensive undertaking, so every effort was made to maximize the electricity generated.

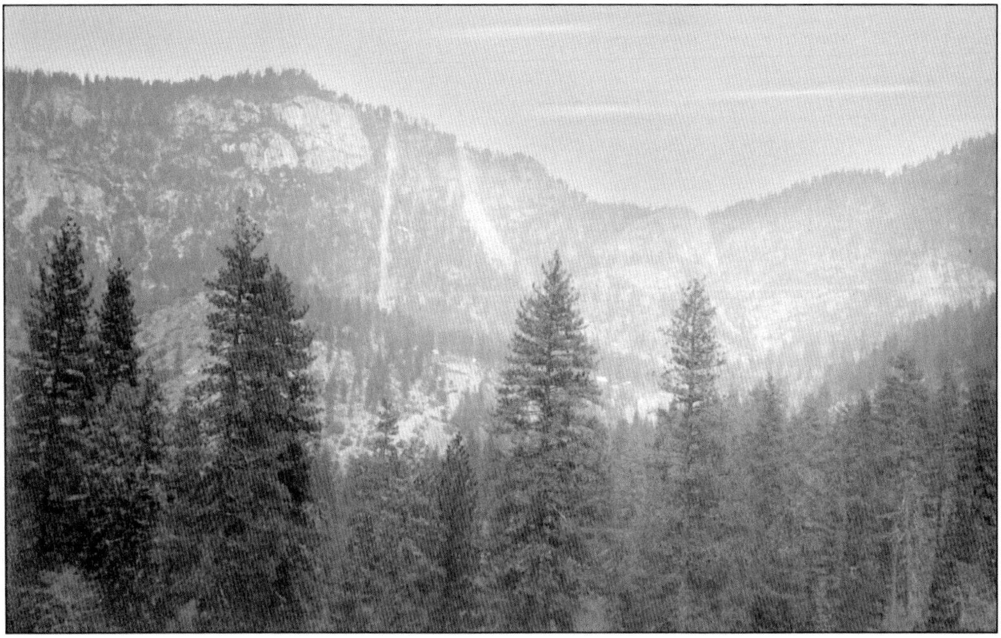

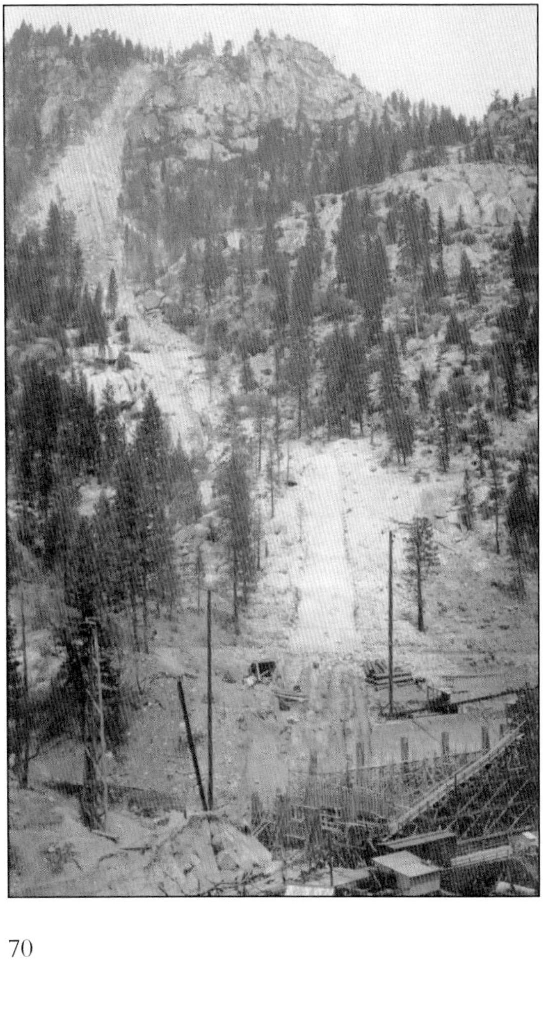

This photograph by Manley White shows the wide path of the penstocks carrying water from Huntington Lake, just over the ridge, to Powerhouse No. 1. The high-pressure pipe used for the penstocks was made in Germany. The sections of pipe were laid uphill from the powerhouse. The lines were kept full of water to keep the metal cool and more stable during construction.

The concrete foundation for Powerhouse No. 1, visible at bottom right, was poured during March 1913. The route of the high-pressure pipeline, or penstock, had been cleared prior to installation. This drop of 2,100 feet delivered 900 to 1,000 pounds of pressure per square inch to the buckets on the waterwheel in the generator.

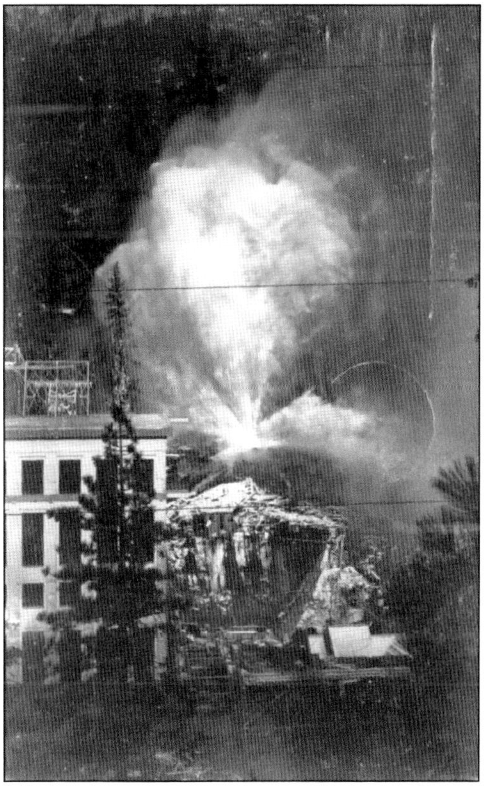

Shortly after going into regular service on November 10, 1913, Powerhouse No. 1 was struck by a disaster. On December 1, a flange joint pulled apart on the penstock just above the powerhouse. The dramatic fountain of water is clearly shown in the photograph at right. What made it worse is that the spray froze on all the surfaces. The gushing water also washed sand and mud down the hill and flooded the powerhouse. The gate at the head of the penstock had to be jacked shut to stop the flow of water through the pipe so repairs could be made. Everyone worked hard to clean up the mess and restore the powerhouse to operation as quickly as possible.

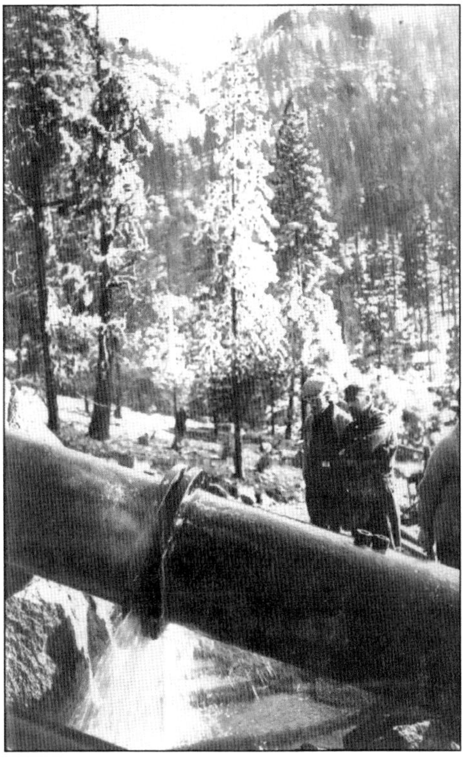

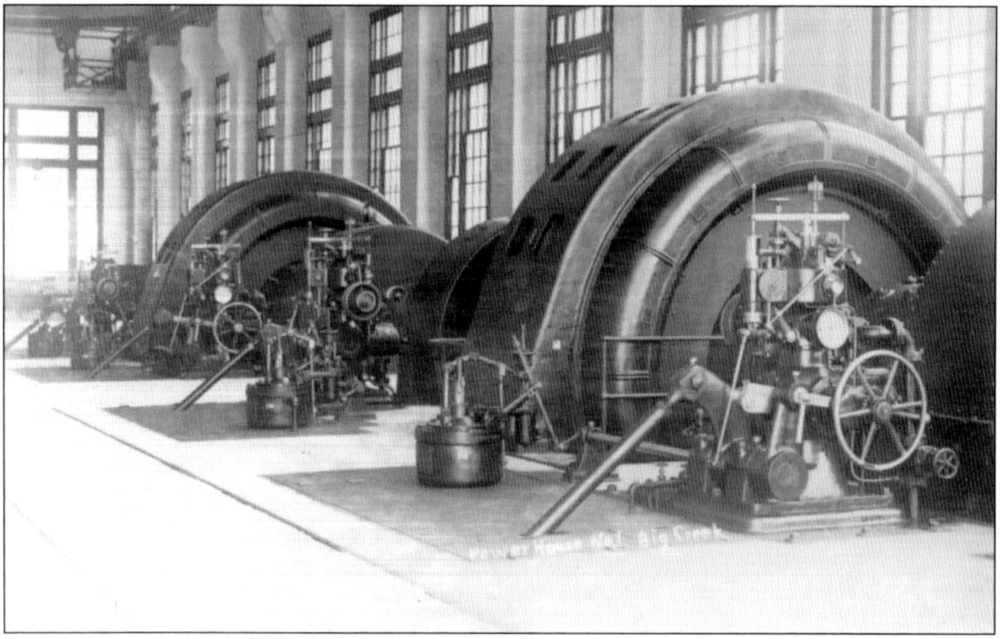

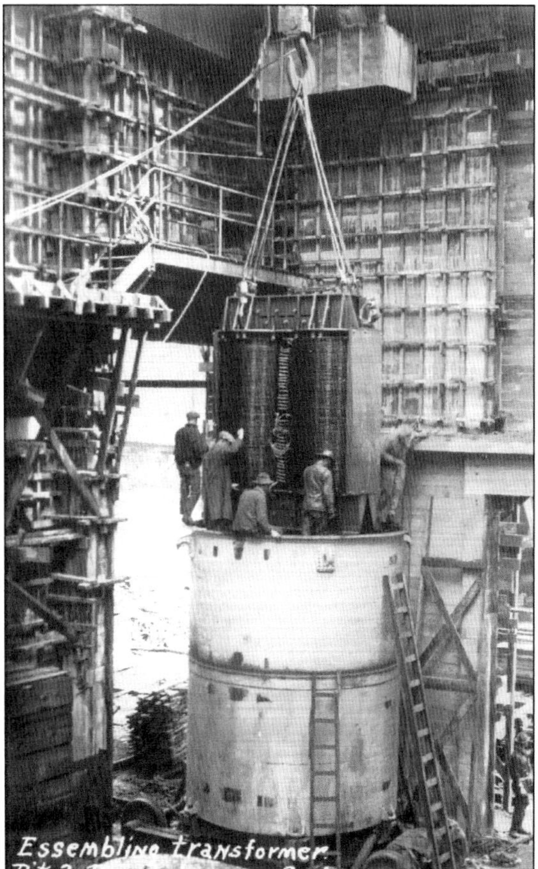

These 23,500-horsepower generators were installed in Powerhouse No. 1 and began delivering power locally on October 14, 1913. Eventually, most of the power from this and other powerhouses was transmitted to Los Angeles to help operate over 1,200 miles of electric railways, also called interurbans.

A transformer is being assembled in this photograph from the Big Creek Hydroelectric Project. Current from the generators, like those shown at the top of this image, was sent through step-up transformers, which increased the voltage. When the voltage was at the correct level, it was sent to the transmission lines leaving the plant. Powerhouse No. 3 had seven 200-kilovolt transformers when it was first constructed in 1923. (Fresno County Public Library.)

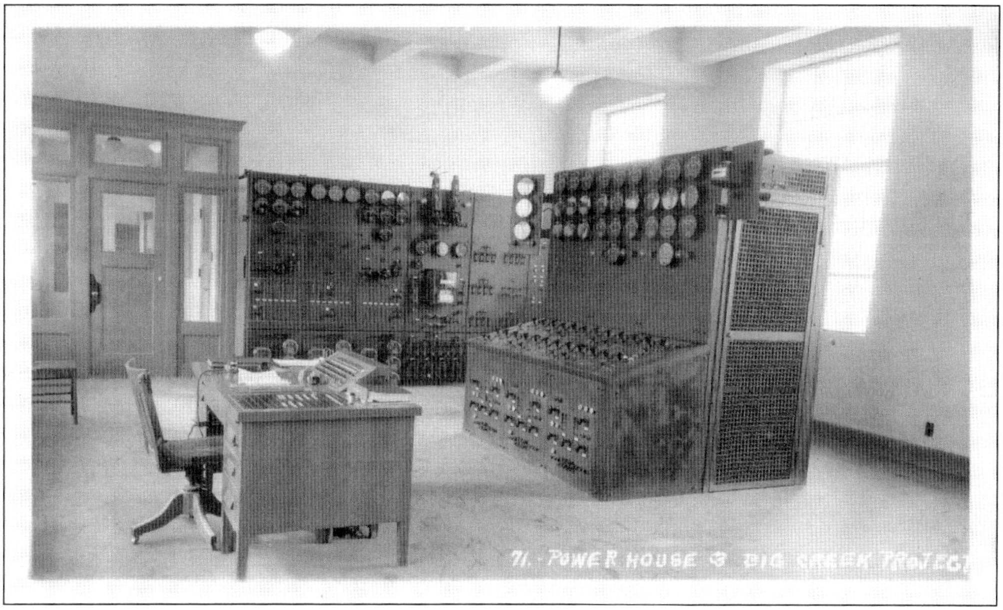

Powerhouse No. 3, located on the San Joaquin River, went into service in 1923. It was referred to as "the Electrical Wonder of the West" because it was the largest hydroelectric plant in the western United States. The control room, with switchboards purchased from Westinghouse, controlled the flow of electric current from multiple generators to multiple transformers and from the transformers to the transmission lines. (Fresno County Public Library.)

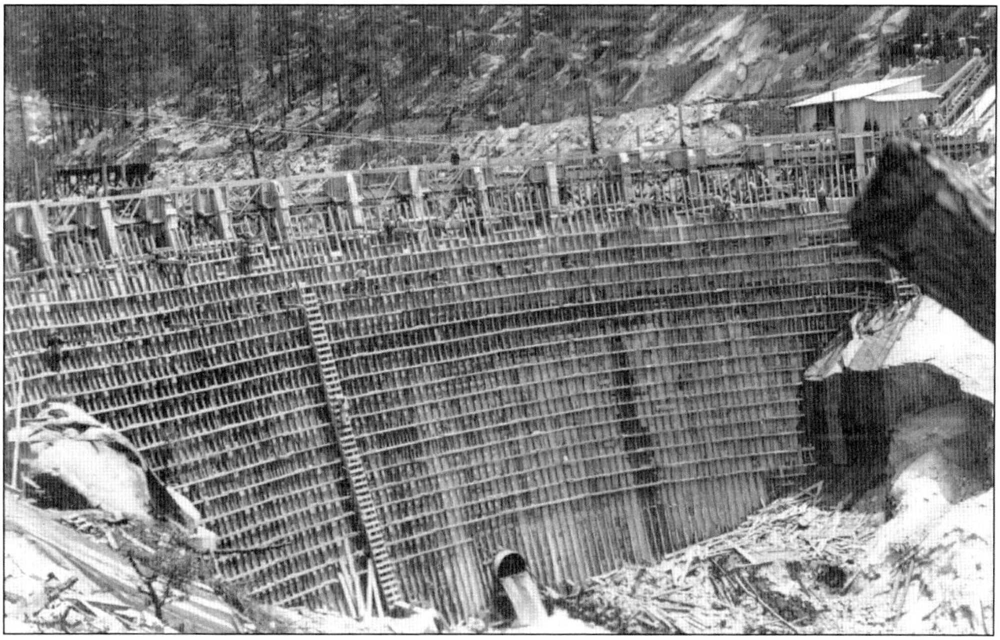

This photograph by Manley White shows Dam No. 4 under construction in 1913. This dam was located on Big Creek just below Powerhouse No. 1, and from here, the impounded water was diverted into a four-mile tunnel that ended at Powerhouse No. 2. There, the Big Creek water was once again used to generate electricity.

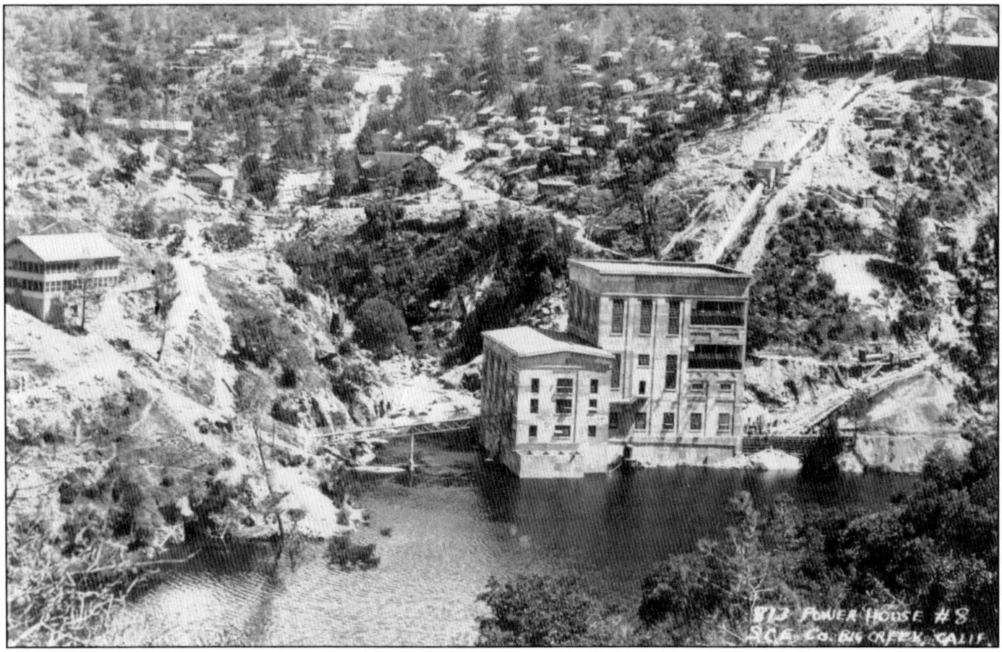

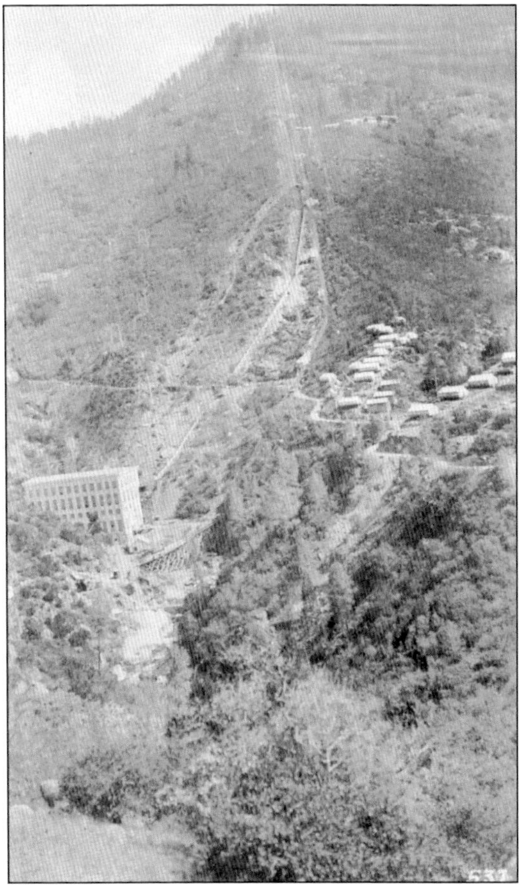

Powerhouse No. 8 was built between Nos. 2 and 3 as part of the Big Creek Hydroelectric Project. It was served by the San Joaquin & Eastern Railroad using a two-mile incline. Dam No. 5 was built below Powerhouse No. 2 to form a forebay for No. 8. The first concrete was poured May 12, 1921, and 90 days later, it was generating power.

Powerhouse No. 2 is shown in this real-photo postcard mailed from Big Creek in 1923. Camp 7 is visible at right, and Incline No. 2 can be seen coming down the steep slope to the same side. The penstock, at left, carried water that came through the tunnel from Dam No. 4, which was below Powerhouse No. 1, where the water had already been used to generate electricity.

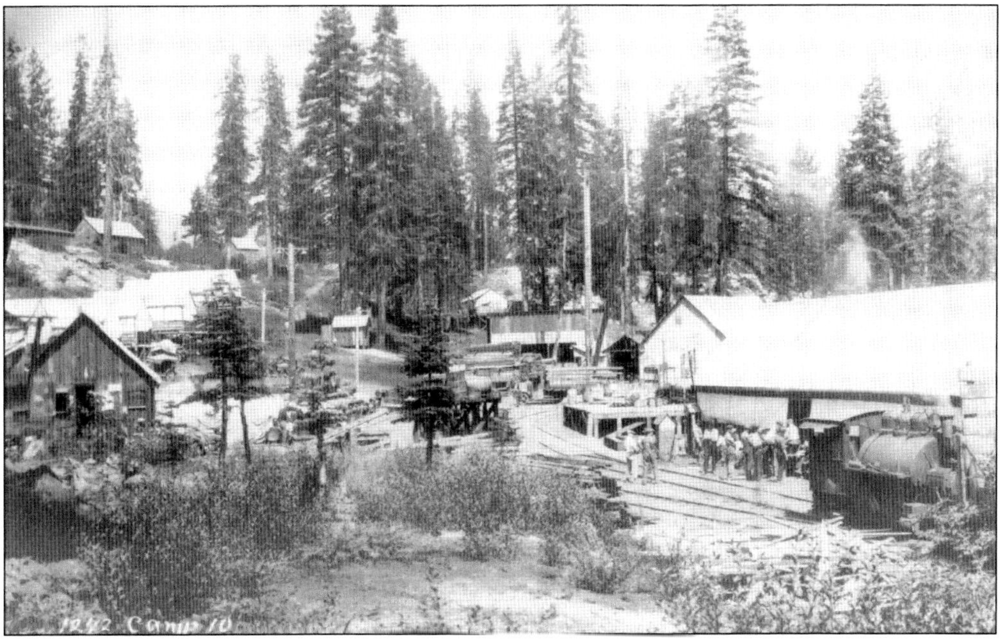

Camp 10 was one of the many camps established throughout the vast and rugged area of the Big Creek Hydroelectric Project. Southern California Edison realized that having camps near each job site was more efficient and economical. However, the logistics of supplying the camps with construction supplies and food was difficult. A construction locomotive is visible at right.

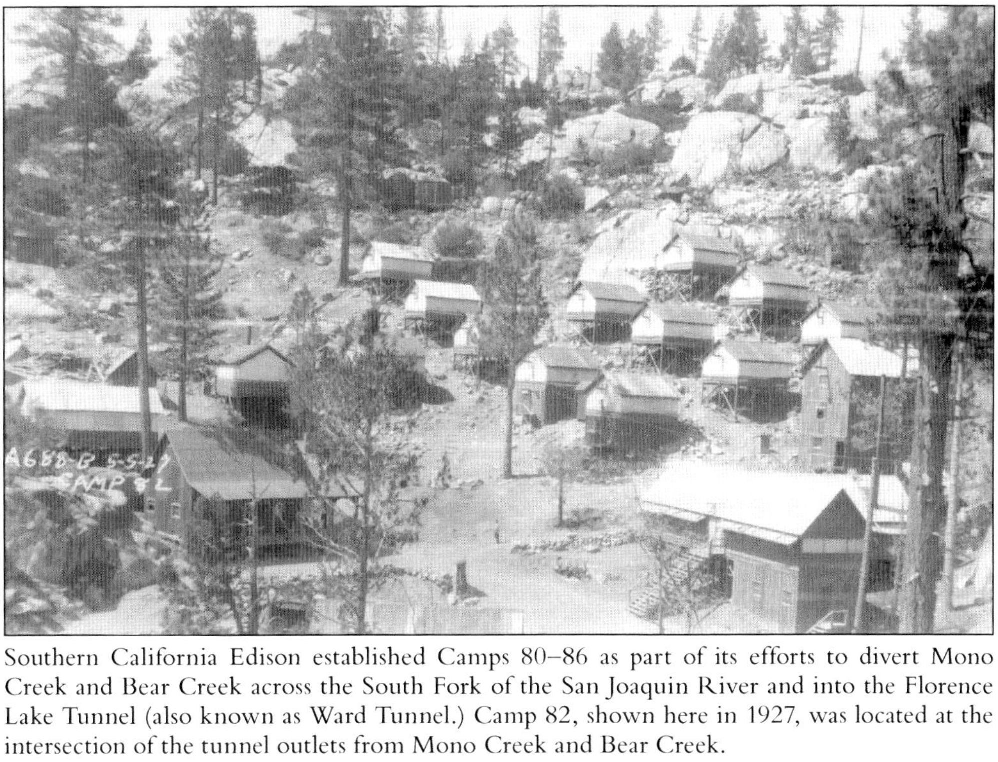

Southern California Edison established Camps 80–86 as part of its efforts to divert Mono Creek and Bear Creek across the South Fork of the San Joaquin River and into the Florence Lake Tunnel (also known as Ward Tunnel.) Camp 82, shown here in 1927, was located at the intersection of the tunnel outlets from Mono Creek and Bear Creek.

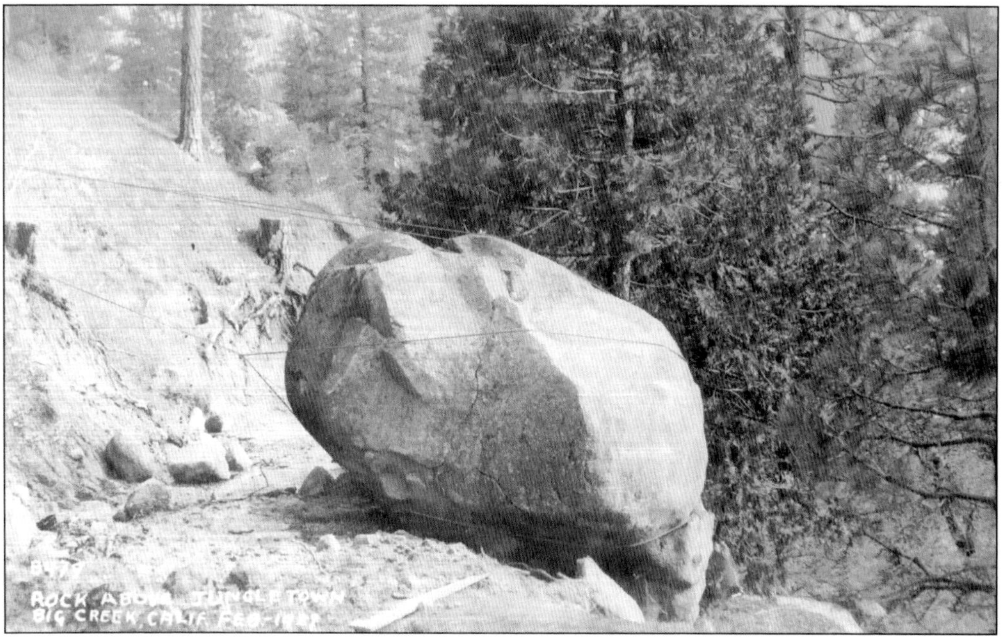

This large granite boulder, resting precariously on the road above "Jungle Town," must have been considered a threat to the camp near Big Creek. Someone installed cables to hold the boulder in place and keep it from rolling farther downhill.

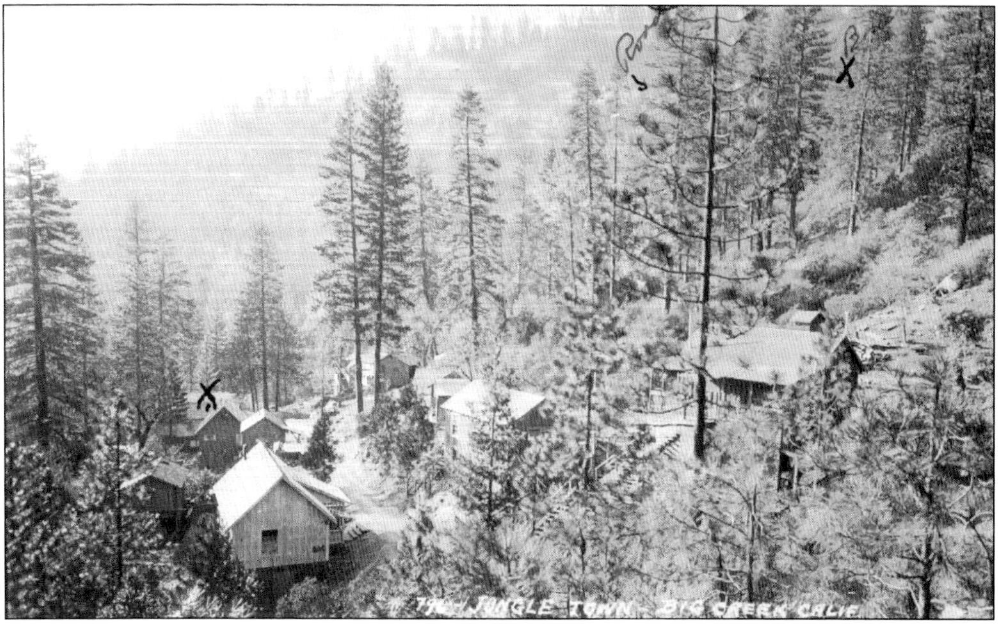

This assortment of cabins perched on the hillside was known as "Jungle Town" and probably served as housing for workers on the Big Creek Hydroelectric Project. Near the top right, someone has written "road" and "boulder," which refers to the large granite boulder in the previous photograph. Both cards are by Murphy's Art Shop in Big Creek.

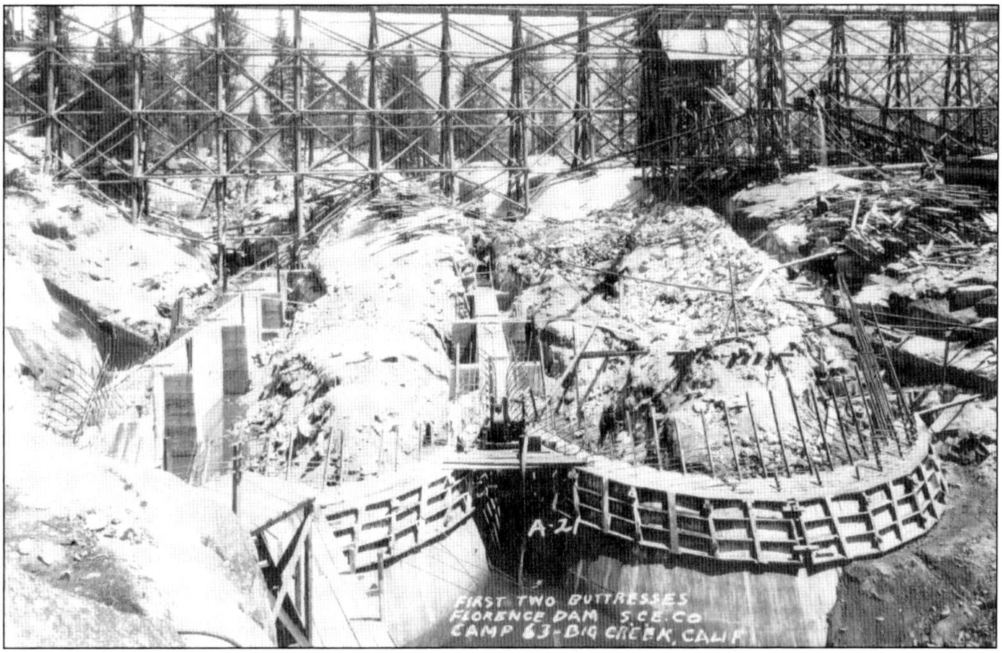

The Florence Lake dam was built in upper Jackass Meadow on the South Fork of the San Joaquin River at an elevation of about 7,000 feet. Both the site and design for the dam were selected after extensive studies and careful consideration. This was a very remote location, so the cost of transporting construction material from the railhead at Cascada became a major factor. It was decided that the rails from constructing the Florence Tunnel could be removed and used to reinforce the concrete. Also, the granite removed from the tunnel could be crushed for aggregate. The first two buttresses of the multiple-arch Florence Dam were photographed by Murphy's Art Shop shortly after the first concrete was poured on March 4, 1925. There would eventually be 58 buttresses, or arches.

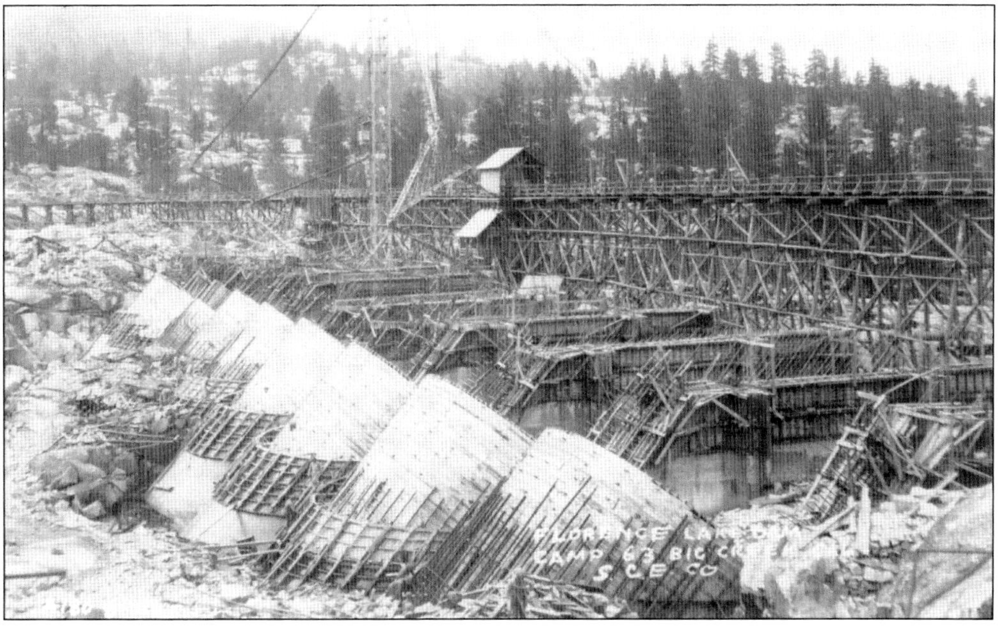

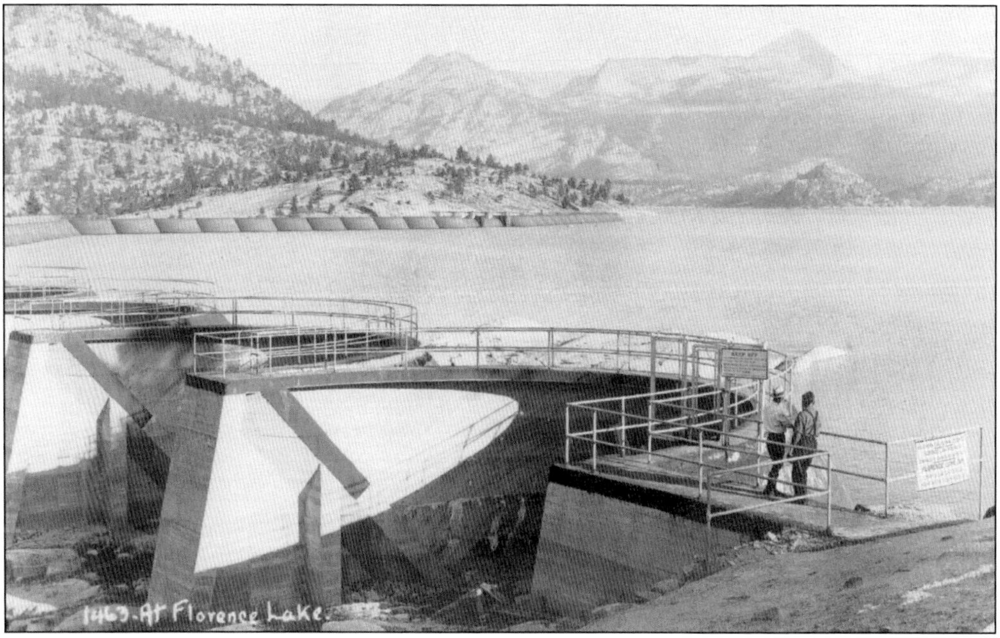

The Florence Lake Dam, at 3,200 feet long, was the longest dam of its type ever built when it was completed on August 15, 1926. Construction on the dam began after the Florence Lake Tunnel (also known as Ward Tunnel) was completed. The arch design is credited to John S. Eastwood, who also designed the dam at Hume Lake for the Hume-Bennett Lumber Company. In 1925, a sawmill was moved from Camp 61 at the entrance to the tunnel to upper Jackass Meadow. As trees were cut to clear what would become the lake, they were sent through the sawmill, and the lumber was used in construction of the dam. The lake has a storage capacity of over 64,000 acre-feet of water.

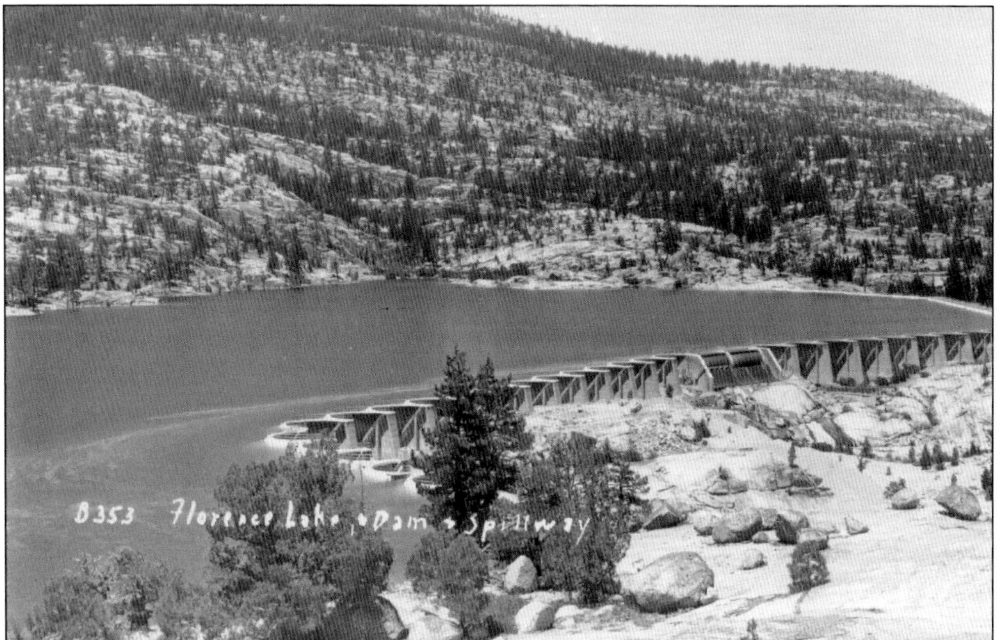

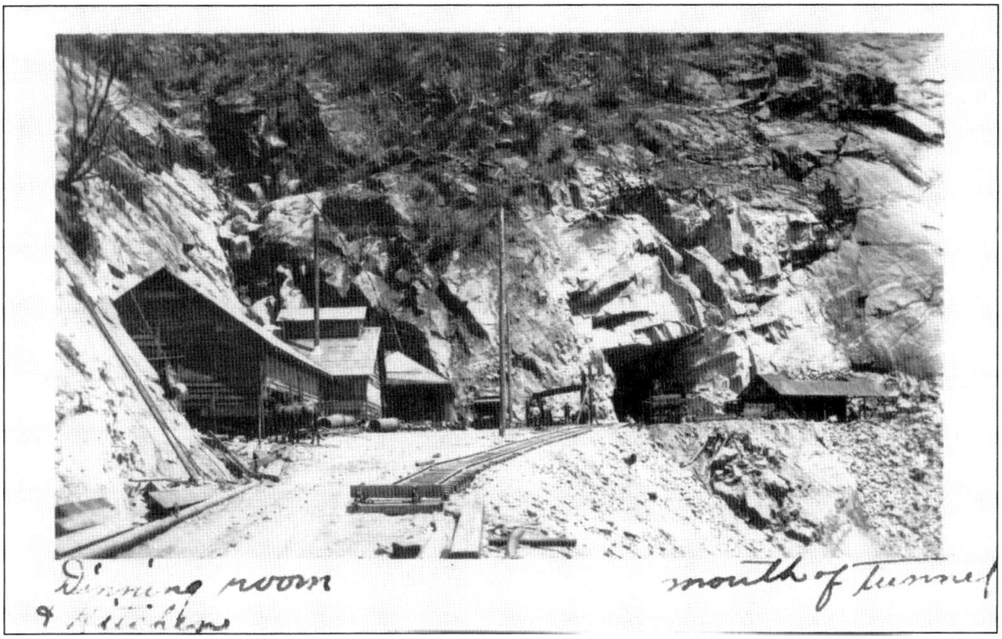

The north portal of the Florence Lake Tunnel was on the Florence Lake side of Kaiser Ridge. Camp 60, which was kept open year-round, was at this end of the tunnel. The entire Big Creek Hydroelectric Project employed about 5,000 people. Feeding these hungry crews was a huge task that involved getting food to these remote locations and preparing and serving the meals.

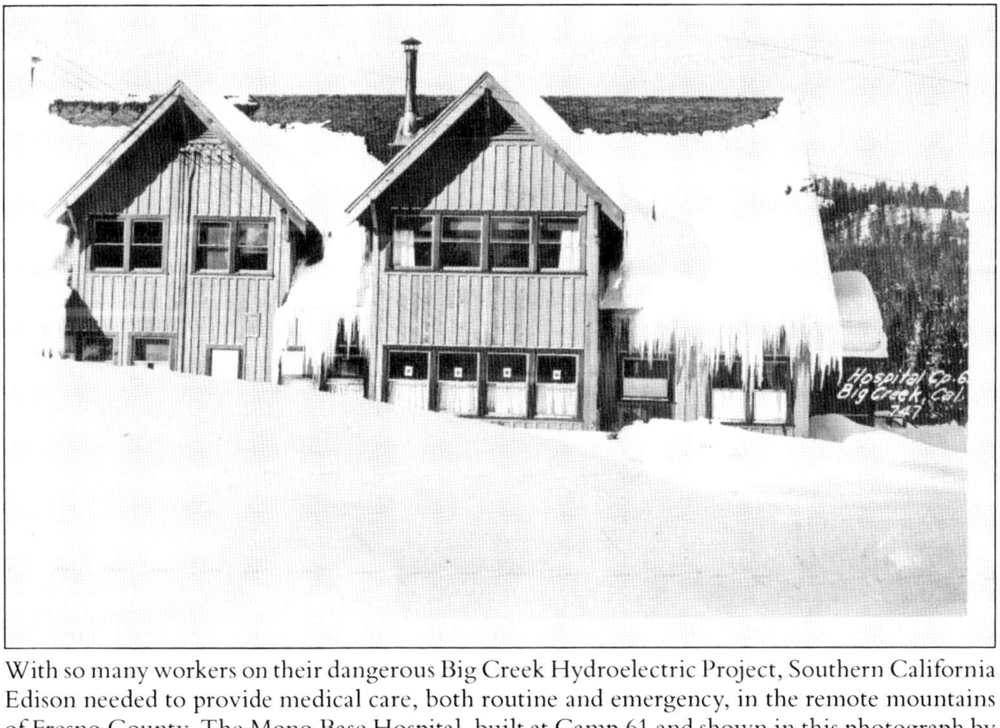

With so many workers on their dangerous Big Creek Hydroelectric Project, Southern California Edison needed to provide medical care, both routine and emergency, in the remote mountains of Fresno County. The Mono Base Hospital, built at Camp 61 and shown in this photograph by Murphy's Art Shop, served all the camps on the Huntington Lake side of Kaiser Pass.

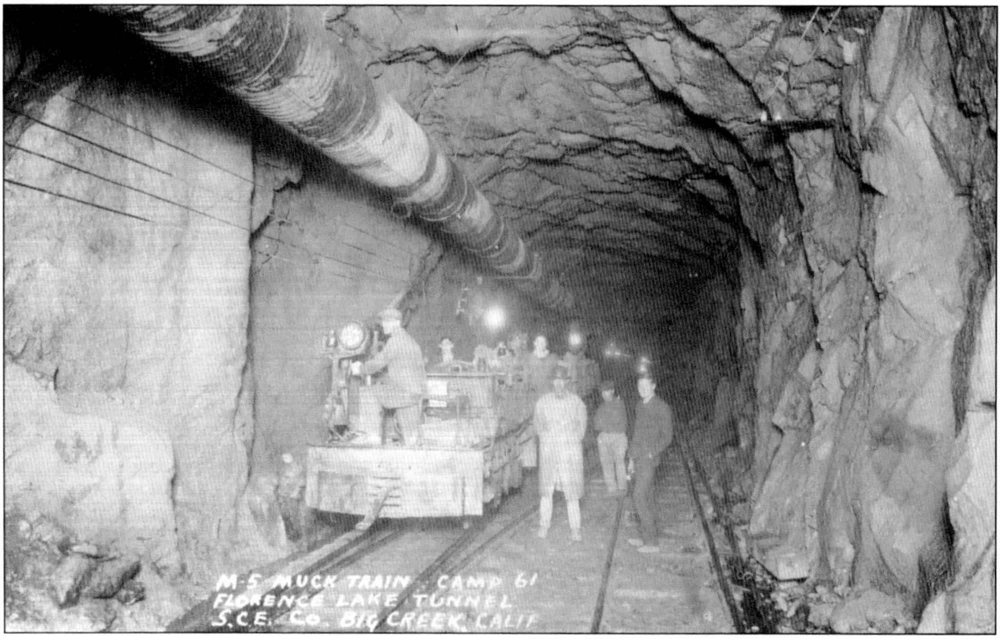

A lot of rock was hauled out of the 15-by-15-foot, 6.5-mile-long Florence Lake Tunnel. The muck trains used an adit, which was completed in February 1922, and stayed very busy hauling out rock during construction. The project took four and a half years to complete, even though construction was year-round with three eight-hour shifts.

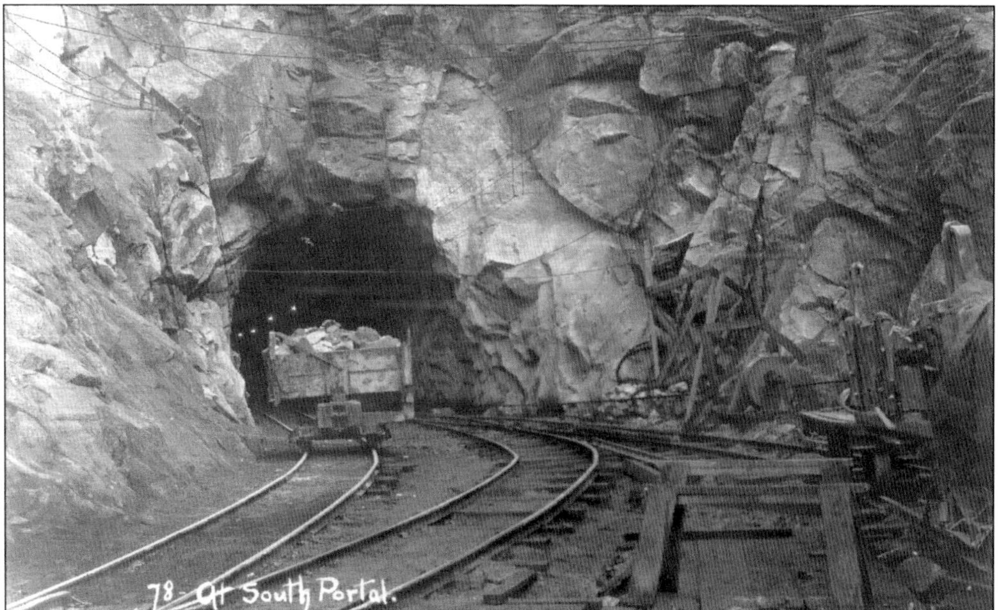

The south portal of the Florence Lake Tunnel was on the Huntington Lake side of Kaiser Ridge. Camp 60 was at this end of the tunnel. A special, small power shovel that moved on rails was used in the cramped space to load blasted rock into the muck cars like this one.

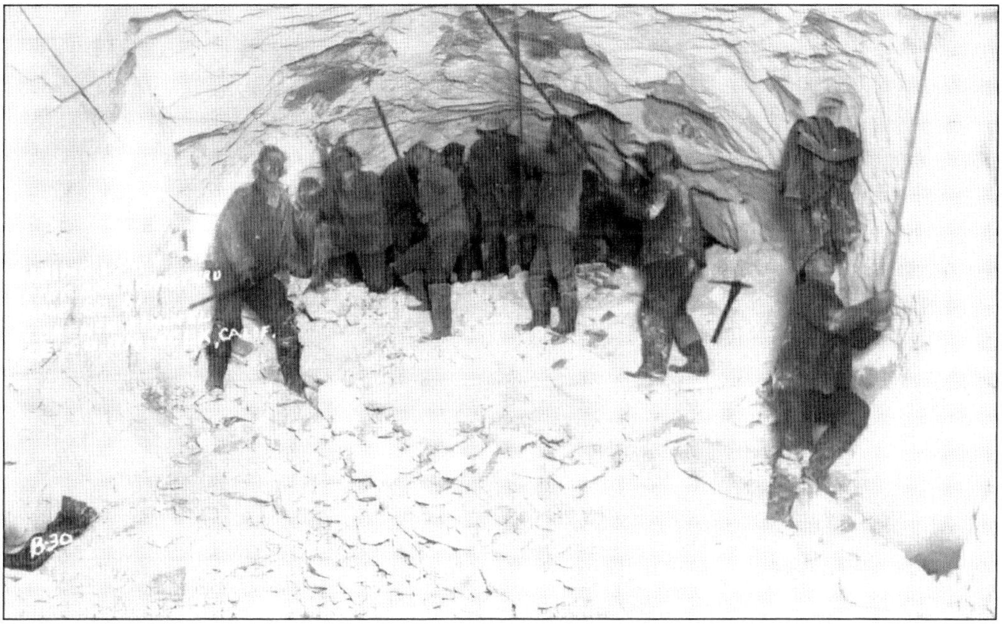

The Florence Lake Tunnel was constructed under Kaiser Ridge to transport water from Florence Lake to Huntington Lake. The final breakthrough on the tunnel occurred on the night of February 18, 1925. A relieved crew is shown "baring down after breaking thru." In 1936, Southern California Edison renamed the tunnel the Ward Tunnel after their former president, George Clinton Ward (1863–1933.)

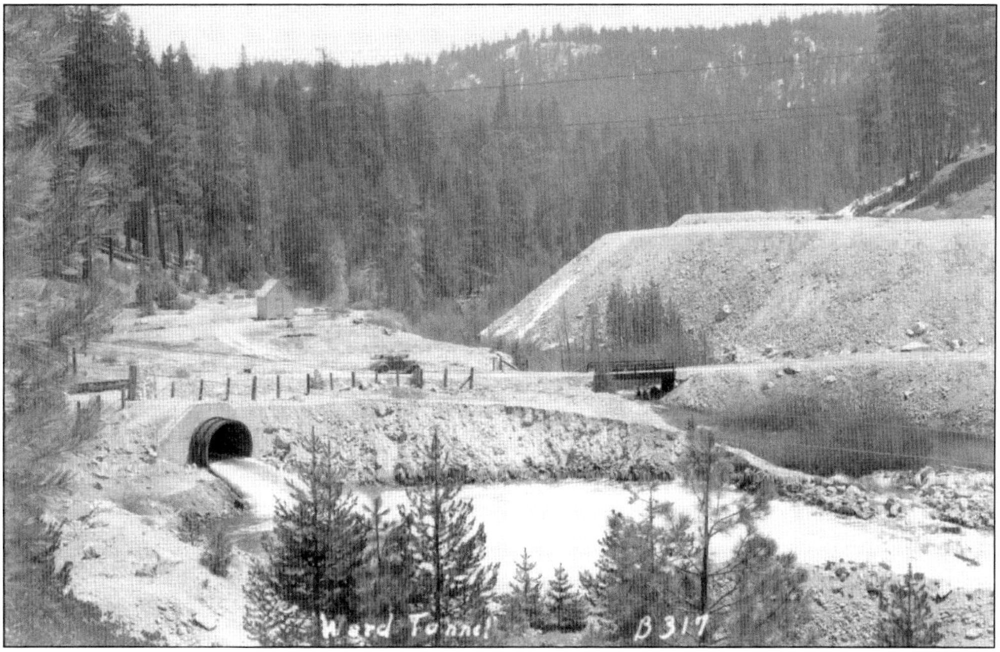

The first water was sent through the tunnel on April 13, 1925. Previously, however, the existing railroad in the tunnel had been used to haul material for the construction of Florence Lake Dam. The trial wooden flume, shown on the following page, was eventually replaced with the metal pipe shown here.

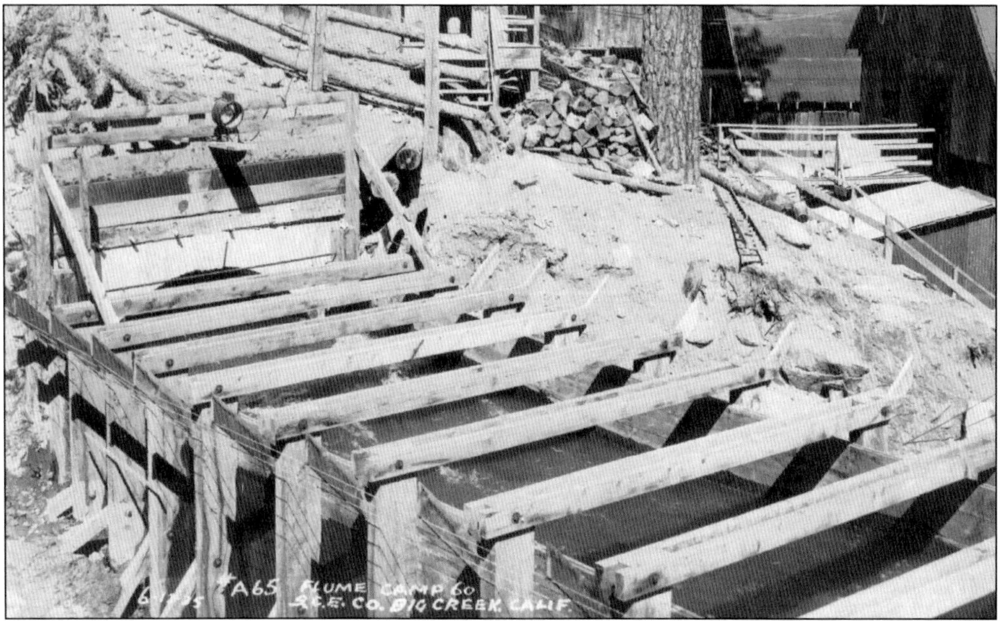

Camp 60, just above Huntington Lake, was the outlet for the Florence Lake Tunnel. The first water was released through the tunnel on April 13, 1925. However, there was concern that the large flow of water would undercut the glacial material at the outlet, so this 1,000-foot wooden flume was constructed. The flume is shown on June 12, 1925, in this photograph by Murphy's Art Shop.

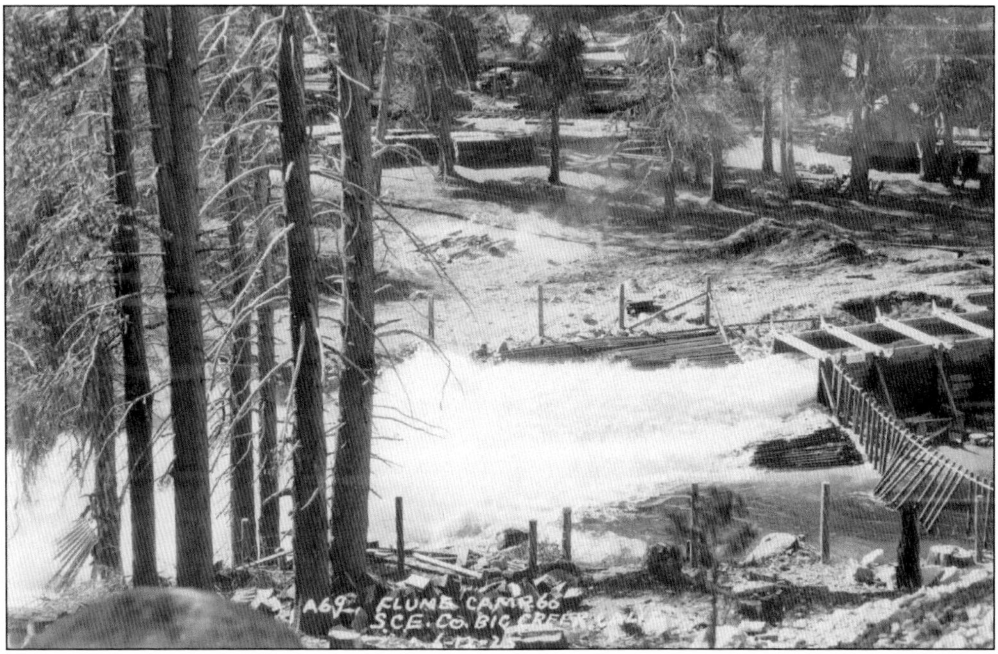

The end of the 1,000-foot flume, shown in this photograph by Murphy's Art Shop, discharged onto a mat of metal rails very near the edge of Huntington Lake. Two years of observation showed no erosion or undercutting problems. With that success, the wooden flume was replaced by 300 feet of 12-foot-diameter riveted pipe.

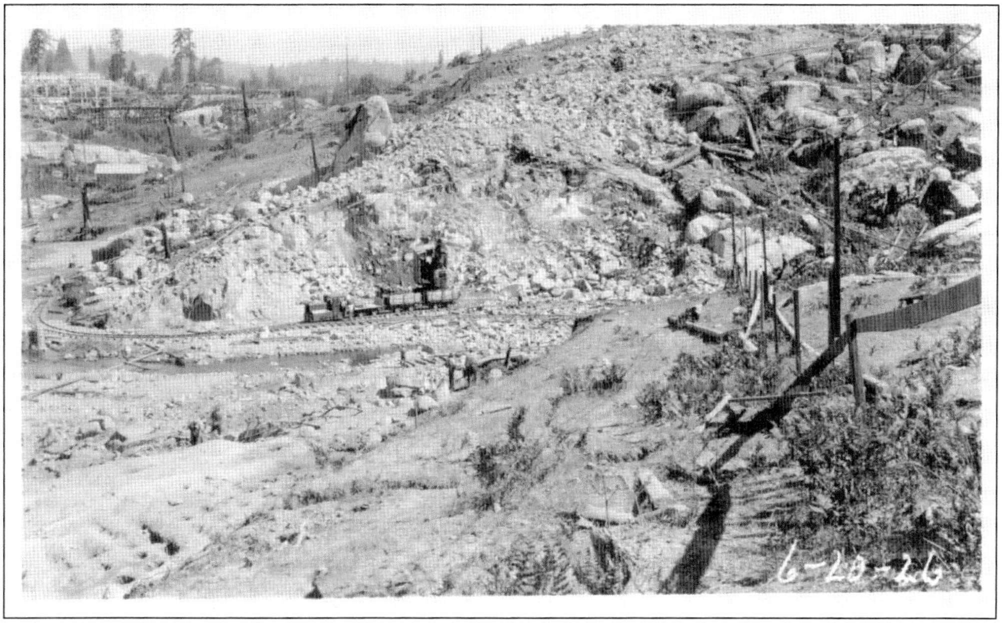

Southern California Edison bought the idle Shaver lumber property in 1919, and site preparation on the new Shaver dam started in May 1926. Dwarfed by the landscape, a trolley locomotive waits on the narrow-gauge track, while the railcars are loaded with rock from the quarry. Loading was done by a steam shovel, and then the rock was taken to a rock-crushing plant for later use in concrete for the dam.

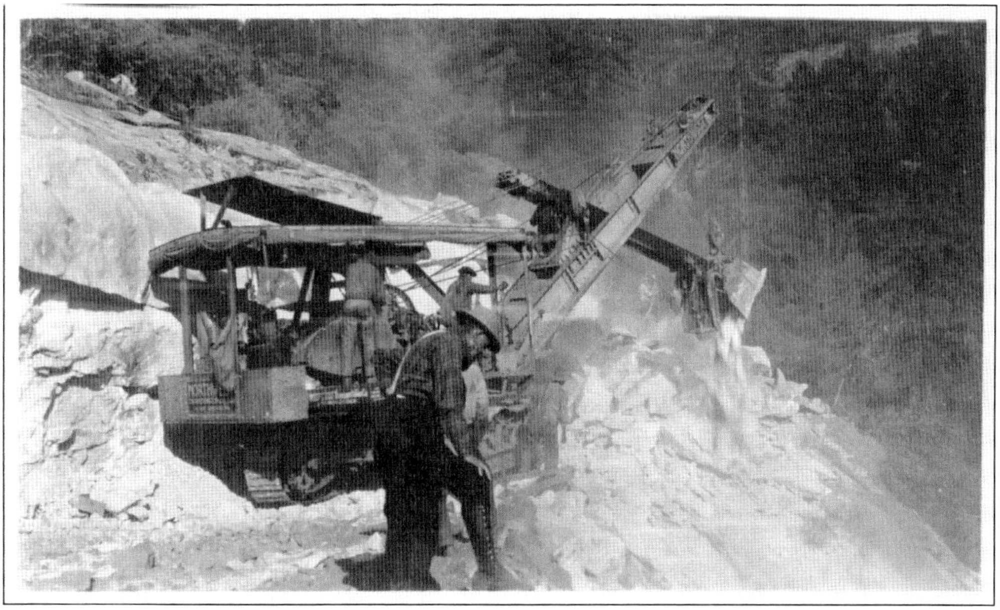

Constructing the 2,200-foot-long dam required a large amount of materials and equipment. Roads and a 4.6-mile-long spur railroad were constructed to the new dam site, which was below the much smaller rock dam built in 1893 for logging operations. In this 1926 photograph, a Northwest Engineering Company power shovel is hard at work.

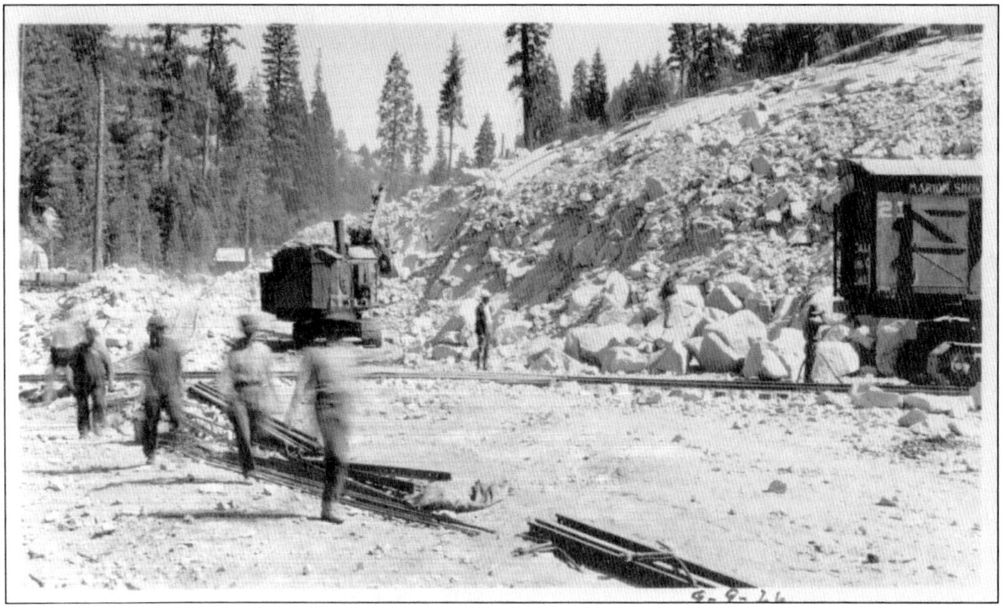

Construction workers walk toward the camera as power shovels noisily work in the background. In September 1926, site preparation work was well under way for the new dam at Shaver. A Marion power shovel with caterpillar tracks is at right, while a steam shovel digs rock in the background. The railroad tracks were for the railcars that moved granite to the crusher.

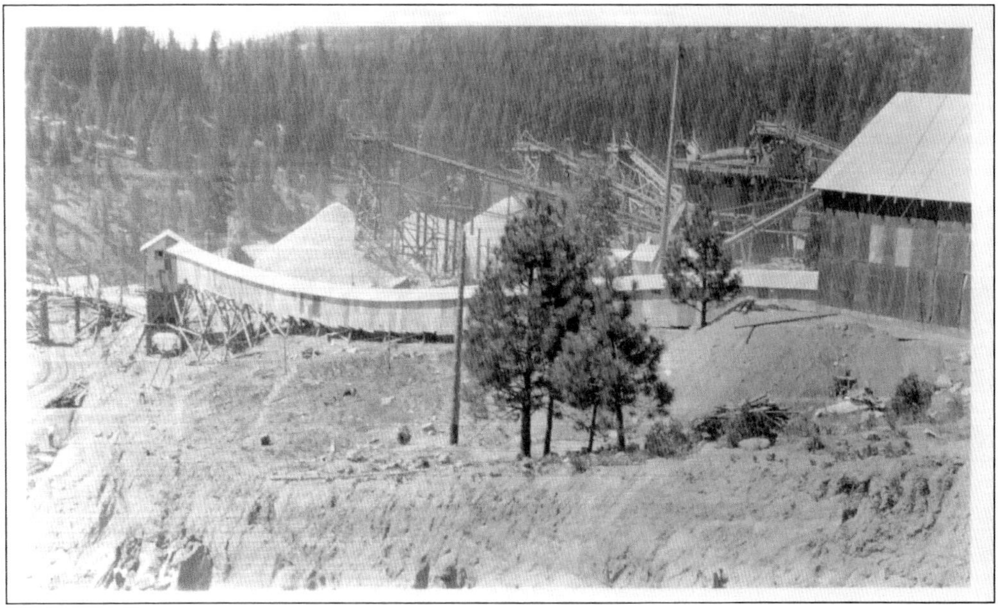

Quarried rock, hauled by narrow-gauge railroad to the crusher at right, was being stockpiled in various sizes for construction of the dam. With a thickness of 125 feet at the base and a maximum height of 183 feet, the dam was going to take a lot of concrete. Making the concrete required a large amount of sand and gravel, which came from the immediate area.

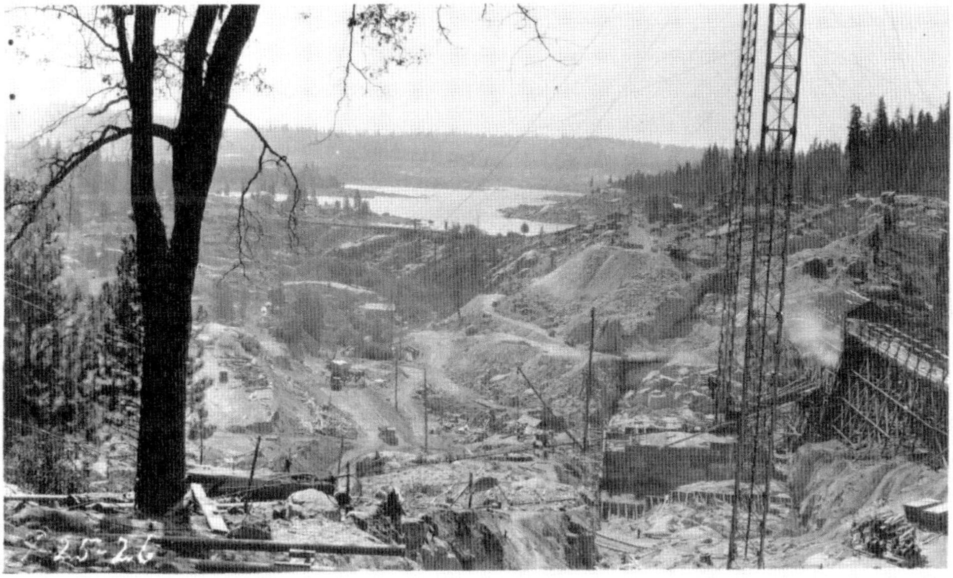

The Shaver dam construction site was a busy place just days after the first concrete was poured on September 21, 1926. The foundation had been excavated to bedrock, which is visible curving around to the right on the far side. The forms, filled with concrete, are also visible. In the background are the first Shaver dam and lake.

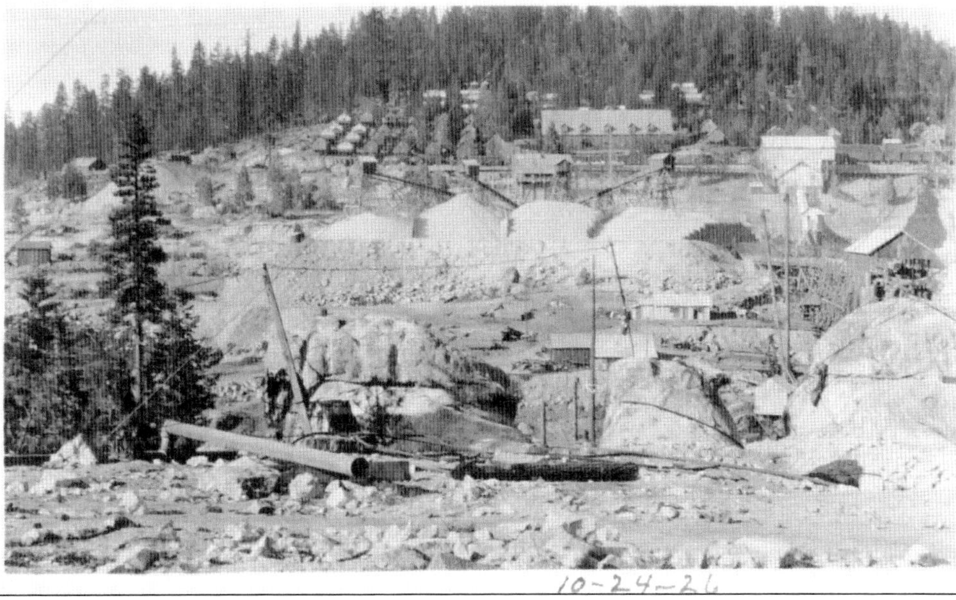

Four piles of crushed rock are visible in this 1926 photograph. Just beyond the rock-crushing plant are the railroads. The narrow-gauge railroad brought rock to the crusher, and the standard-gauge railroad brought all manner of supplies, including food, to the construction camp. The large mess hall, with seating for several hundred men, also had sleeping quarters upstairs. Bunkhouses and other support buildings are also visible on the hillside.

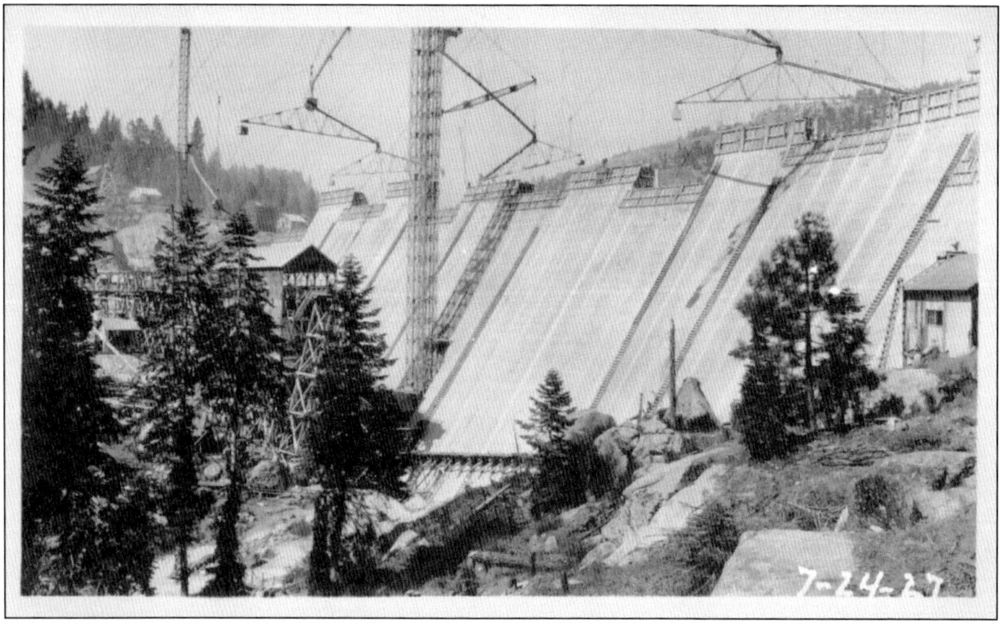

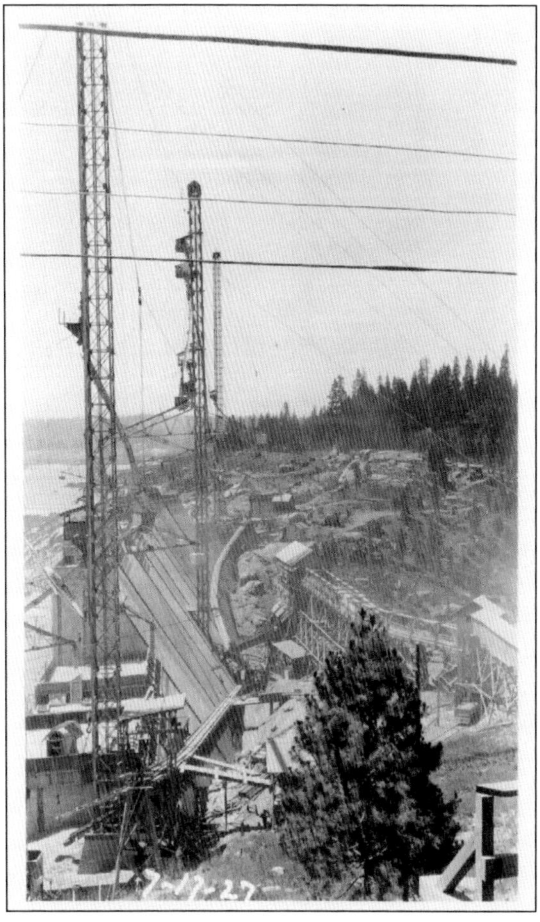

This view, looking up at the dam, gives a good idea of just how big this project was. The photograph was taken a few months before the structure was completed. It is a concrete gravity dam, which is stable because the weight of the concrete resists the pressure from the 135,000 acre-feet of water that became Shaver Lake.

Due to freezing temperatures, work on the dam was halted December 4, 1926. With the arrival of spring, work resumed April 1, 1927. Construction had progressed well by the time this photograph was taken in the middle of July. The dam was built in 50-foot blocks, and the steel towers, with all their cable rigging, provided support for the chutes that distributed the concrete.

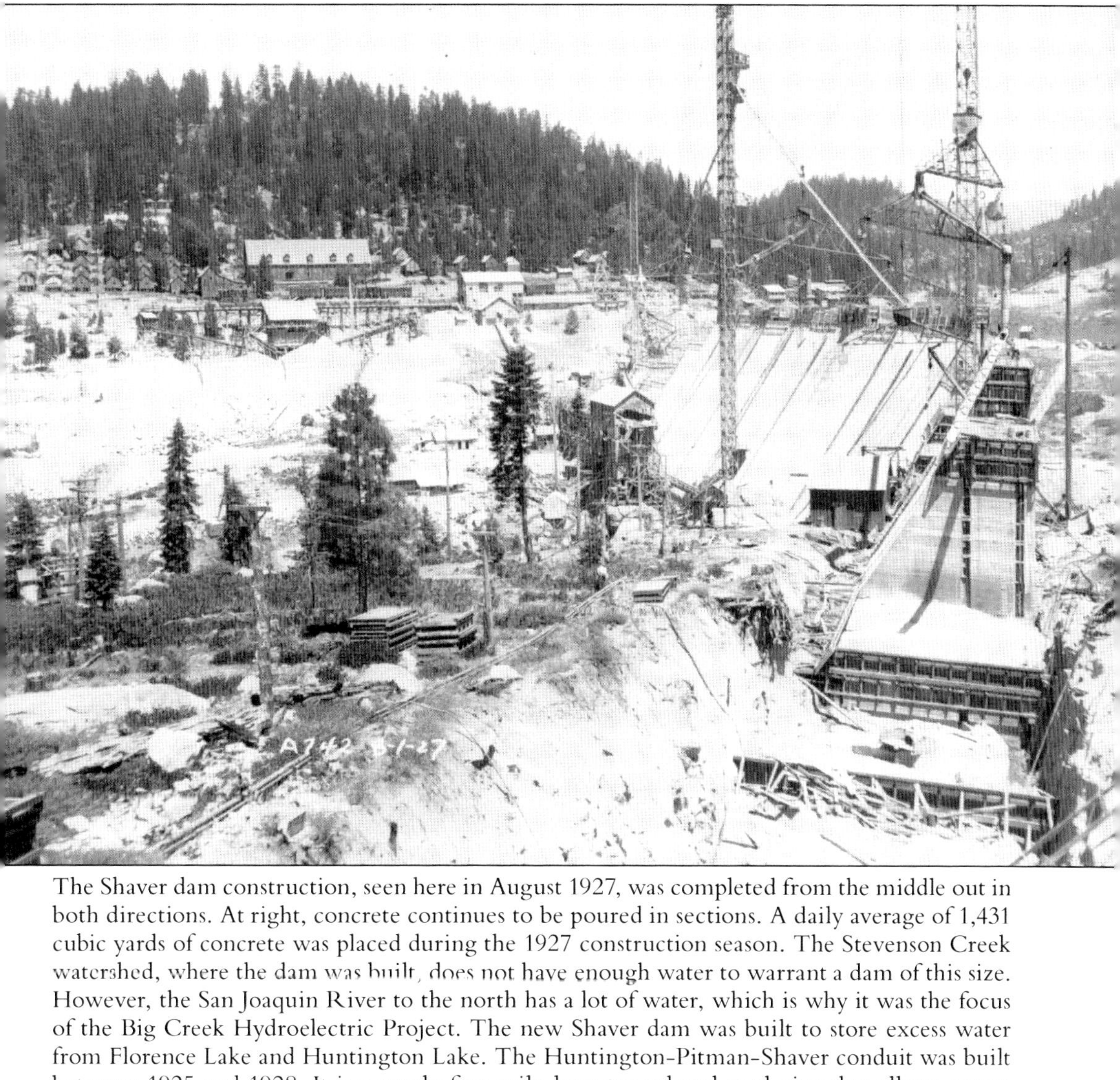

The Shaver dam construction, seen here in August 1927, was completed from the middle out in both directions. At right, concrete continues to be poured in sections. A daily average of 1,431 cubic yards of concrete was placed during the 1927 construction season. The Stevenson Creek watershed, where the dam was built, does not have enough water to warrant a dam of this size. However, the San Joaquin River to the north has a lot of water, which is why it was the focus of the Big Creek Hydroelectric Project. The new Shaver dam was built to store excess water from Florence Lake and Huntington Lake. The Huntington-Pitman-Shaver conduit was built between 1925 and 1928. It is a nearly five-mile-long tunnel and steel pipe that allows excess water to flow from Huntington Lake to Shaver Lake. The water from Shaver Lake is then sent through the Shaver Tunnel and a long penstock to Powerhouse No. 2A on Big Creek.

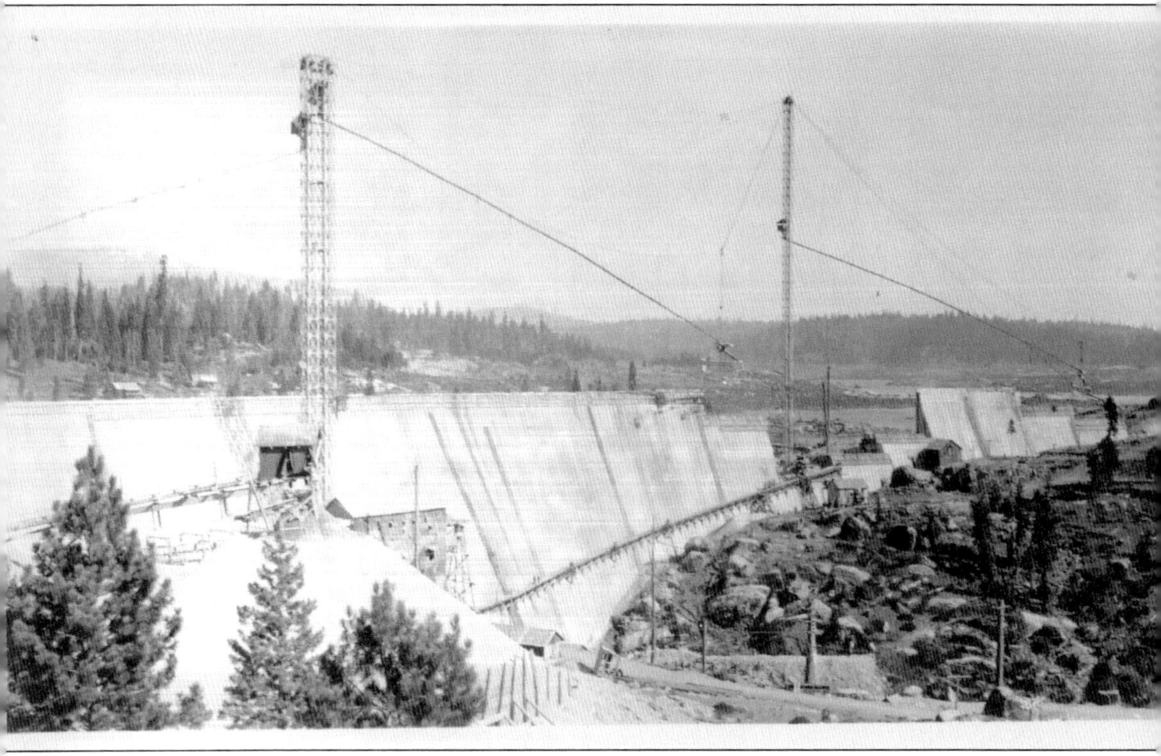

This photograph, taken on August 29, 1927, shows the second Shaver dam nearing completion. Construction on the new dam was completed a few months later on October 23, 1927. One final task was the clearing of the area that would become the reservoir. To accomplish this, the contractor burned all the remaining logging-related structures, including the sawmill, store, and post office. However, when the lake was drained in 2011 so that maintenance could be performed on the dam, metal and other noncombustible remains of the logging operation, such as boilers and an engine, were discovered still in place after over 100 years.

Five

TRAVEL

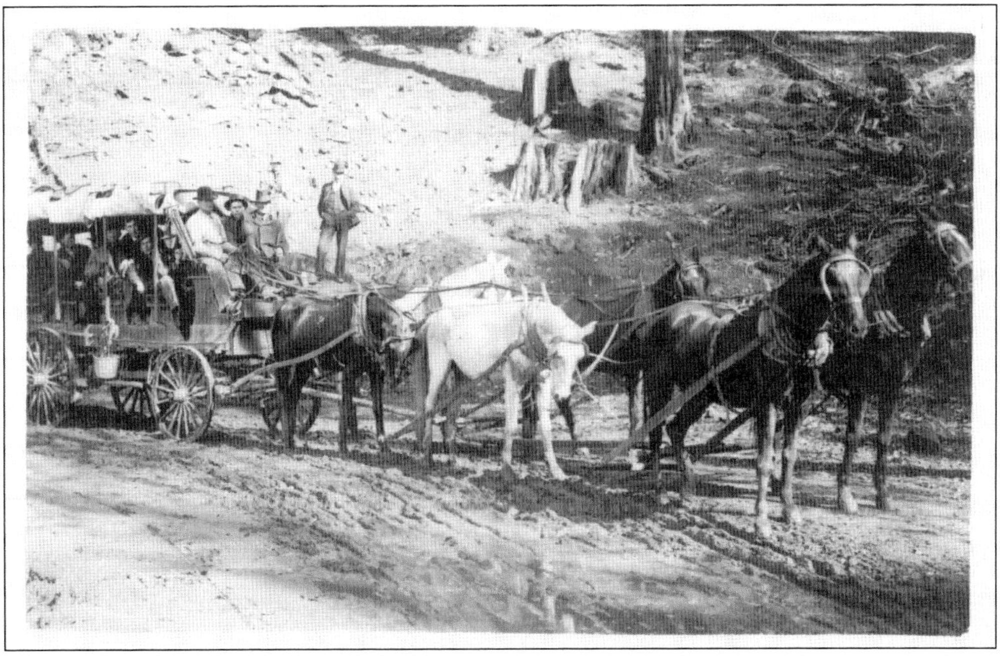

Manley White photographed what he called a "trained stage team" with a full load of passengers. He describes leaving Fresno in a stage pulled by six horses. "We generally had two wild broncs on the tongue and two half broke broncs on the point. This wild team was only drove as far as Clovis." At Clovis, a fully trained team of horses was hitched to the stage for the trip on to Shaver.

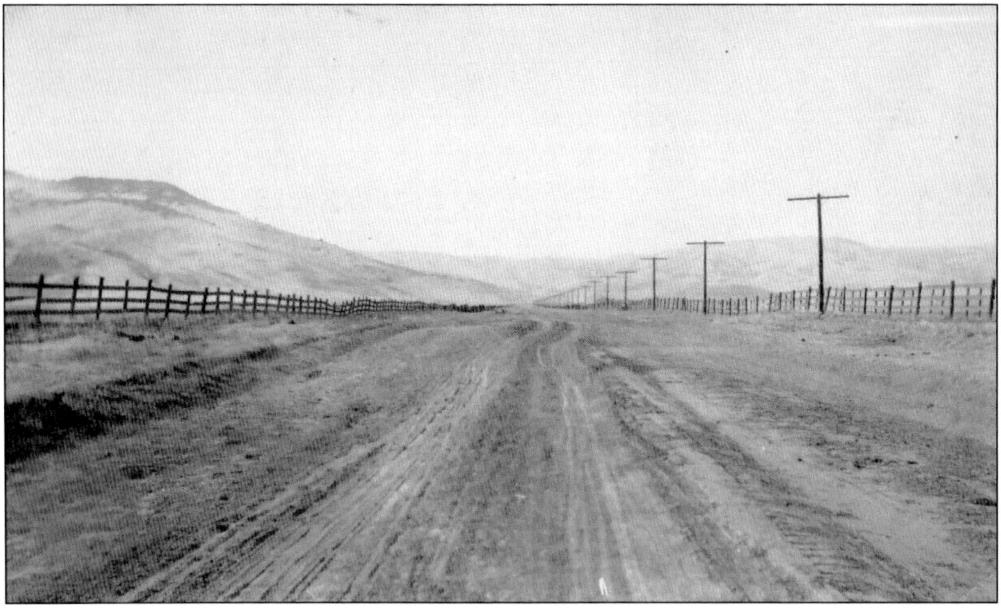

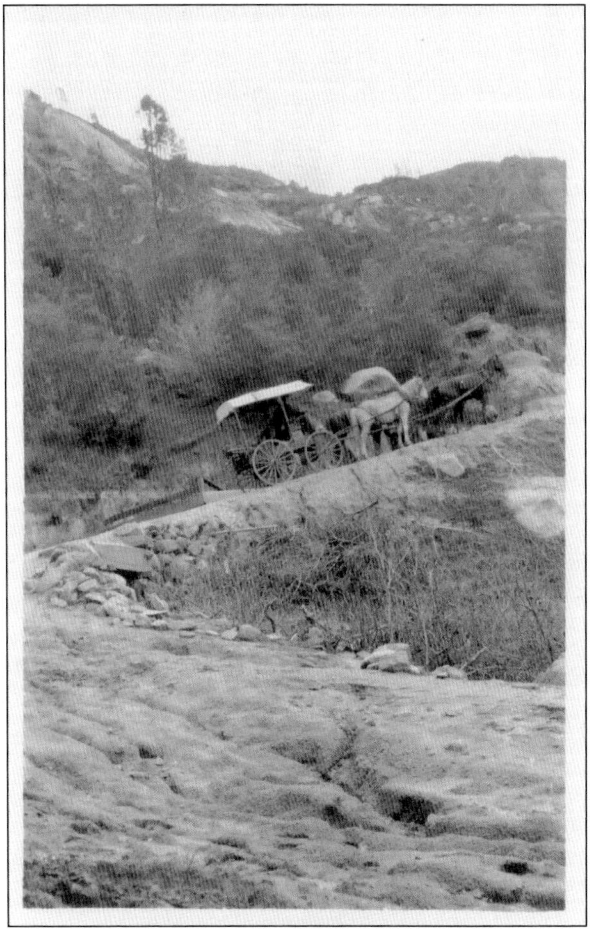

This image looks down a long, straight, lonely road in the San Joaquin Valley toward the distant foothills of the Sierra Nevada. This was the road of miners, lumbermen, laborers, engineers, dance-hall girls, hunters, and more. Now wider and paved, it still leads to the promises of the mountains. Photographer Manley White's stage traveled this road on his first spring trip to Shaver.

"Stage on toll house hill" was Manley White's description of this photograph. The stage stopped for dinner at Academy, where a fresh team of horses was hitched up. The stage continued on to Tollhouse, where it stopped for the night. The following day, with eight horses pulling the stage, they completed the journey to Shaver.

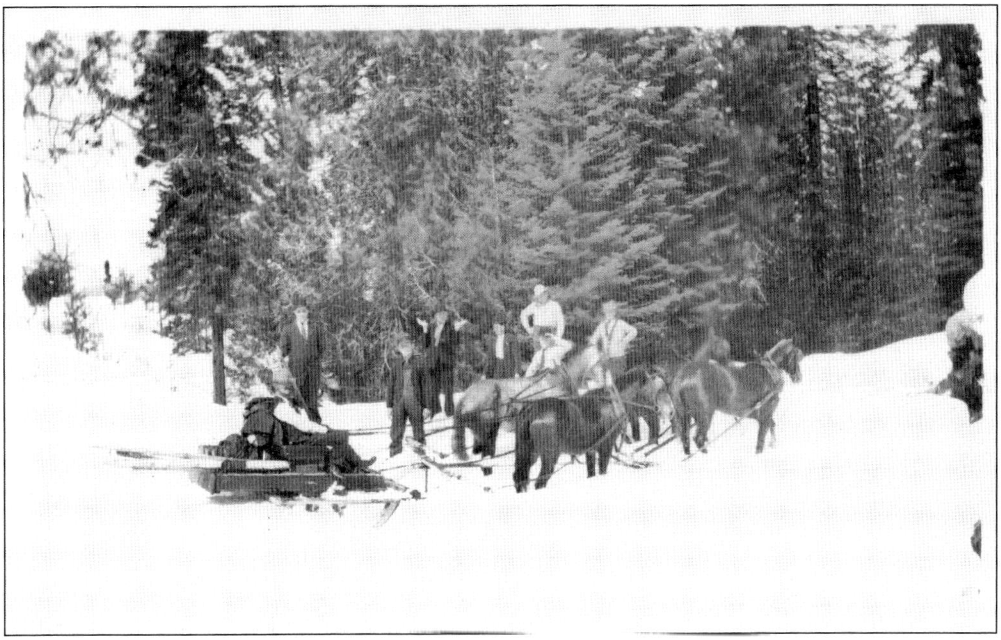

Transportation for Manley White's early spring trip to Shaver changed dramatically at Cressman's, above the Tollhouse grade. "We changed from the stage to Bob Sled, to break the road in. In the Bob Sled were loaded axes, skis, snow shoes, and cross cut saw and the mail for Shaver." For the next 17 miles, they broke trail, cut out trees, and shoveled out the drifts of snow to clear the road to Shaver.

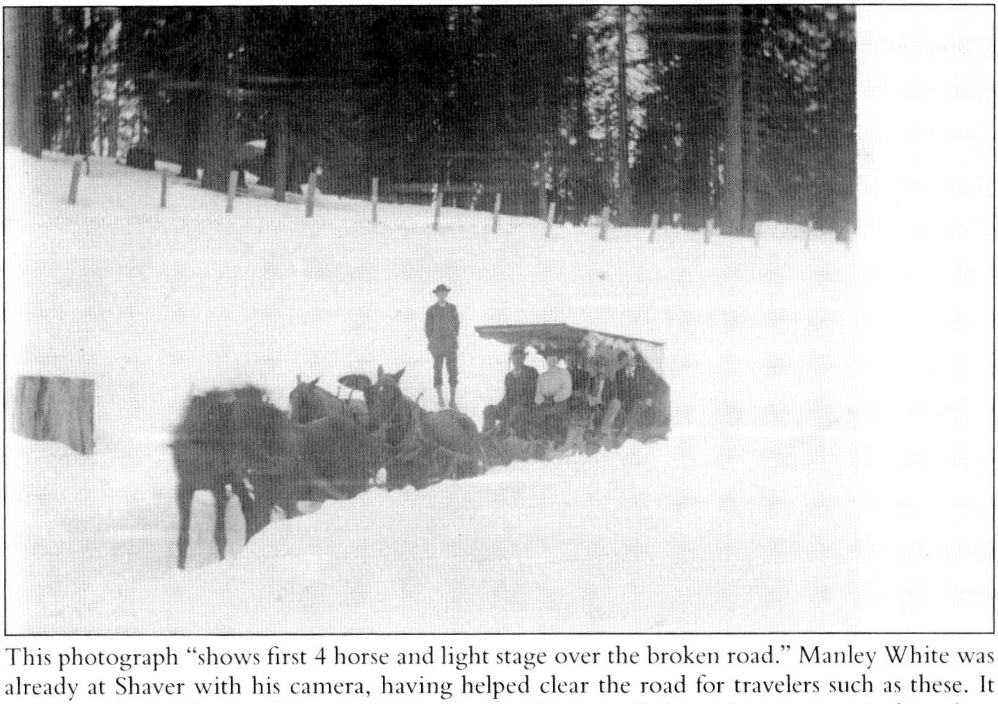

This photograph "shows first 4 horse and light stage over the broken road." Manley White was already at Shaver with his camera, having helped clear the road for travelers such as these. It must have been a long, cold trip in an open stage. These well-dressed passengers, in fancy hats and neckties, were probably not millhands or loggers.

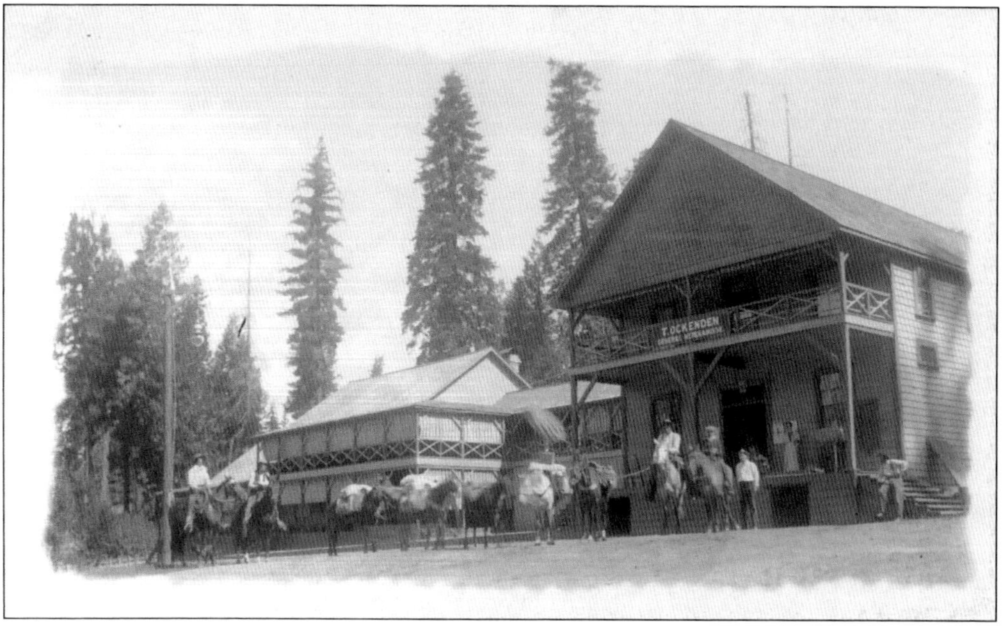

Located just south of Shaver Lake, Ockenden was a popular place, judging by its size. This rambling assortment of outbuildings and stables included a very large two-story structure with a store, post office, and hotel. The striped awnings provided afternoon shade for guests on the hotel veranda. The location and business were named for owner Thomas James Ockenden (1864–1939), an Englishman who came to America around 1886 and was appointed postmaster for Ockenden on July 24, 1893. Thomas Ockenden and his second wife, Mary, later lived in Oakland and Fresno, where he raised and sold cattle.

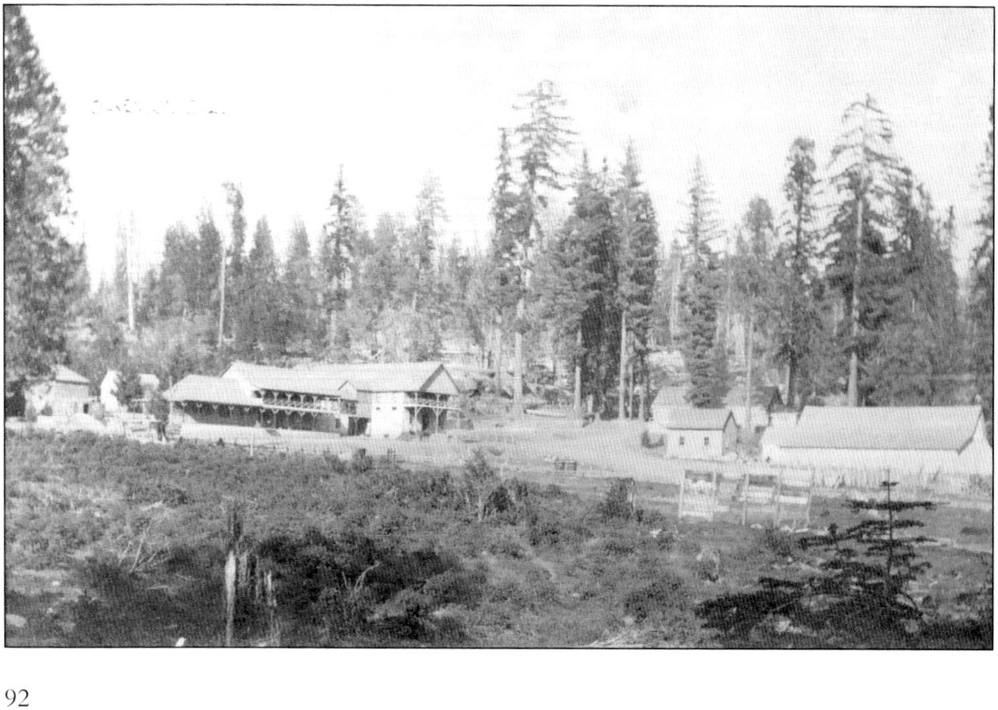

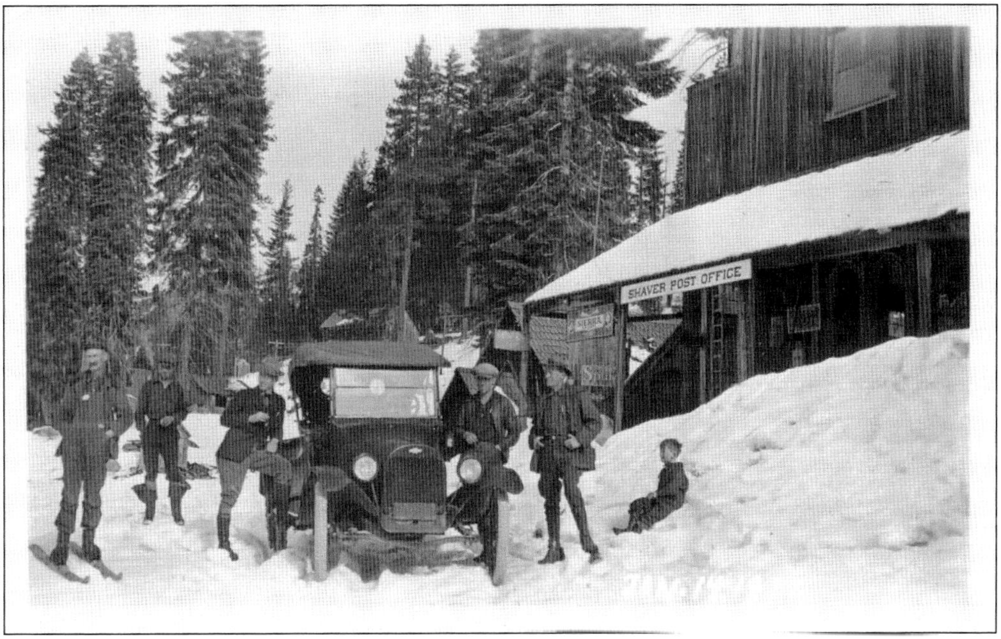

By the end of 1914, all operations at the Shaver sawmill had ceased. The property was sold to Southern California Edison in 1919, and their Shaver Lake Lumber Company again operated the sawmill. Patrick Leedy, who had been appointed postmaster in 1916, was still postmaster and storekeeper in 1922 when these winter customers arrived by automobile and skis.

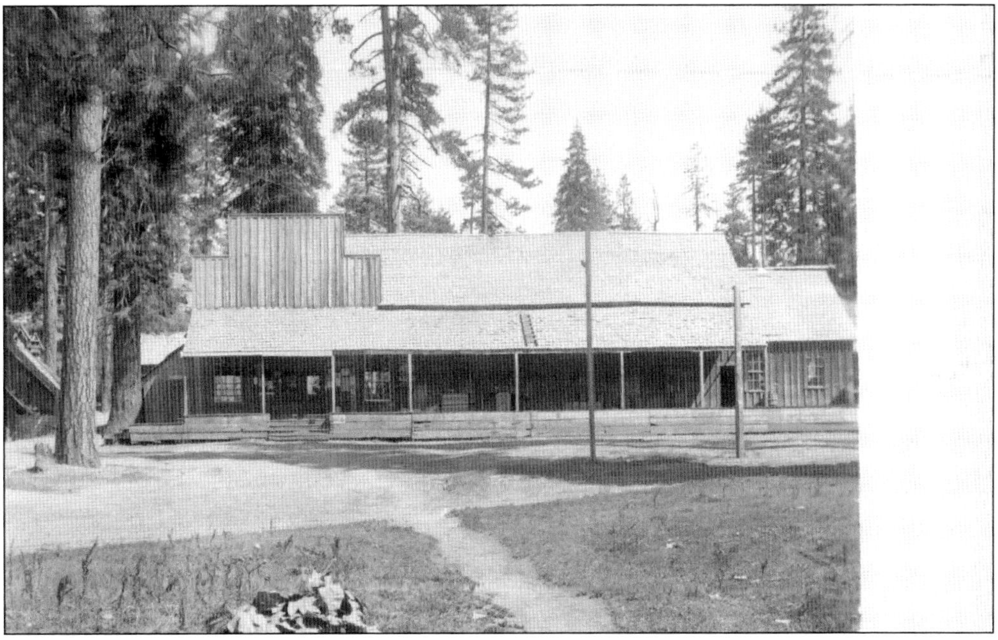

The Shaver store and post office, with its odd false front, was surprisingly quiet when Manley White took this photograph. The proposed name for the post office was *Swift*—in appreciation of Lewis P. Swift, appointed postmaster in 1896—but that name had already been used for another post office. The Shaver store and post office was an important institution in the area because of the large workforce there.

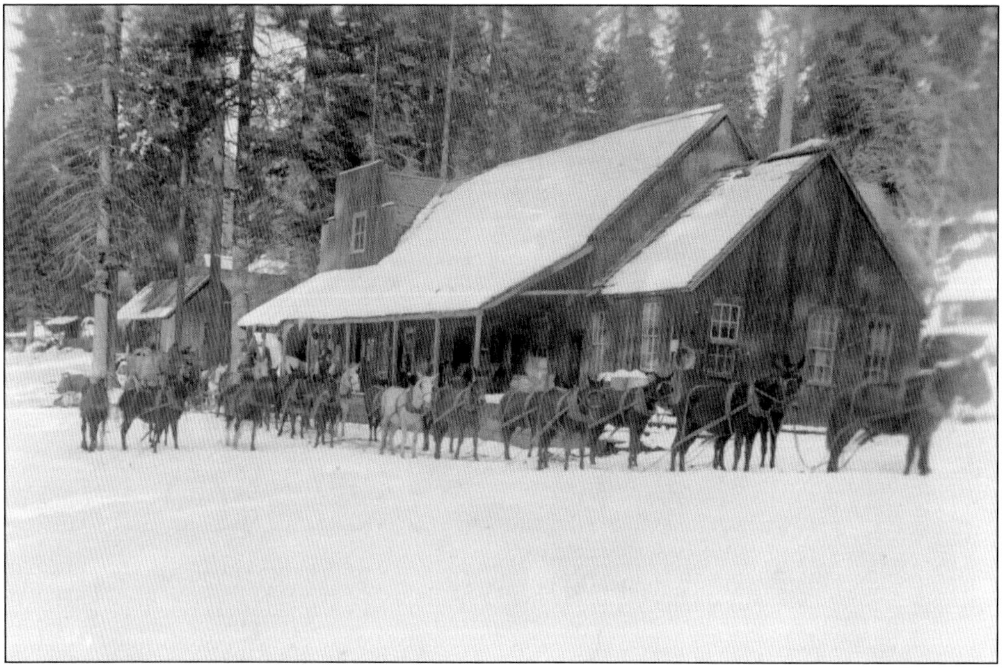

Manley White photographed this large team of mules hauling supplies to the store in winter or early spring. During the summer of 1927, as the larger Shaver dam neared completion, the area that was to become the current Shaver Lake was cleared. That work included burning all remaining structures, including the old sawmill and this store and post office.

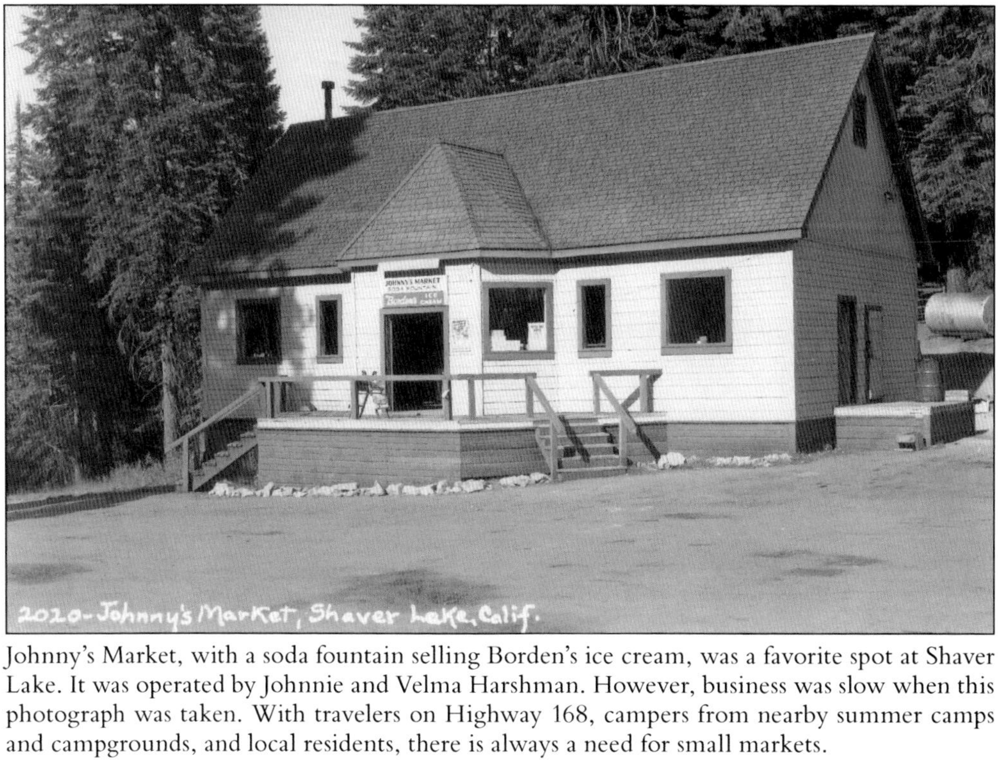

Johnny's Market, with a soda fountain selling Borden's ice cream, was a favorite spot at Shaver Lake. It was operated by Johnnie and Velma Harshman. However, business was slow when this photograph was taken. With travelers on Highway 168, campers from nearby summer camps and campgrounds, and local residents, there is always a need for small markets.

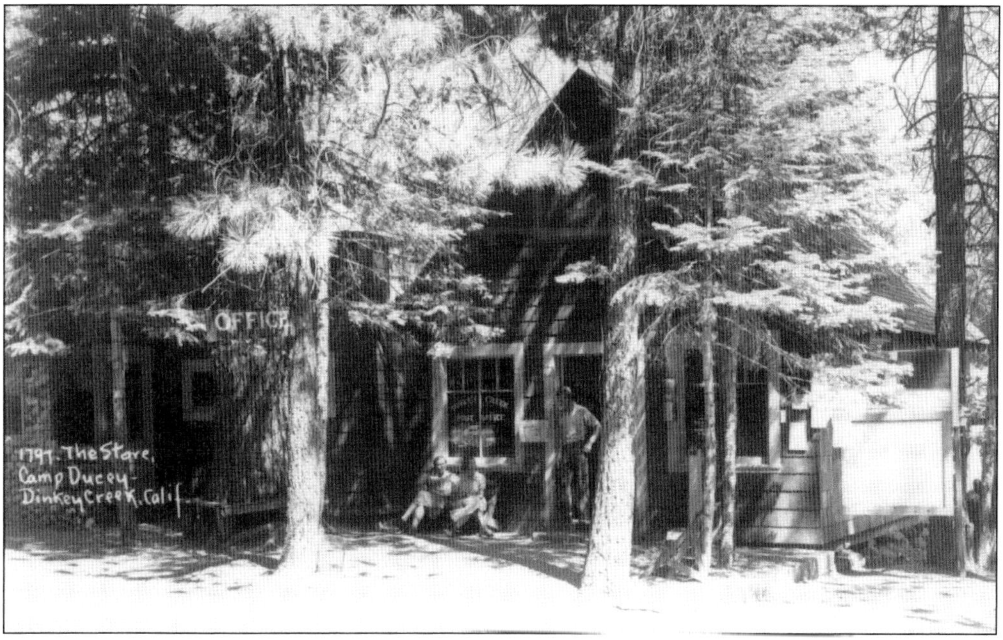

Dinkey Creek, at an elevation of nearly 6,000 feet, is located just east of Shaver Lake. It has long been a summer resort area, with a variety of lodging and campgrounds over the years. The Sierra National Forest currently has a campground there. Ducey's, a name long associated with Dinkey Creek, was originally built by Jack E. Ducey (1892–1964) in 1925. It had a two-story hotel with a dining room—the Buckhorn Café—and a store. In 1937, Ducey sold the resort to Mildred and R.C. Gibbs. The buildings were bulldozed in 1981 as part of the cleanup after the Dinkey Creek fire. Great fishing and swimming in Dinkey Creek and hiking in the surrounding pine- and cedar-covered mountains make for a relaxing vacation in the High Sierra.

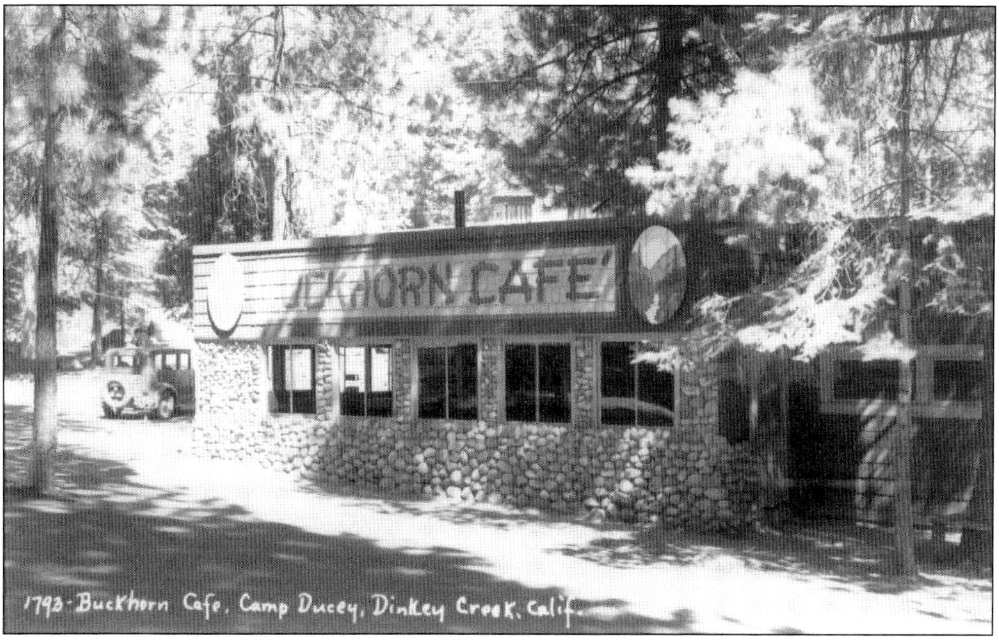

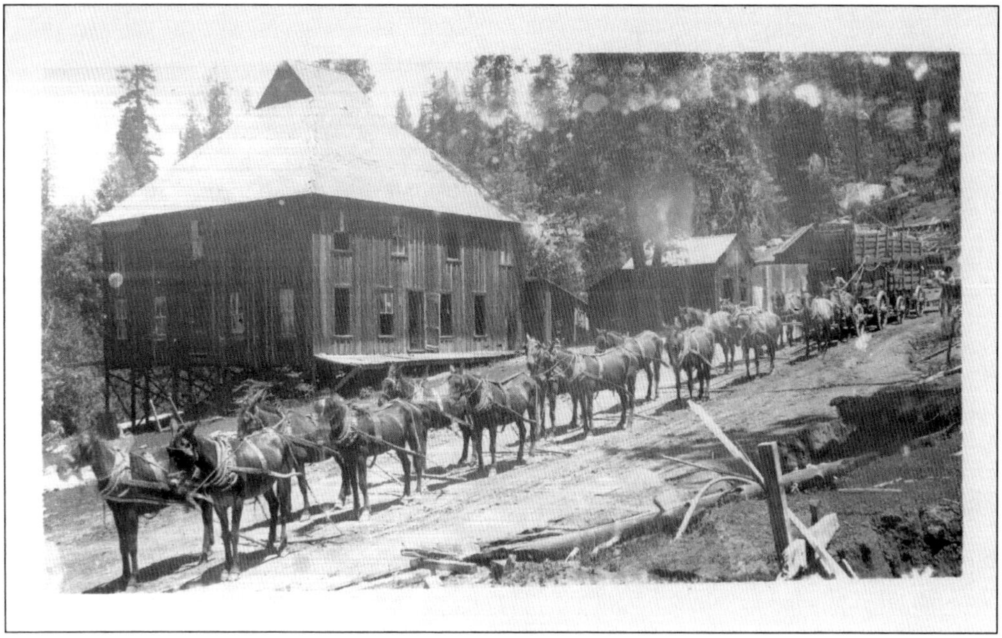

The Old Dalton's Hotel, shown here, was located on Pine Ridge on the way to Meadow Lakes. Bill Elanton is driving this very large mule team, which is pulling two freight wagons into the Sierra to support various businesses, mostly related to logging. Meadow Lakes was located about six and a half miles west-southwest of Shaver Lake.

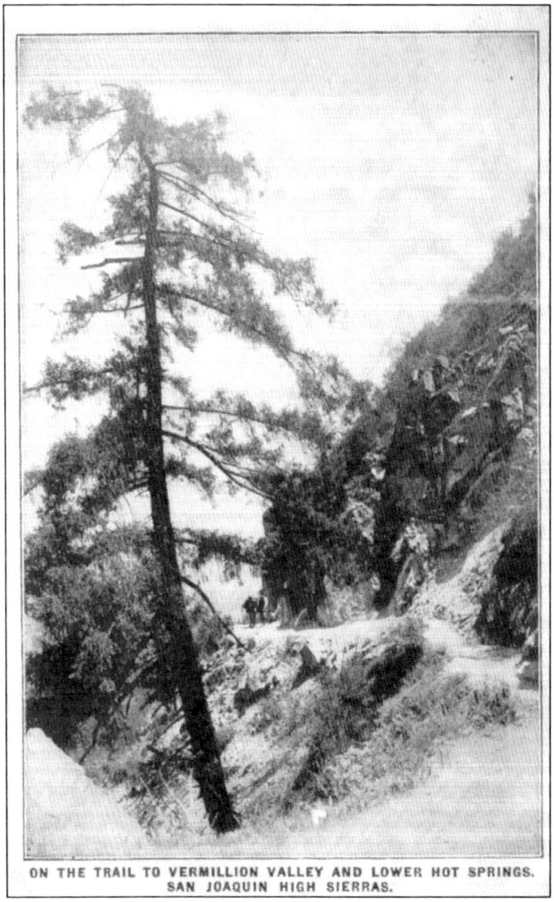

ON THE TRAIL TO VERMILLION VALLEY AND LOWER HOT SPRINGS. SAN JOAQUIN HIGH SIERRAS.

Before the Kaiser Pass Road was built to access Florence Lake, there was only a trail to Vermillion Valley and Lower Hot Springs, now known as Mono Hot Springs. Mono Creek was impounded by the Vermilion Valley Dam in 1954, as part of the Big Creek Hydroelectric Project, to create Lake Thomas A. Edison. This postcard was published by Huntington Lake Lodge and mailed from Big Creek in 1917.

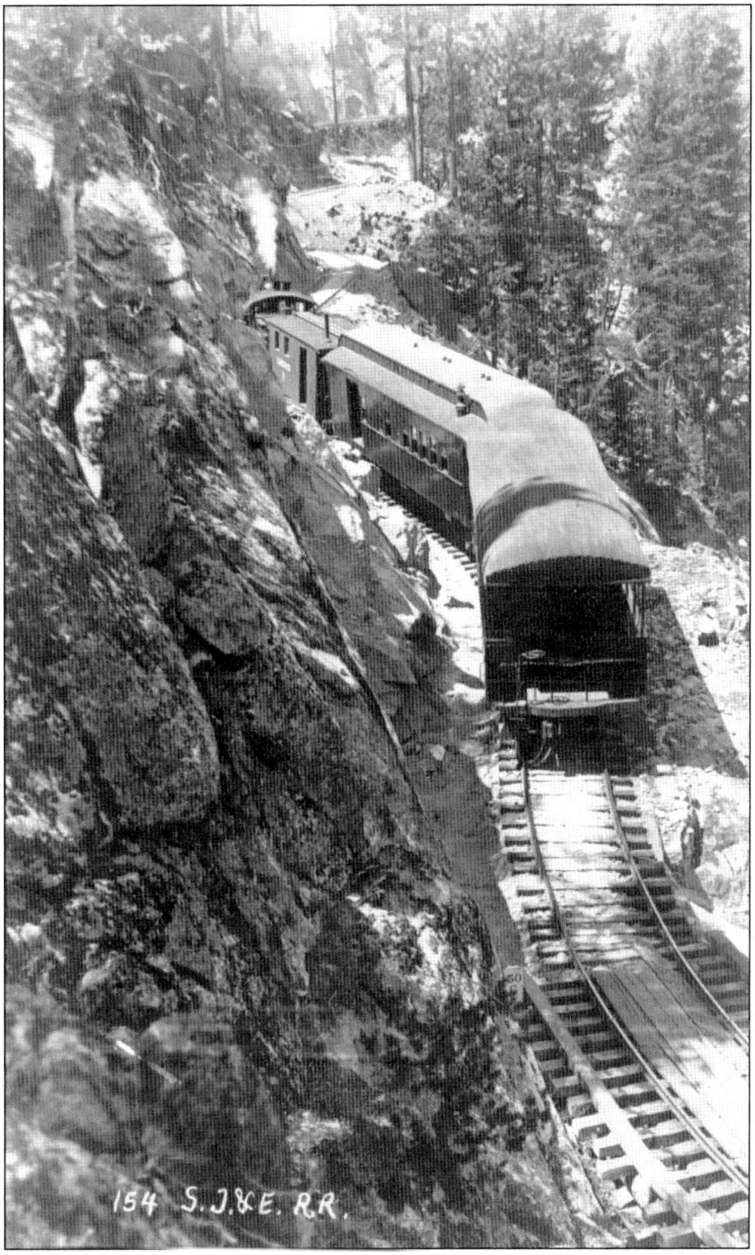

The San Joaquin & Eastern Railroad (SJ&E) was built by Pacific Light & Power in 1912 to haul construction materials into the mountains for the Big Creek Hydroelectric Project. Ground was broken on February 5, 1912. All the work was manual and involved the use of teams and scrapers, wheelbarrows, and hand drills. A crew that averaged 800 men worked seven days a week for at least 10 hours a day to build the railroad up the steep western slope of the Sierra Nevada. The last spike was driven on July 10, 1912. Completed in just over five months, the 56-mile-long railroad quickly earned the nickname "Slow, Jerky, and Expensive." The cost of construction was $1,175,000. There were 1,078 curves on the original rail line, some reaching 60 degrees, and there were 255 grades, some as steep as 5.2 percent. Regular train service to Cascada began on August 1, 1912.

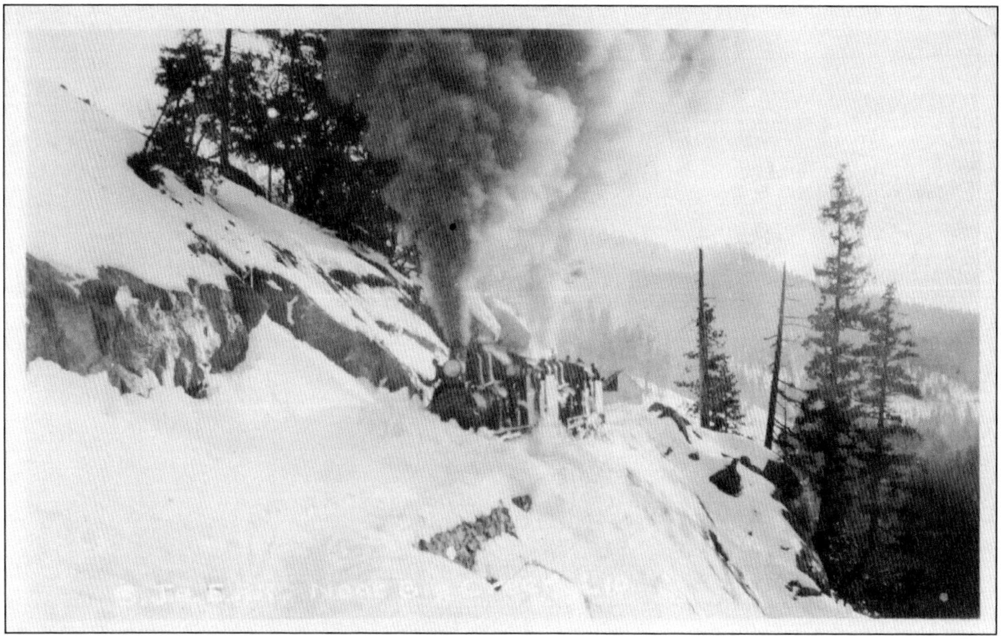

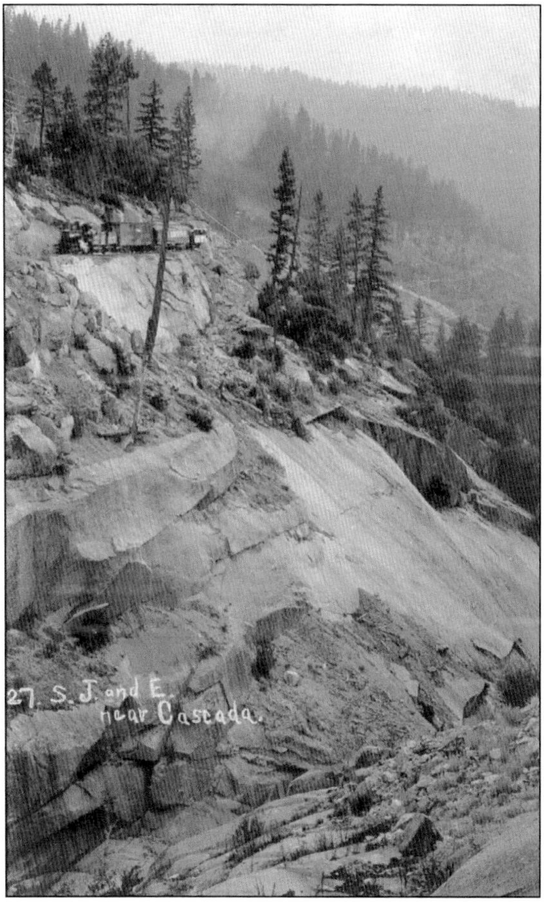

Operating a railroad in the Sierra Nevada was not easy, especially in winter. This SJ&E train, with two locomotives belching smoke, is pushing through the snow to get to Cascada. At an elevation of nearly 5,000 feet, Cascada (renamed Big Creek in 1926) was the destination for workers and supplies during the Big Creek Hydroelectric Project. It was also used by tourists traveling into the mountains for recreation.

The views from sections of the San Joaquin & Eastern Railroad, including this location near Cascada, must have been spectacular. The SJ&E commonly ran mixed trains, and this one appears to have an open excursion car at the end. This real-photo postcard by Robert A. Parker, who had studios at Big Creek, Huntington Lake, and Fresno, was mailed from the Big Creek Post Office in 1922.

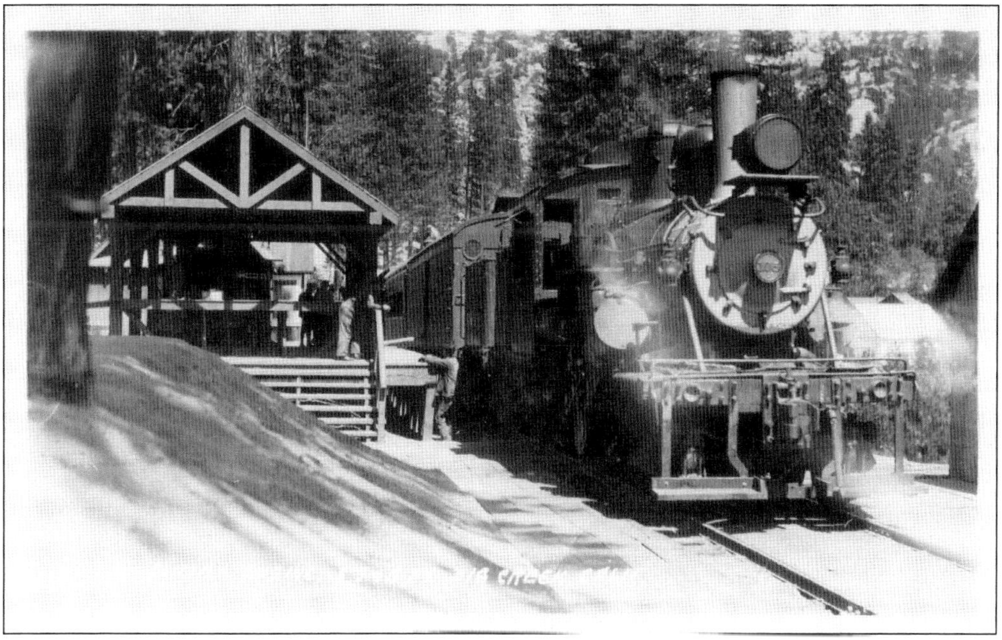

The San Joaquin & Eastern Railroad's Climax engine 105 is shown at the Cascada station. The SJ&E purchased this engine new from the Climax Manufacturing Company of Corry, Pennsylvania, in 1917. This photograph was taken between 1921 and 1930, when the railroad was leasing the baggage car (immediately behind the locomotive) from Southern Pacific. Passenger service to Big Creek was discontinued on May 1, 1930.

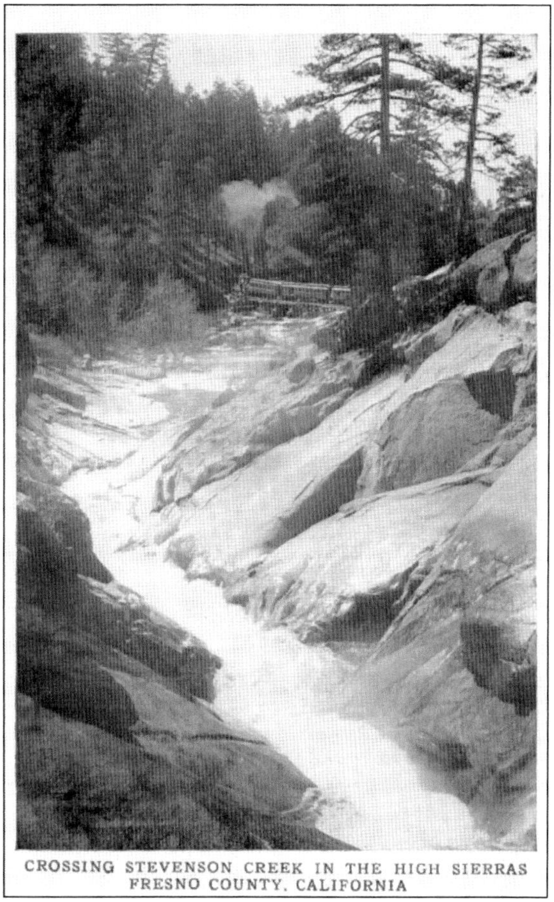

This printed postcard, showing a San Joaquin & Eastern Railroad train crossing Stevenson Creek, was published by Huntington Lake Lodge. The opening of the lodge in July 1915 reflects the shift from logging and hydroelectric development to tourism. The SJ&E welcomed sightseers and tourists on their line, as shown by their use of observation and open excursion cars.

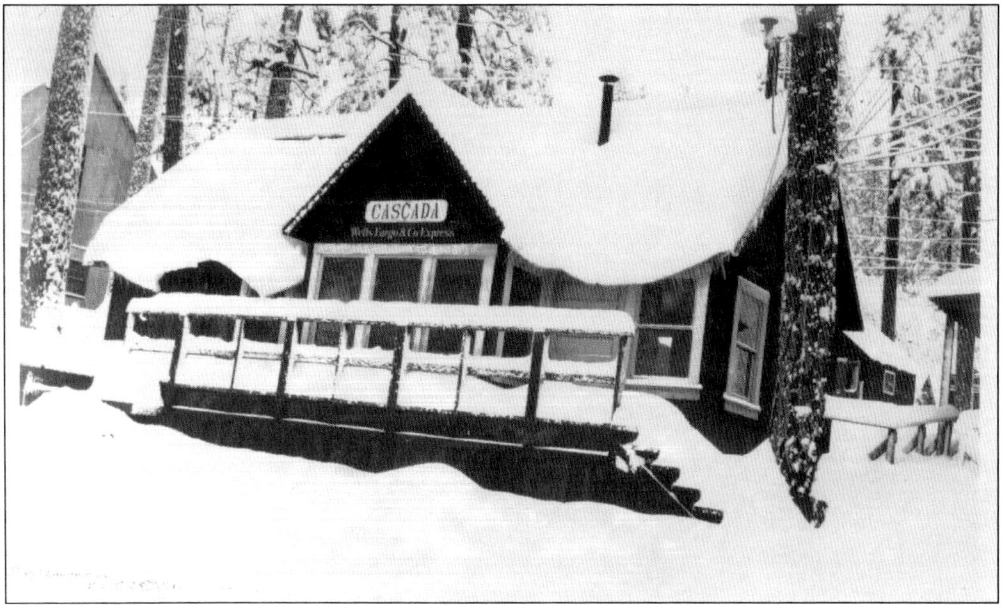

The Cascada station was at the terminus of the San Joaquin & Eastern Railroad. Cascada was also the headquarters for the Pacific Light & Power Company when they started the Big Creek Hydroelectric Project in 1911. When the post office was established in 1912, it was called "Big Creek," but the town remained Cascada until 1926, when the name was finally changed to Big Creek as well.

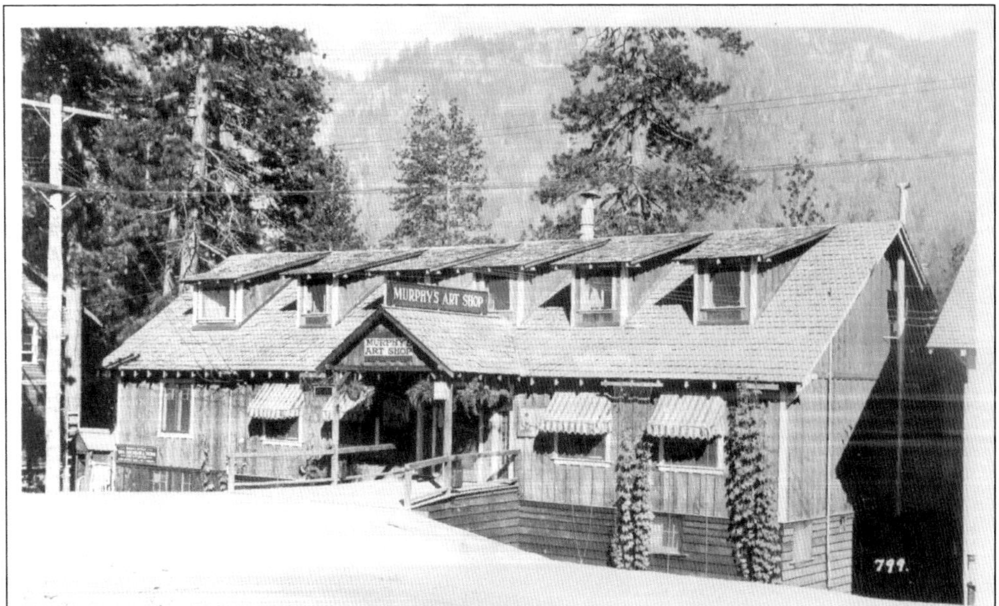

Walter L. Murphy owned and operated Murphy's Art Shop in Big Creek. He was in Big Creek by 1920 working as a stenographer for the Southern California Edison storekeeper, but he quickly recognized a business opportunity and opened this photography business. Unfortunately, a fire burned the building and several others on October 29, 1930. Later, this became the site of the Big Creek Church.

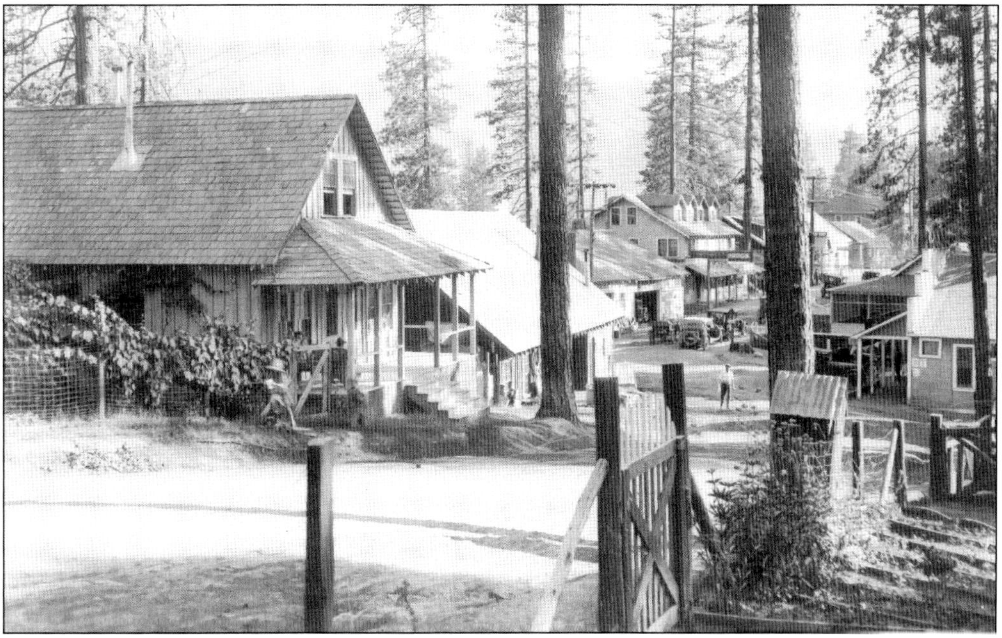

This is a good view of Cascada's main street in 1924. On the left side of the street were the home of A.O. Smith; Mile High Garage; L. Solomon's Service Station and Garage (with the large open door); and Harriman & Tiffany's building, which housed a drugstore, dentist's office, café, and shoe-repair shop. Aggergaard's General Store was on the right side of the street.

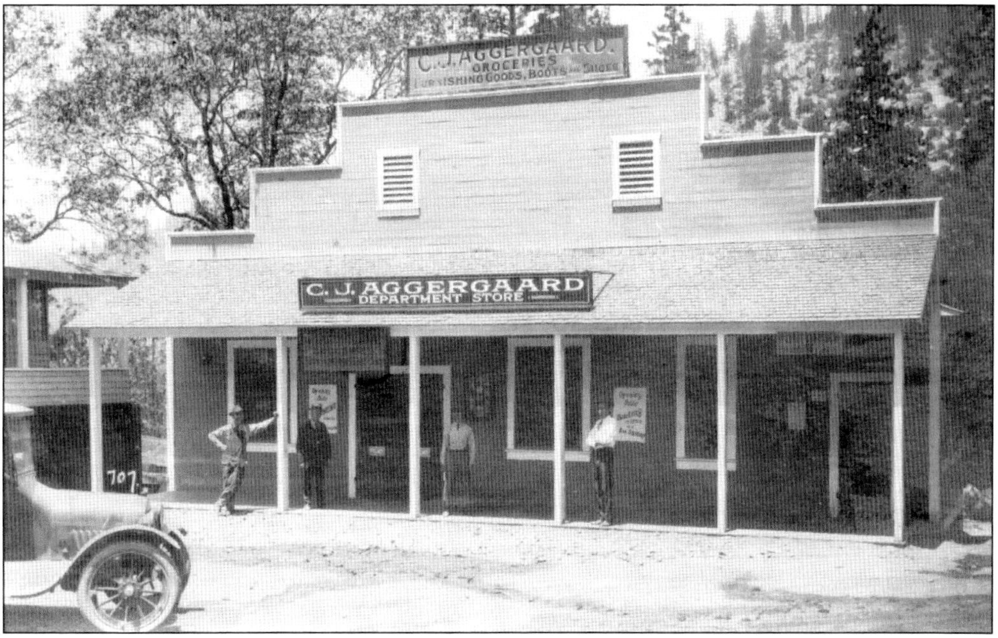

Frank Imhoff (1876–1974) and Christian Jensen Aggergaard (1873–1935) bought the store in Cascada in 1916, and Aggergaard became the sole owner in 1921. They must have jammed a lot into a small space to have groceries, a department store, and the Big Creek Post Office all in this one building. It must have been a busy place. The building burned on October 29, 1930. (Fresno County Public Library.)

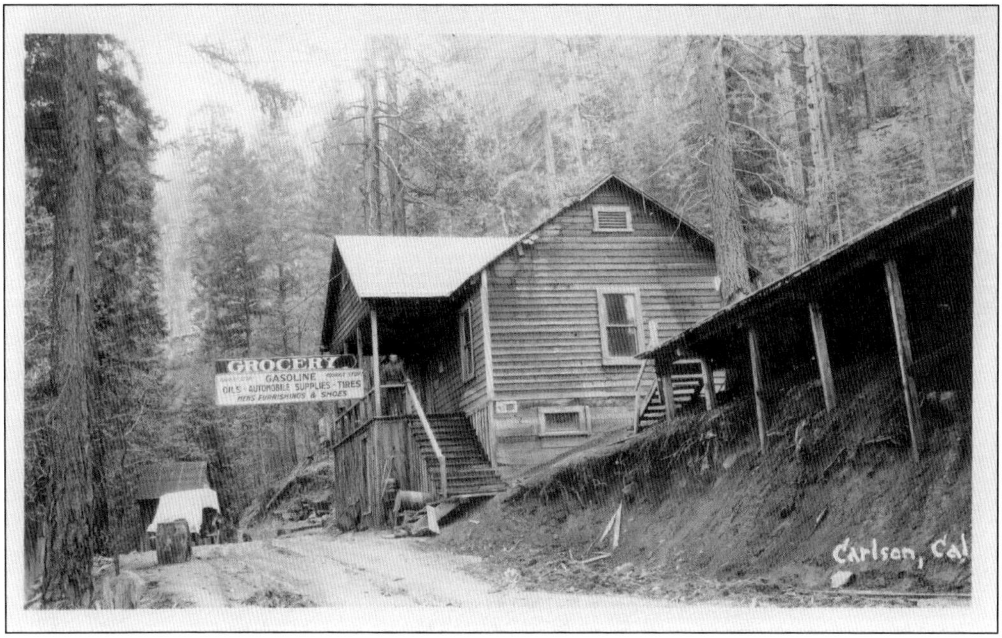

The Carlson Hotel and Resort was built in 1880 near what would become Cascada (Big Creek). Around 1916, the hotel was sold and became the Sierra Chautauqua, complete with a post office that opened in 1918. The name was changed to Camp Sierra in 1924. Camp Sierra lives on, still providing lodging, dining, and meeting facilities.

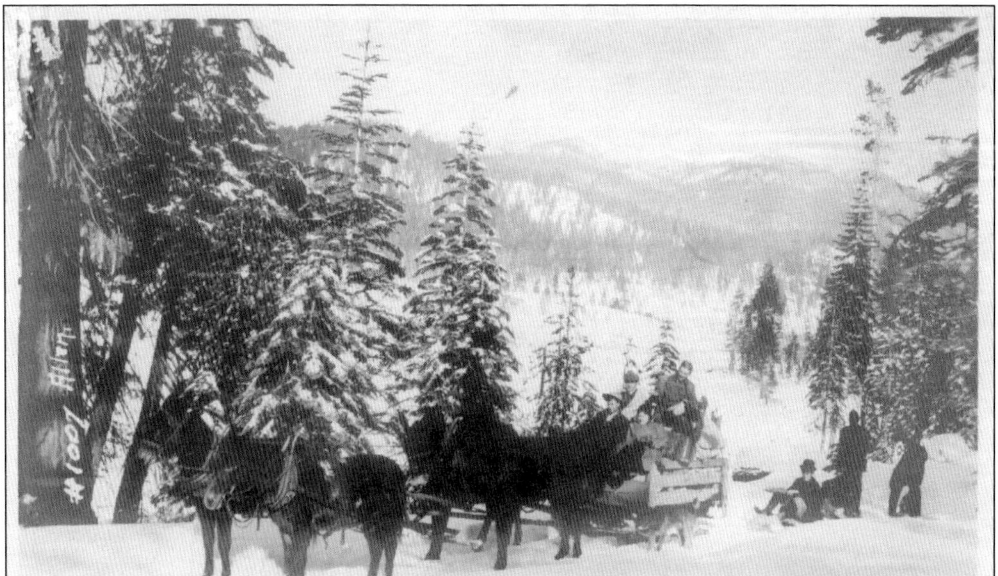

Travel was very difficult in the Sierra Nevada in winter, but the commercial activities of logging and hydroelectric development required some level of year-round activity. In this photograph, four mules pull a rather large load of people and supplies from Big Creek, the terminus of the San Joaquin & Eastern Railroad, to Huntington Lake.

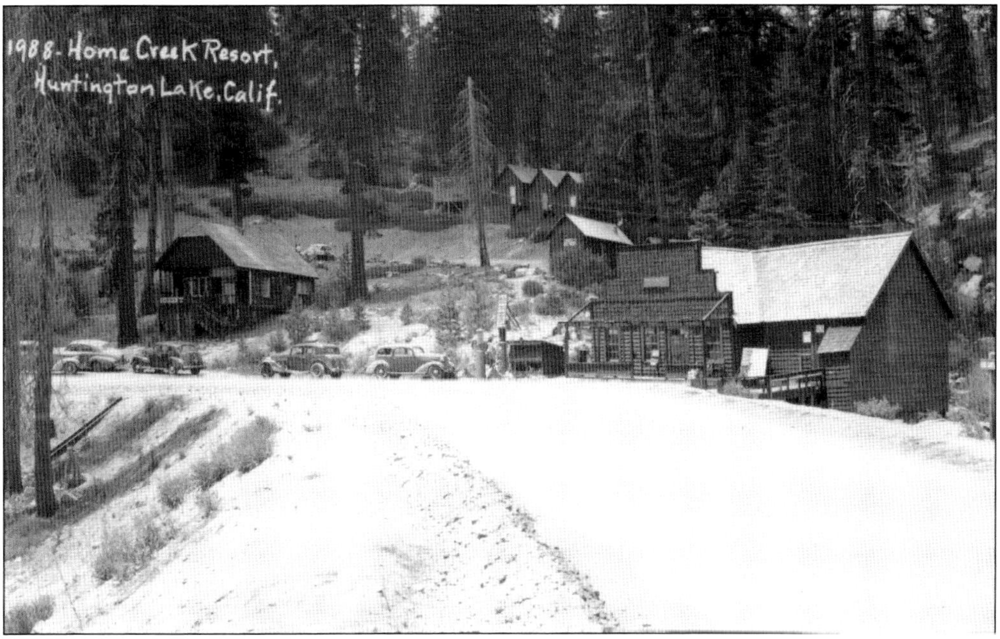

Home Creek Resort was an early resort on Huntington Lake. Home Creek flows into the northwest end of the lake. When a road was built along the north shore of Huntington Lake, a post office soon followed. The name of the resort was later changed to Huntington Lake Resort, and it remains in operation today.

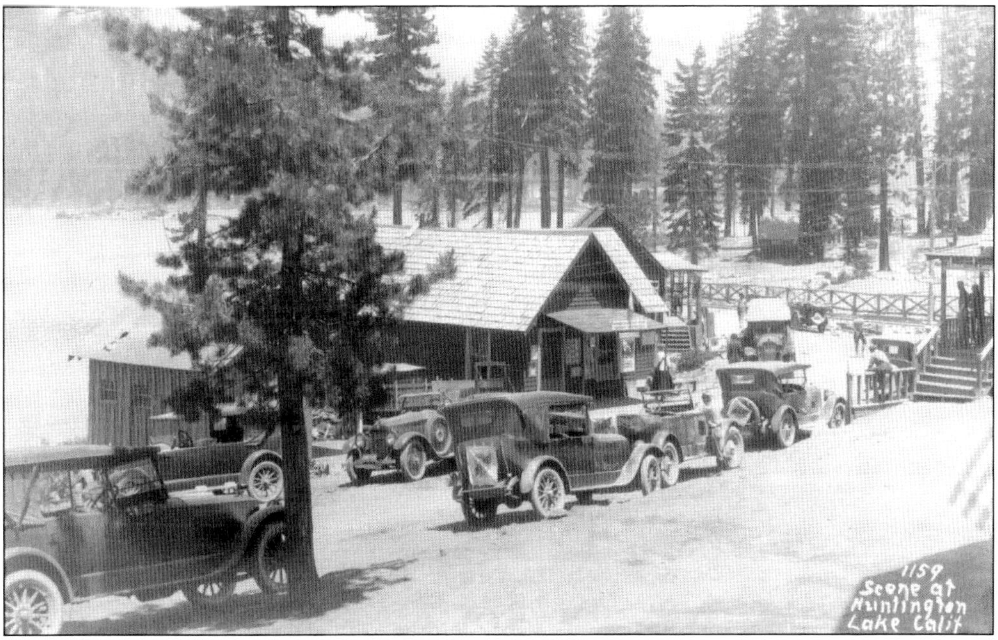

This summer photograph shows many touring cars that have made the trip to Huntington Lake. Achilles C. Mudge had his photography business in this building. Other businesses, such as a store that sold candy, at right, sprang up at this location near the west end of the lake.

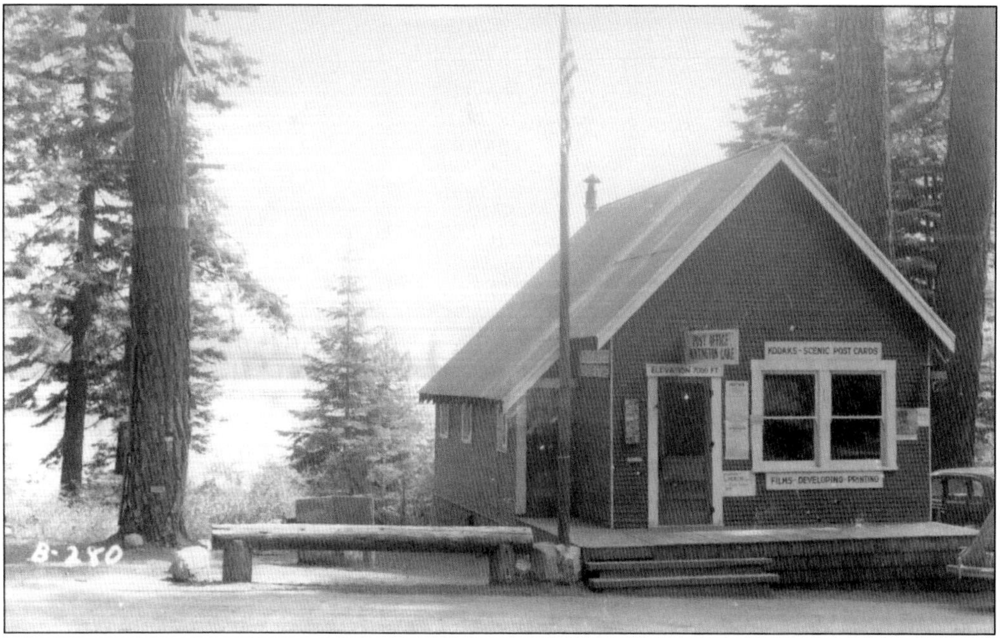

The Huntington Lake Post Office was near the west end of the lake. Achilles C. Mudge was the postmaster from 1918 to 1931, and he also operated Mudge's Photo Art Store out of this building. To the right of the door is a 1942 government poster with "Instructions to All Persons of Japanese Ancestry" regarding their evacuation to "relocation centers" during World War II.

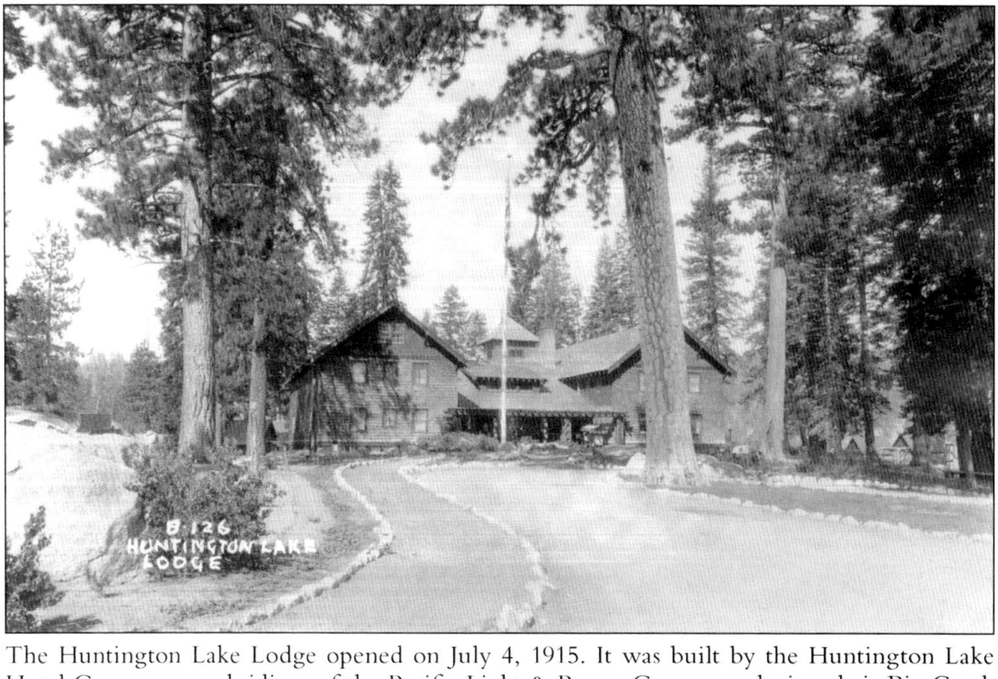

The Huntington Lake Lodge opened on July 4, 1915. It was built by the Huntington Lake Hotel Company, a subsidiary of the Pacific Light & Power Company, during their Big Creek Hydroelectric Project. Located on the south shore of the lake and near the west end, it was accessible by road from the railhead at Cascada. The lodge closed in 1931 and was torn down in 1949.

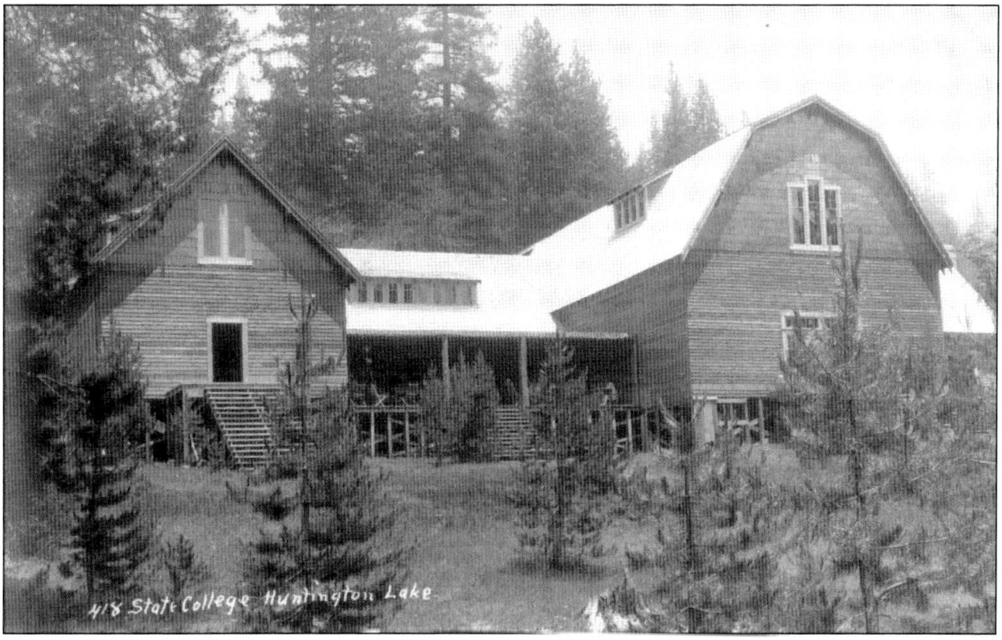

In 1914, the Fresno State Normal School held their first summer school at Huntington Lake. The inaugural class was a large group of young women who had to use bunkhouses and mess halls left behind after construction of the Big Creek Hydroelectric Project. In 1916, the summer school established permanent quarters near the Huntington Lake Lodge, where it operated until 1926. It then moved to a large tract at Lakeshore on the north side of the lake, where it operated until 1949. Established in 1911, the Fresno State Normal School became the Fresno State Teachers College in 1921, Fresno State College in 1934, and California State University, Fresno in 1972.

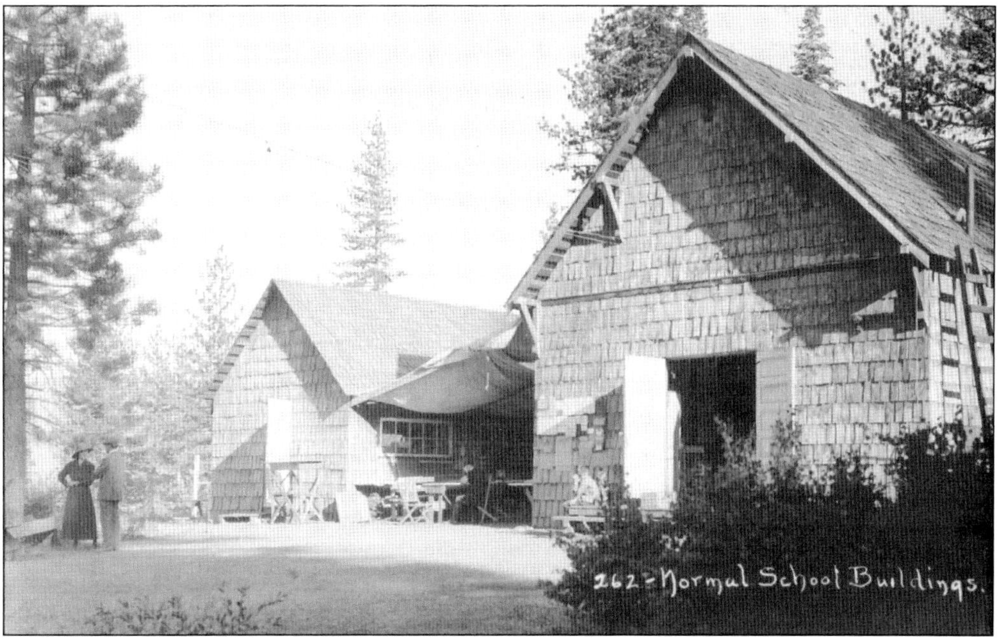

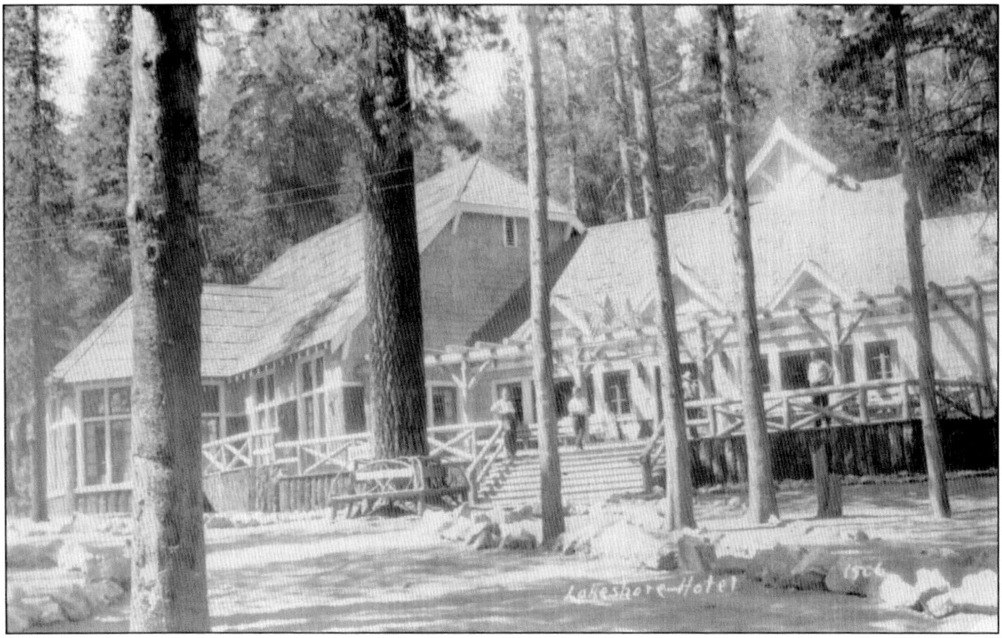

Lakeshore Resort has long been a popular business near the east end of Huntington Lake. In 1922, Harry Allen built a general store, a hotel, and some cabins. The property has changed hands numerous times over the years and been known for brief periods as Alpine Village and Canadian Village. The resort was boarded up and abandoned for several years until Stephen and Melinda Sherry bought the property in 1987. It now retains its rustic character and continues to provide a restaurant, a variety of lodging, and a large hall. The real-photo postcard above, by Mudge's Photo Art Store, was mailed from the Lakeshore Post Office in 1931.

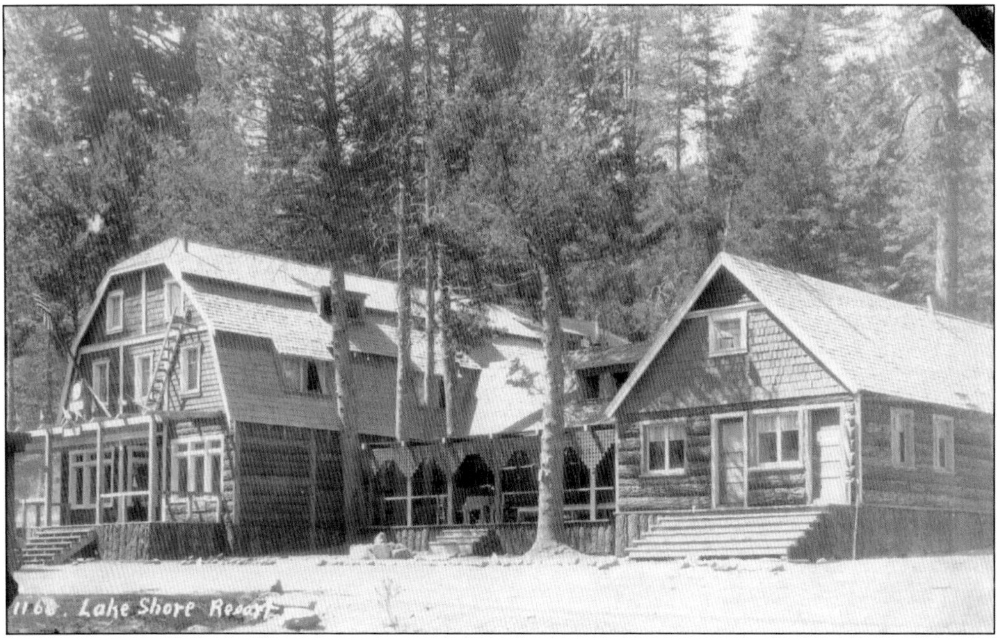

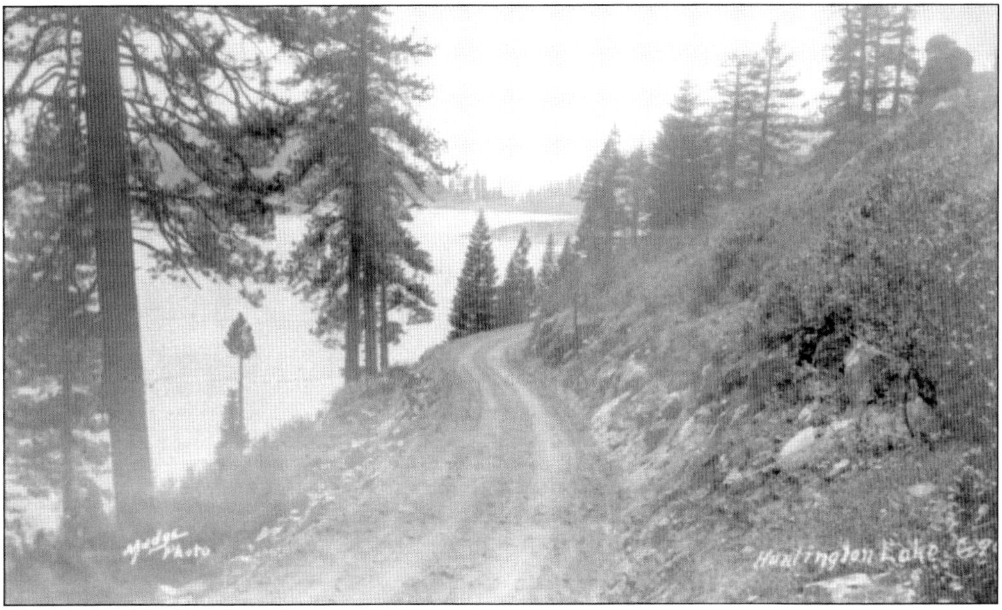

Huntington Lake was filled in 1913, but this road along the north shore was not built until 1920. The lake was named for Henry E. Huntington (1850–1927), a principal stockholder in the Pacific Light & Power Company of Los Angeles, which built the Big Creek Hydroelectric Project. He is best known today for creating the Huntington Library, Art Collections, and Botanical Gardens in San Marino, California.

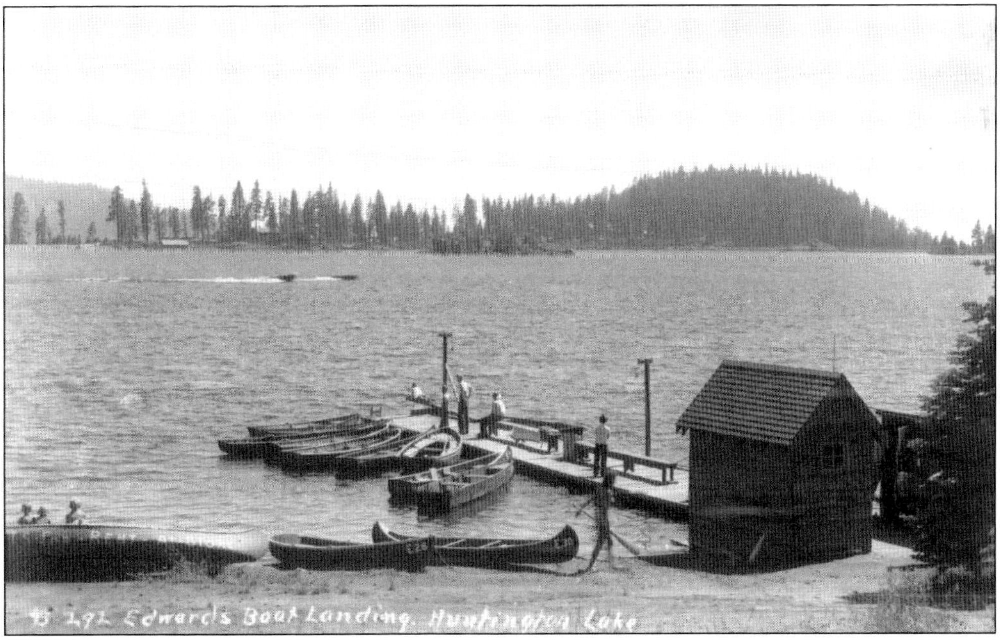

Edwards Boat Landing, located on Huntington Lake, appears to have only rented canoes. Boating has always been a popular sport, as evidenced by the two motorboats in the distance, and Huntington Lake is one of California's premier sailing lakes. Nearly five miles long, it has a peculiar thermal effect that produces consistent westerly winds in the afternoon. The High Sierra Regatta had its 60th anniversary in 2013.

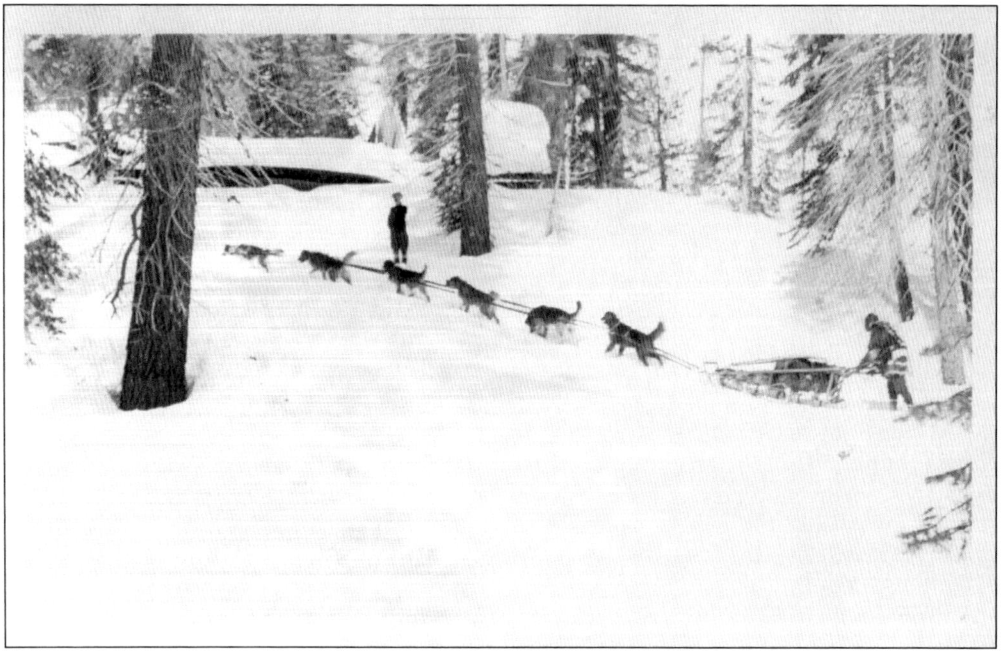

Jerry Dwyer and his dog team from Alaska were hired by Southern California Edison in 1920. They hauled mail and supplies, including medicine, from Camp 60, at Huntington Lake, over Kaiser Pass to Camp 61. The Florence Lake Tunnel was a major year-round project for Southern California Edison, and winter snow made other means of transportation over the pass impossible. The team made the 12-mile-long trip over the pass one day, then returned to their base at Camp 60 the next day. When Dwyer's lead dog, Babe, died in 1922, she was buried at Kaiser Pass in the grave shown below. Two other dogs from the team, Whiskey and Trim, were also buried at Kaiser Pass. Jerry Dwyer left the area in 1927 following completion of the tunnel.

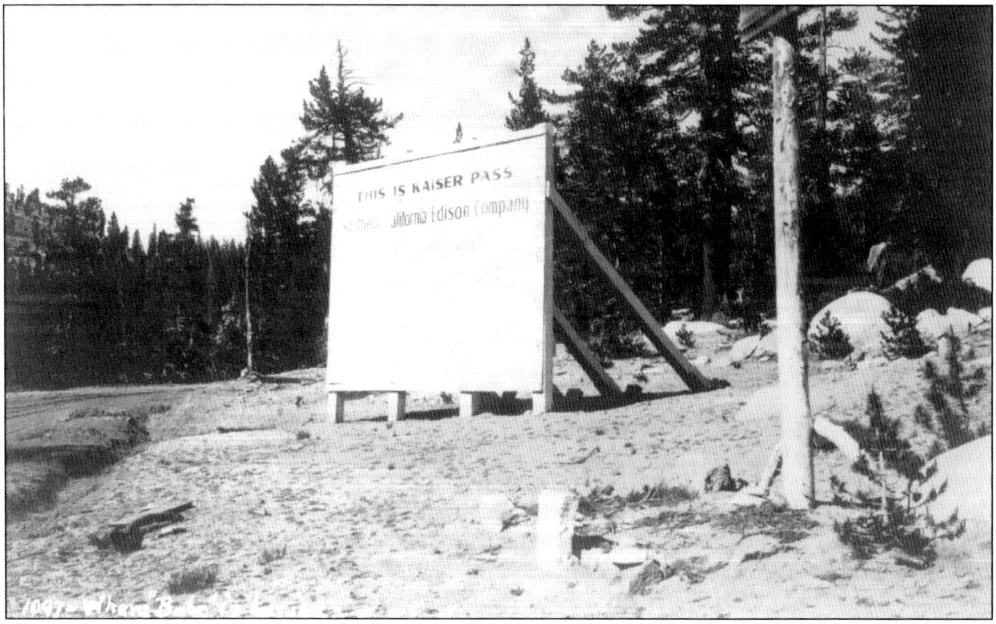

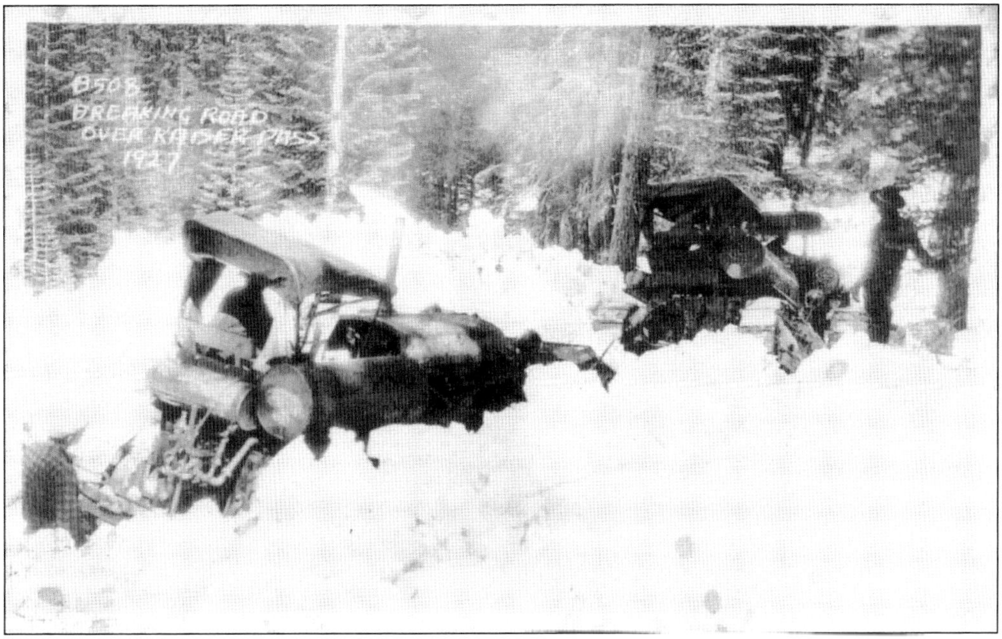

Construction on the road over Kaiser Pass, elevation 9,184 feet, started in 1920 as part of the planned Florence Lake development and tunnel construction. Two caterpillar tractors appear to be struggling to get over the road in 1927. The road has not changed much in over 90 years—it is still steep, winding, exposed, full of potholes, and not much wider than one lane.

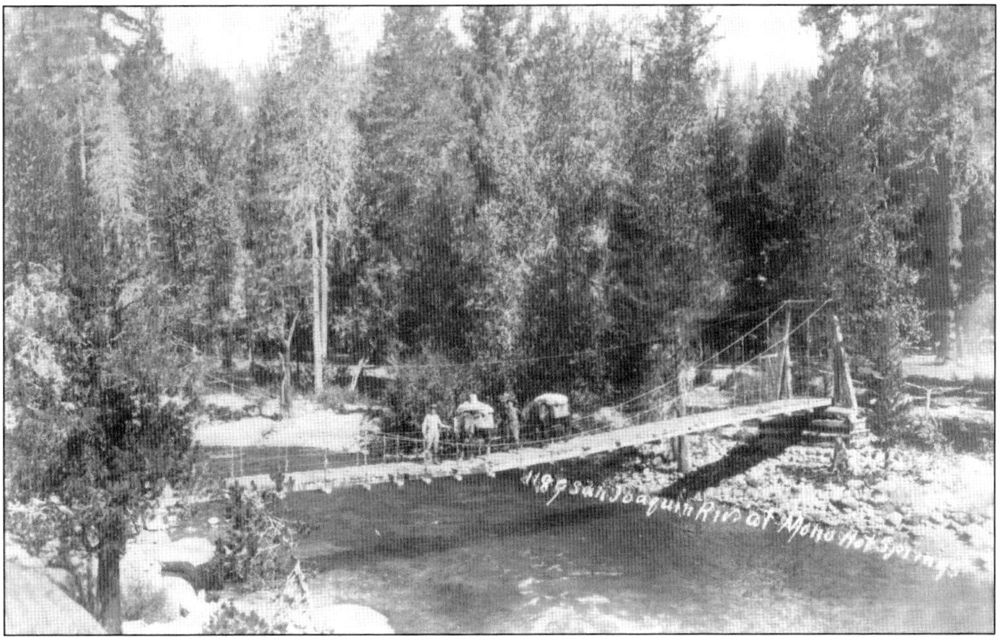

Two men and their pack mules take advantage of an early suspension bridge across the South Fork of the San Joaquin River at Mono Hot Springs. This was a remote location high in the Sierra Nevada before the Kaiser Pass Road was built. Historically known as Lower Hot Springs, Mono Hot Springs currently has a resort, post office, campground, and, of course, hot springs.

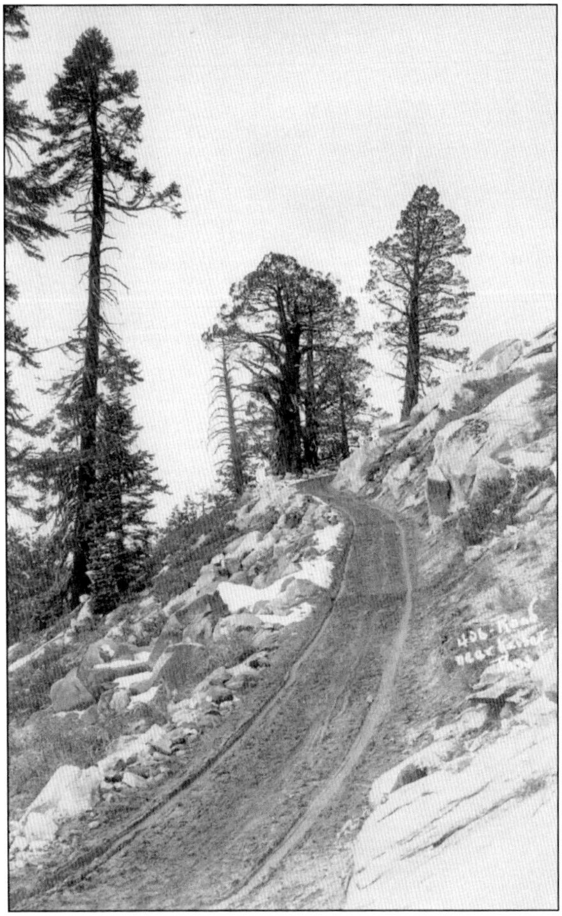

The early Kaiser Pass Road is shown in this photograph by Robert A. Parker. The 11.5-mile-long road, connecting Huntington and Florence Lakes, was built in about two months by men using mules, plows, scrapers, and a steam donkey engine. It is now paved but has otherwise not changed much since 1920. The road is under the jurisdiction of the US Forest Service.

The mountain roads were dangerous, and the early automobiles unreliable. The driver of this touring car ended up "over the grade near Hume." The roads were narrow, winding, and steep in places, and accidents were not infrequent. There seems to be no shortage of help up on the road, but it looks like they are still trying to figure out what to do about the car.

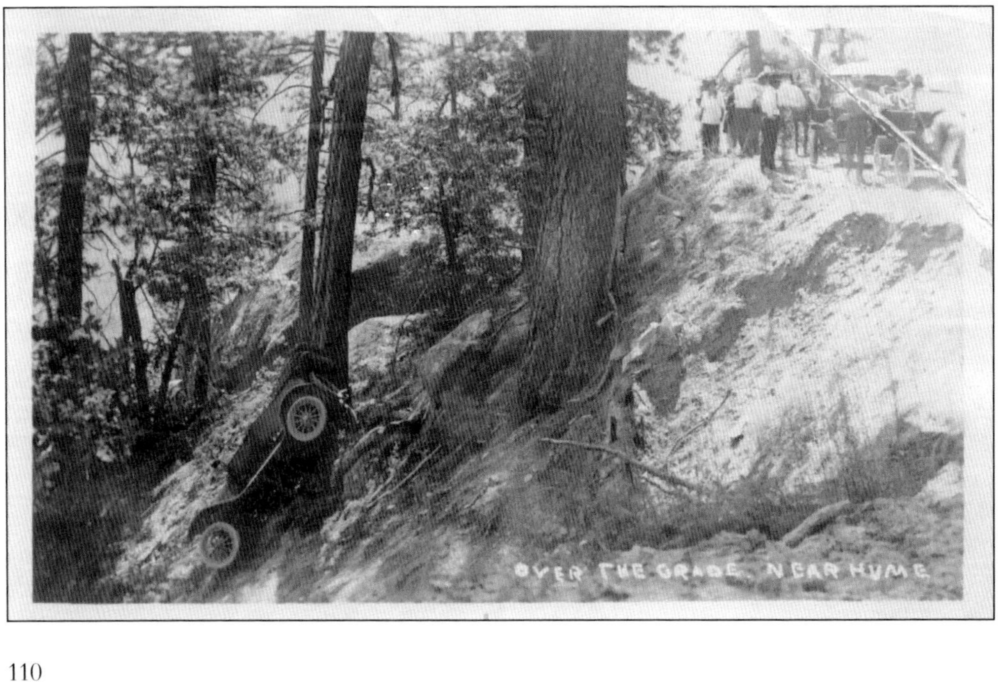

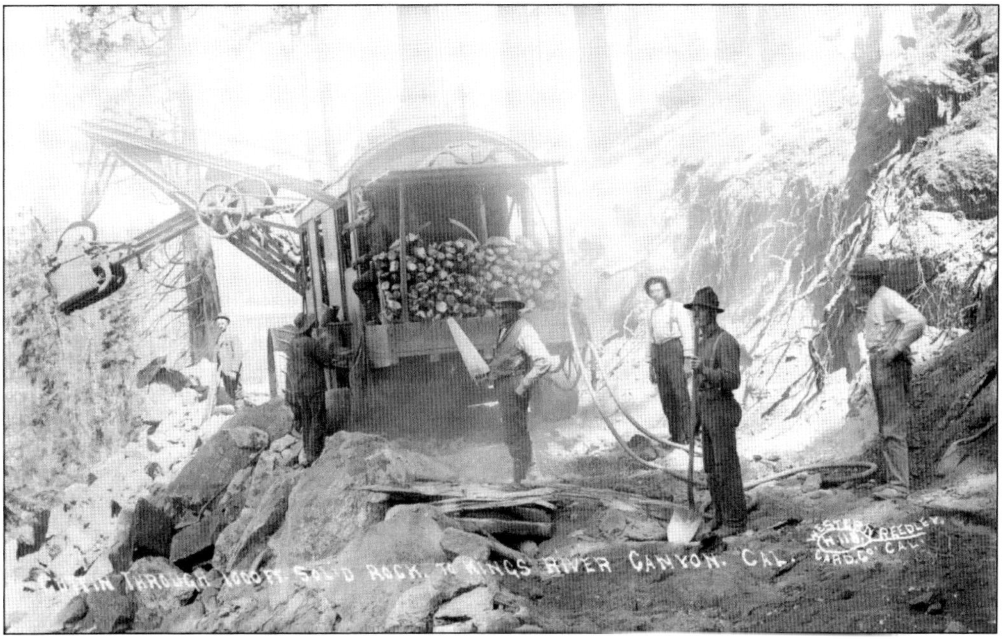

In 1912, the government constructed a road into Kings Canyon. The contractor used a steam shovel to get through the granite rock. The photograph above, captioned "Cutting through 1,000 ft. solid rock," shows wood stacked on the back to fuel the boiler. The steam shovel has wheels rather than a caterpillar track. The photograph below shows the steam shovel at Inspiration Point in Kings Canyon. Previous roads were built in 1889 by the Kings River Lumber Company and in 1894 by Fresno County. By 1912, logging was giving way to tourism. Sequoia National Park and General Grant National Park were established in 1890, in part to protect the giant sequoias from logging. General Grant was later included in Kings Canyon National Park when it was established in 1940.

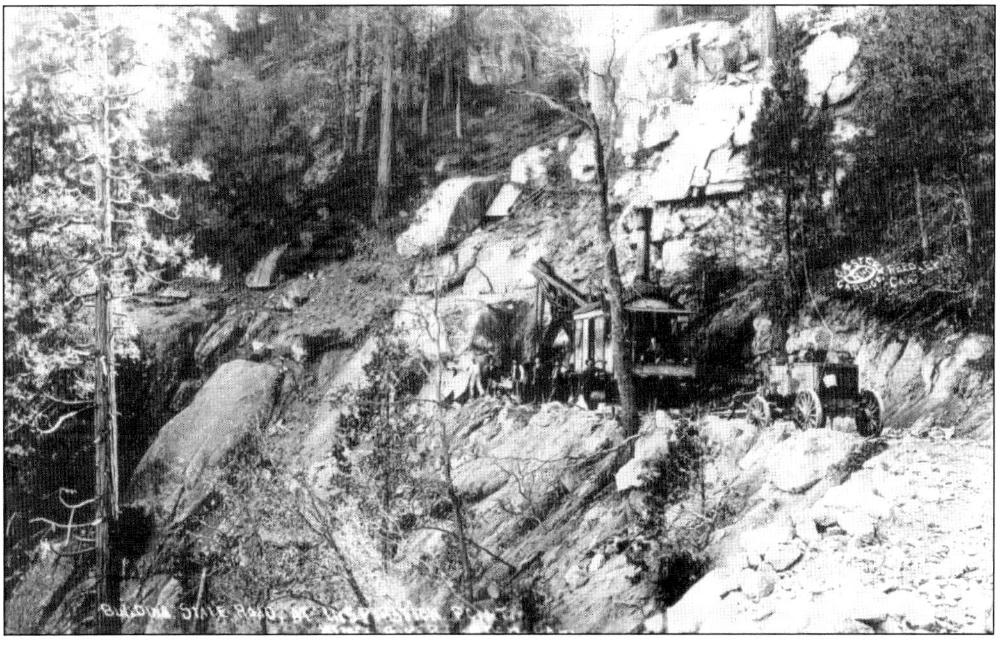

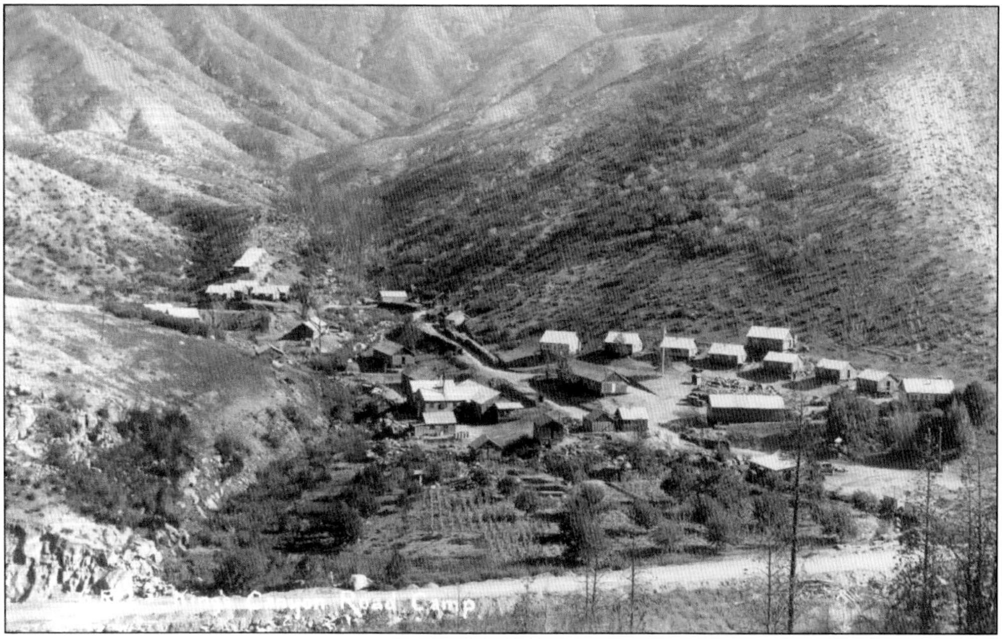

During the 1912 construction of the road to Kings Canyon, a support camp was built in the foothills to provide housing for the workers. It almost certainly had a mess hall for meals as well as offices for the construction company. Workers would have been needed to operate and provide wood for the steam shovel in addition to clearing and leveling the road surface.

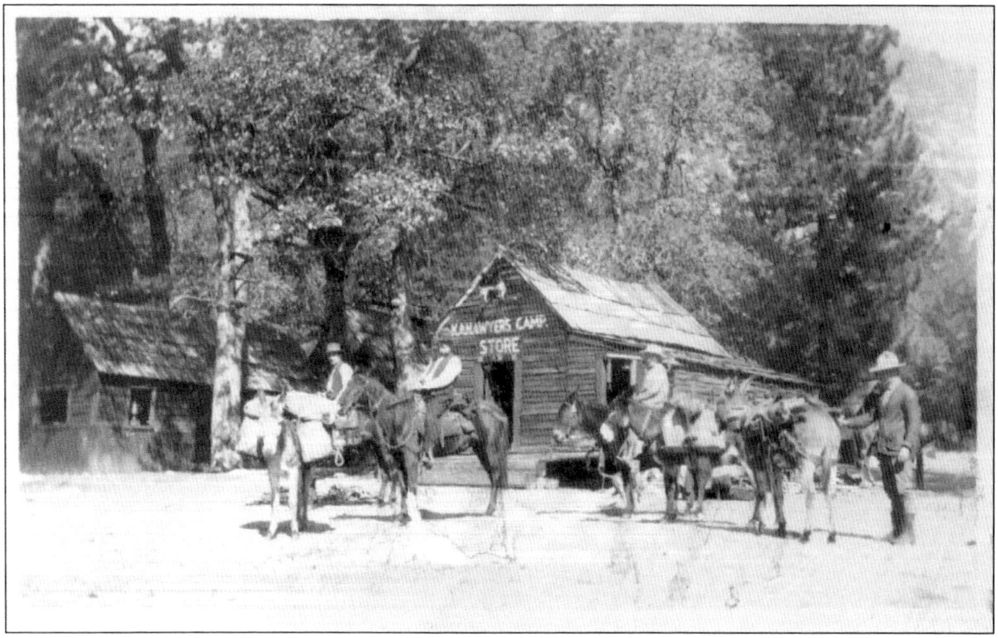

The rustic Kanawyer's Camp was operated by Peter Apoleon "Pole" Kanawyer (1849–1908) and his wife, Viola (1858–1948), in the Kings River Canyon. In addition to the store, they operated pack trains. The horses and pack mules shown here are certainly loaded and ready for a trip. Viola was postmistress at Millwood from 1900 to 1902. After Pole's death in 1908, she continued to operate the camp until 1917.

Six

People

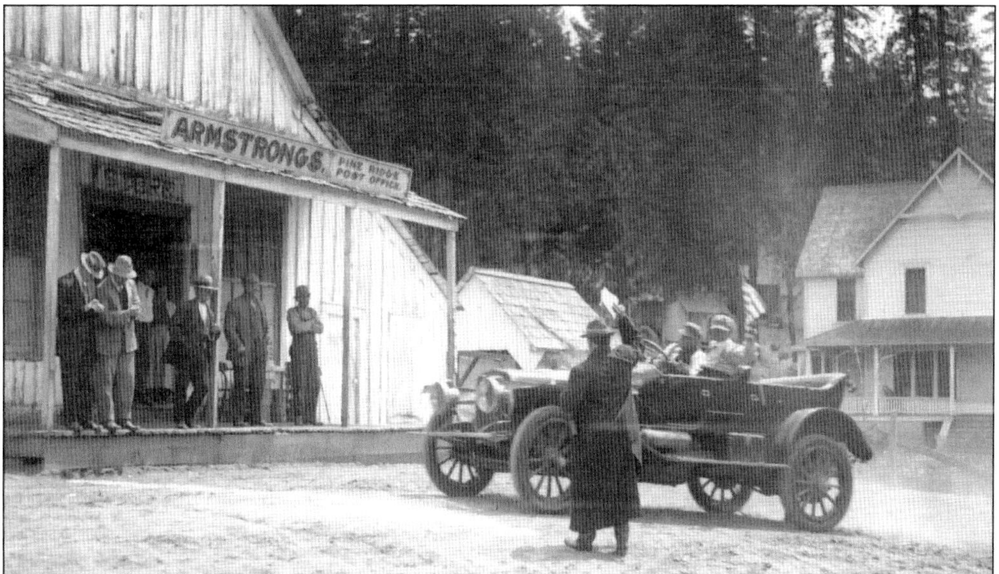

Onlookers at Armstrong's Store at Pine Ridge watch the finish of an early automobile race. This eight-mile race took place annually from 1910 until about 1935; it began at Tollhouse and went up the steep Tollhouse grade. Each car had a passenger who kept the elapsed time. John W. Armstrong operated this store and post office, which was located about one mile above Cressman's.

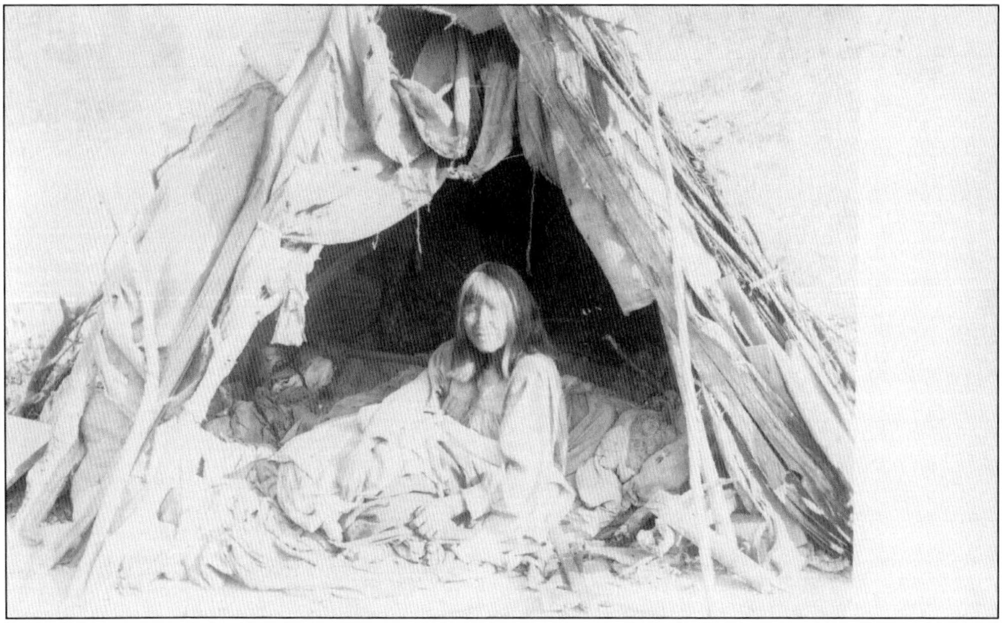

Native Americans lived throughout California, but their population quickly declined with the establishment of the Spanish missions and the onslaught of the California Gold Rush. The Western Mono, or Monache, lived in the foothills of the central Sierra Nevada. The woman shown above was 104 years old, according to a note photographer Manley White wrote on the back of the postcard. These photographs were probably taken at a camp or *ranchería* between Clovis and Tollhouse, near the road to Shaver. On the back of the postcard shown below, White wrote, "Indian bride and groom and there [sic] home." They probably slept on mats inside the shelter of wood poles and incense cedar bark and cooked outside, as evidenced by the pails. They even had a dog that would not stand still for the camera.

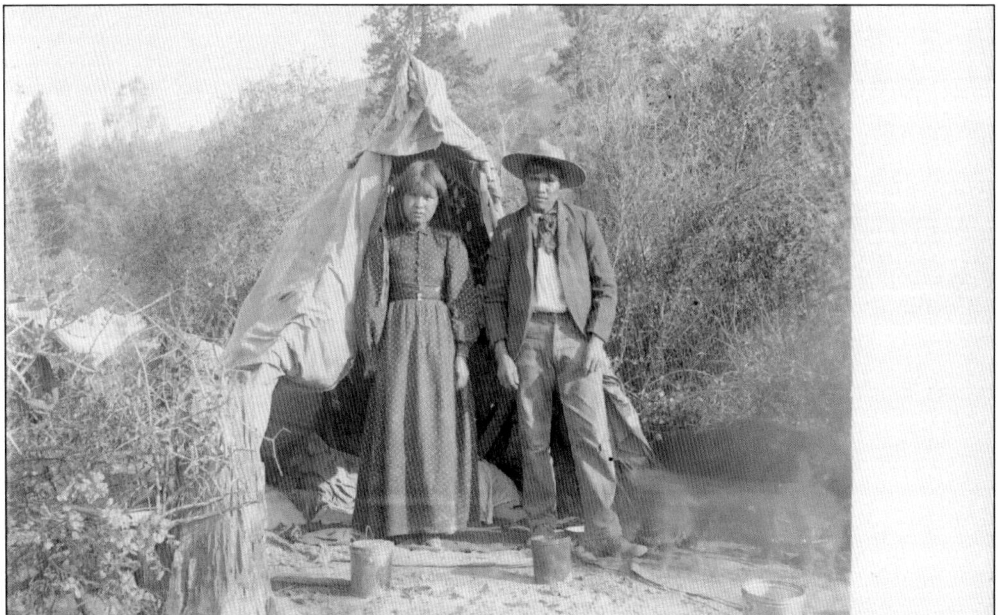

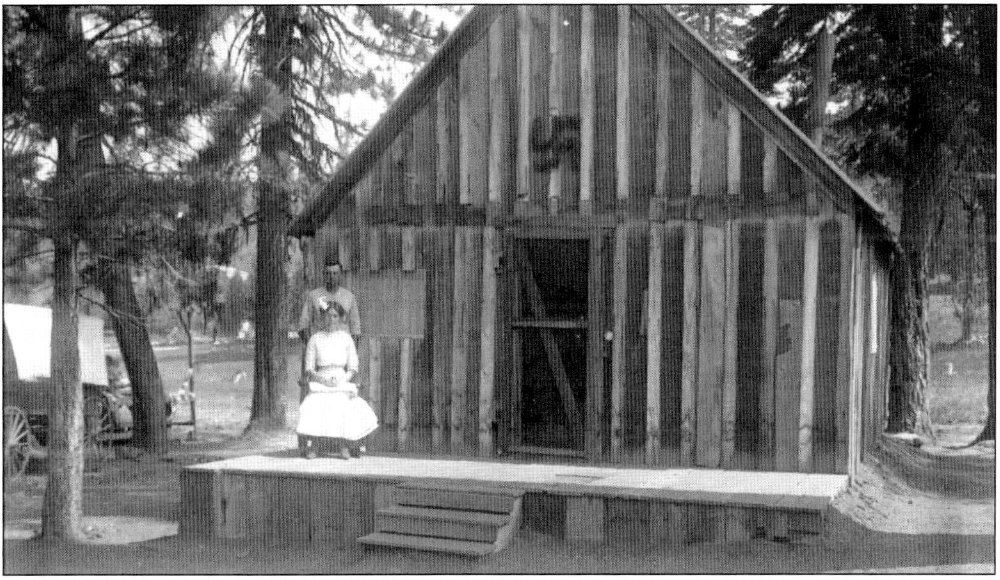

These two photographs are from a series of glass-plate negatives made by Manley White, probably at Shaver. The young couple is living a Spartan life in their small mountain cabin. The man appears to be a logger or millhand. Most of those workers were single men, but there was housing available for couples. For recreation, it seems that he enjoyed hunting and fishing, and they both appear to enjoy reading. They could even read the walls and ceiling of their cabin, which are papered with various newspapers, including the *Fresno Herald*. Unfortunately, the couple and their location are not identified. The cabin backs up on a large meadow, and there is a horse-drawn wagon to the left. They have embellished the front of the cabin with a swastika, which, at that time, was a good luck symbol.

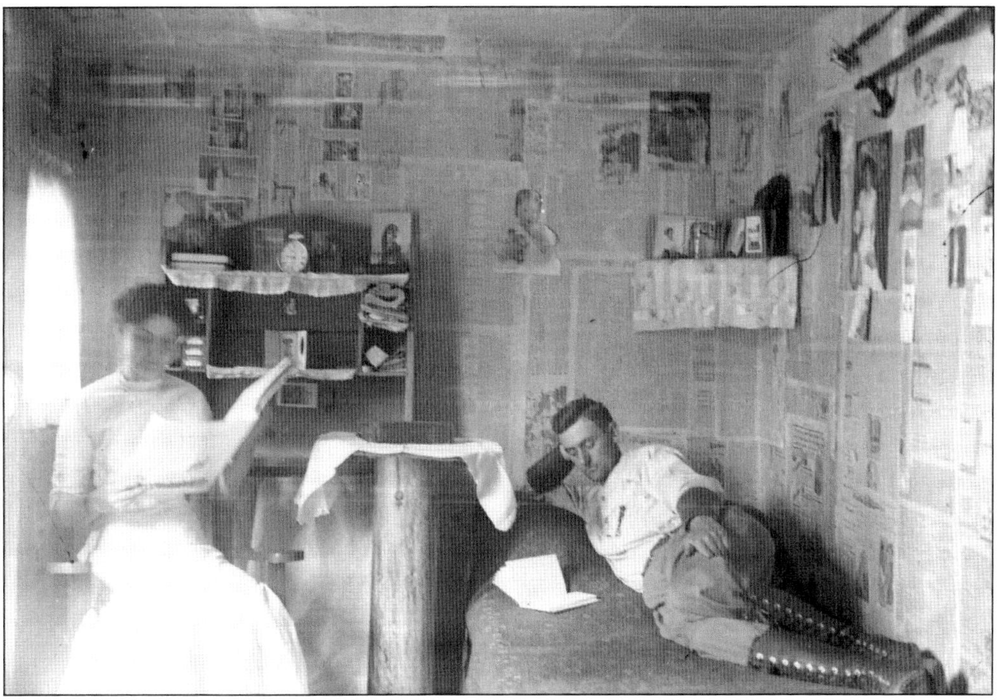

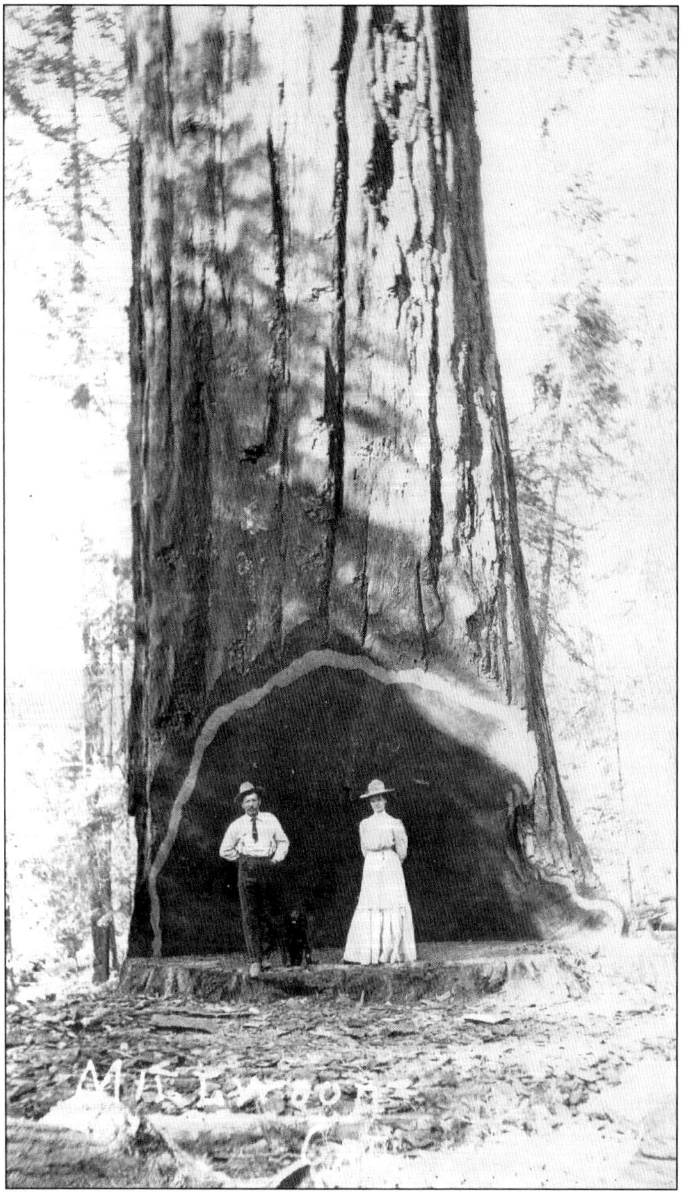

Loggers and tourists loved to pose with the giant sequoias (*Sequoiadendron giganteum*) being cut in the Sierra Nevada. This well-dressed couple stands in an undercut, which the loggers, working in teams, chopped for many days to make. Due to the buttress at the base of the massive sequoias, loggers built platforms where the buttress ended and the diameter of the tree was smaller. The loggers stood on the platform high above the ground and eventually completed the undercut. Then, two sawyers, working from the opposite side of the tree, cut into the tree with a very long two-man crosscut saw. They used steel wedges to prevent the tree from settling onto the saw blade. Eventually, wedges were used to slowly force the tree to fall toward the chopped side. The mammoth trees were so heavy and their wood so brittle that they often shattered when they hit the ground. It was a very time-consuming and wasteful process, and though the lumber companies kept cutting, they made little or no profit from their destructive effort.

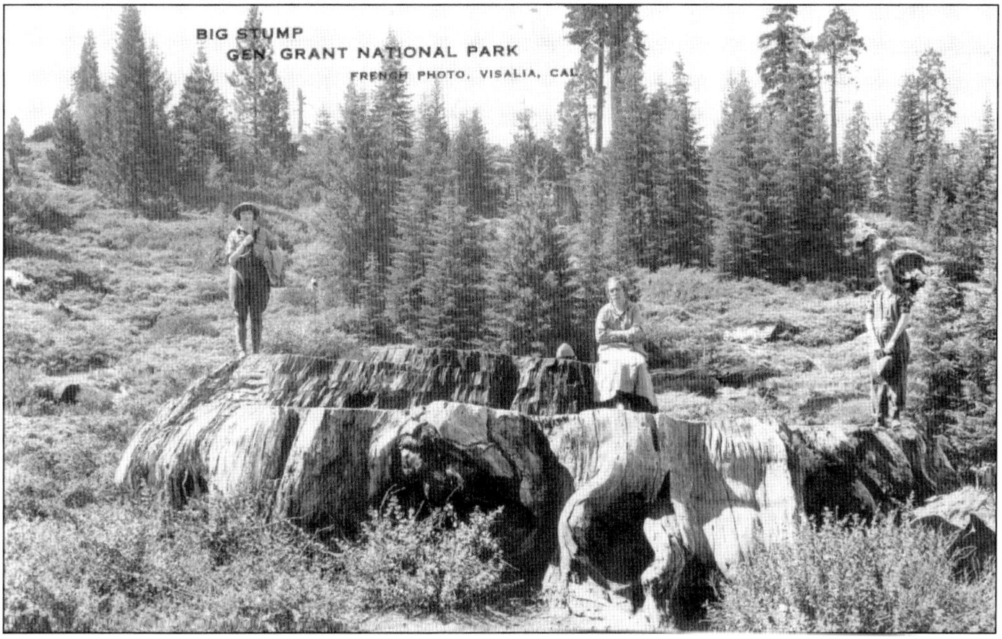

Big Stump Basin contains the remains of giant sequoia trees logged by Smith Comstock's lumber company over 100 years ago. The loggers quickly learned that giant sequoias were brittle and usually shattered when they hit the ground. The lumber does resist rot, so it was often split into fence posts or grape stacks for vineyards in the San Joaquin Valley. These postcards show the stump of the Mark Twain Tree, which reportedly took 13 days to fell in 1891. A slice of its trunk was sent to the American Museum of Natural History in New York City, and another slice went to the British Museum of Natural History in London. After logging, the area became part of General Grant National Park, which later became part of Kings Canyon National Park.

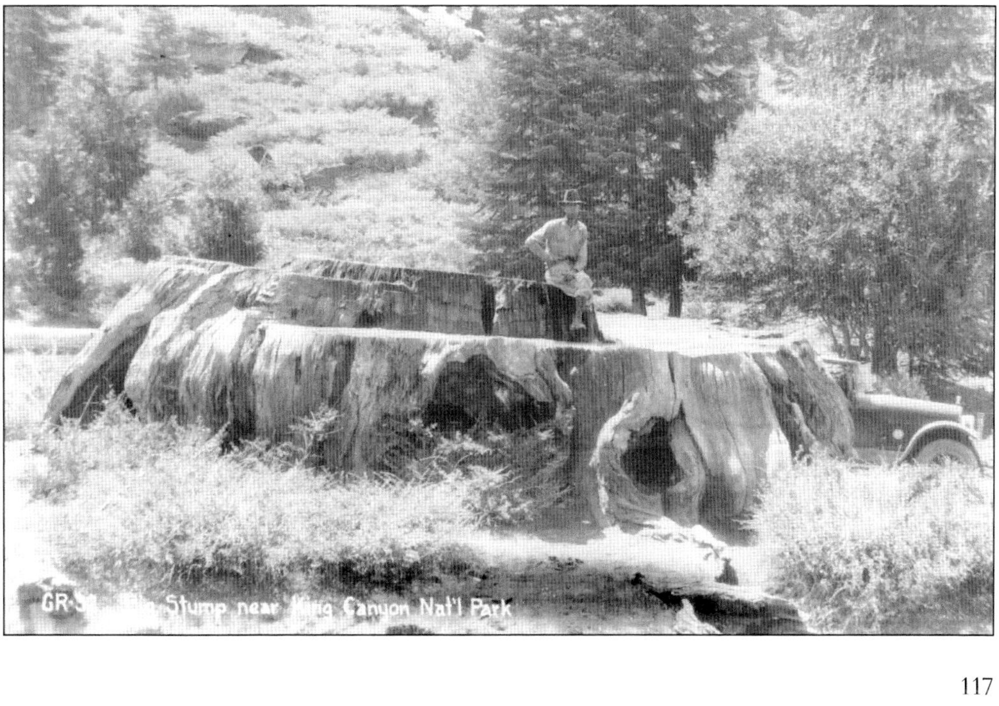

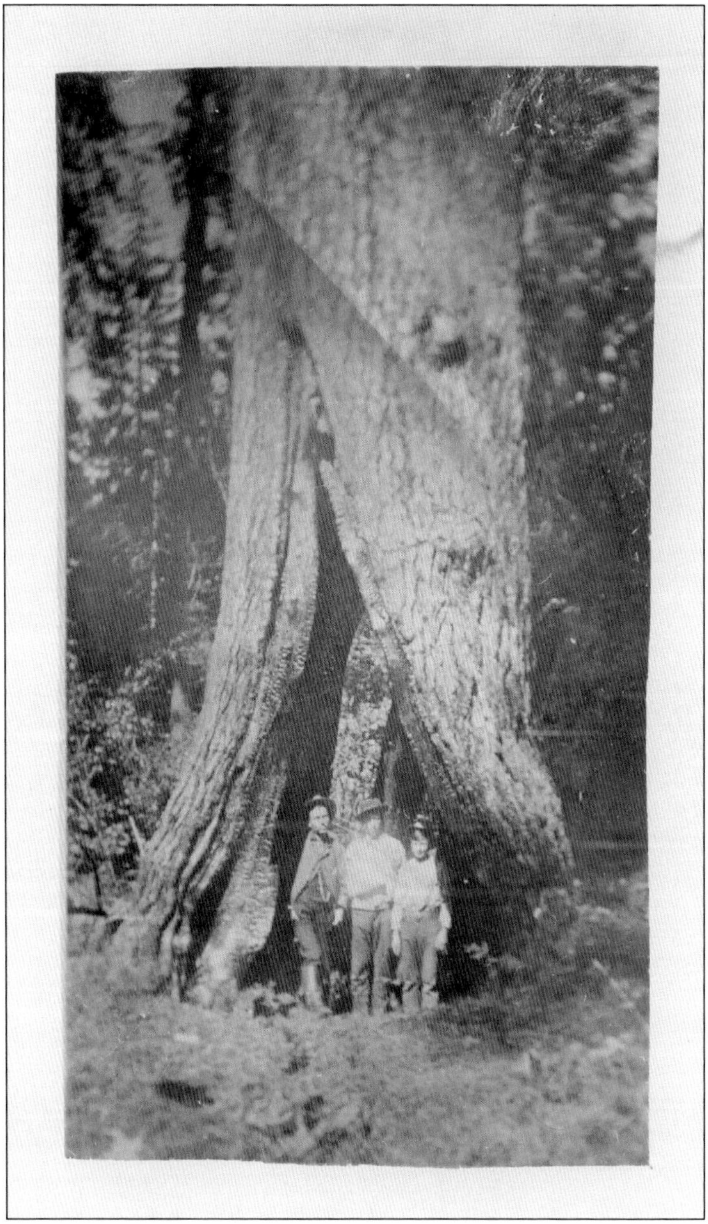

This photograph, taken around 1884, shows what was reportedly the "largest pine tree on Pine Ridge." It was cut down in 1888 and used to make shakes. As seen in the logging photographs in this book, there were many very large white pine, sugar pine, cedar, and fir trees in the Sierra Nevada. According to *A Sawmill History of the Sierra National Forest: 1852–1940* by Bert Hurt, there were at least 117 mills in Fresno County alone that produced over one billion board feet of lumber from over 54,000 acres. Posing in front of the tree above are, from left to right, John S. Eastwood, James McCardle Jr., and Charles "Charlie" McCardle. Eastwood (1857–1924) is the engineer credited with being the first to recognize the power possibilities that became the Big Creek Hydroelectric Project. The father of the two McCardle boys, James McCardle Sr. (1833–1898) was born in Ireland and came to California during the Gold Rush. At the time of this 1884 photograph, McCardle and John Smyth owned the largest sawmill on Pine Ridge.

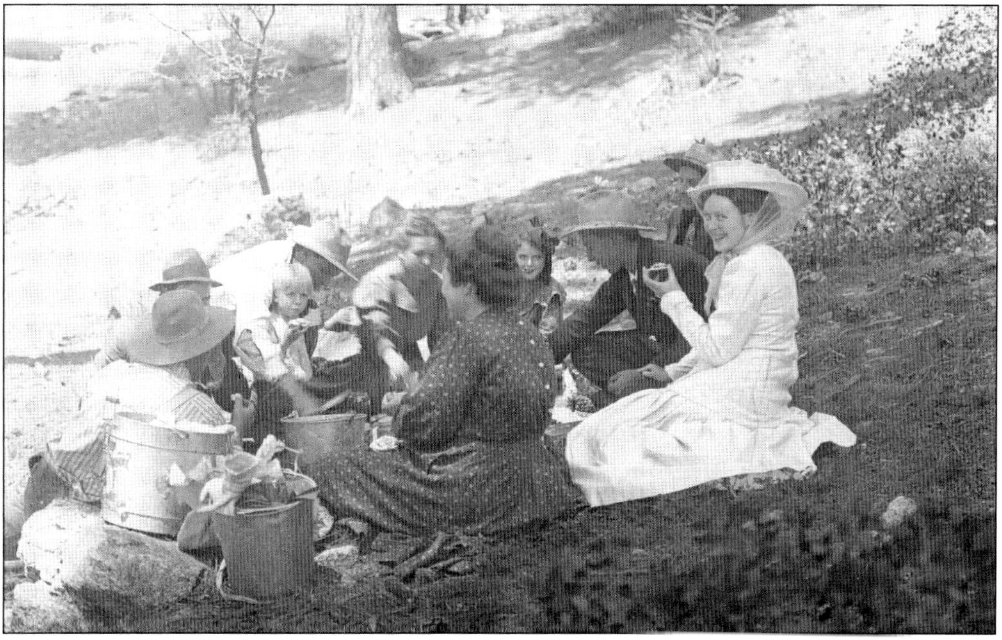

With several buckets of food, these families seem to be enjoying their summer picnic in the Sierra. Although most of the logging-camp workers were single men, there were individual cabins available as housing for couples. The logging-camp work was seasonal, so it was possible for families who lived in Fresno and nearby cities to spend the summer in the mountains.

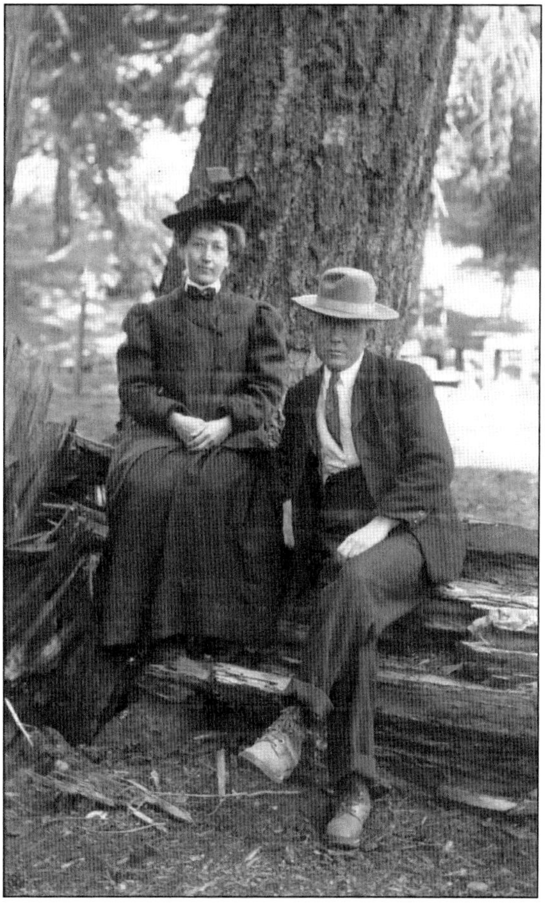

This very well dressed couple seated on a log were obviously not working at the Shaver sawmill. Even though getting to the mountains was time consuming, there was always a steady flow of tourists. With various development projects and the construction of the San Joaquin & Eastern Railroad, travel was easier, and company executives made periodic visits to inspect the progress of the work.

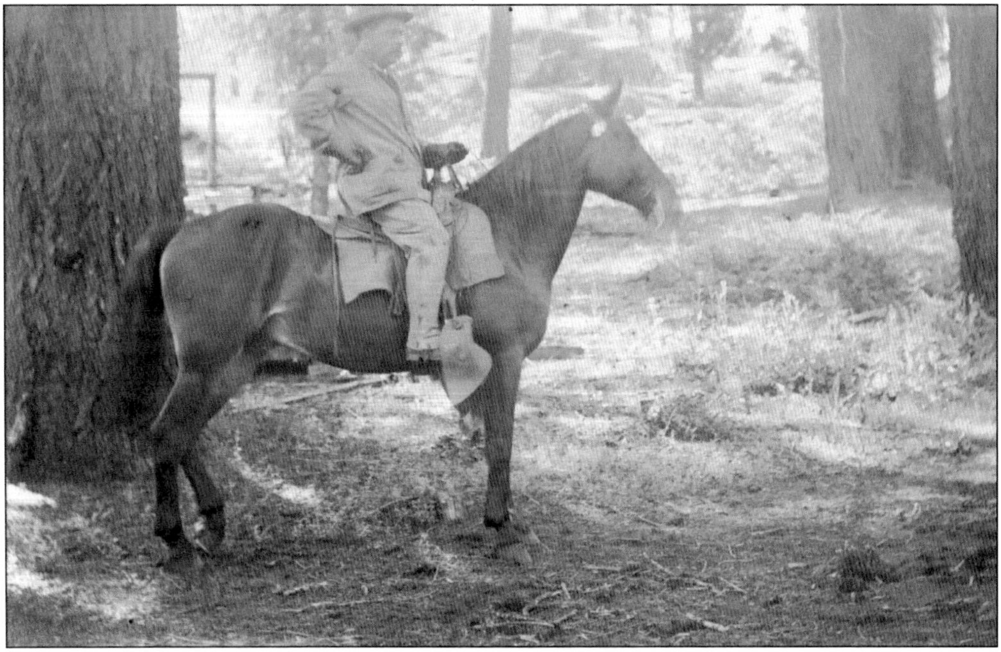

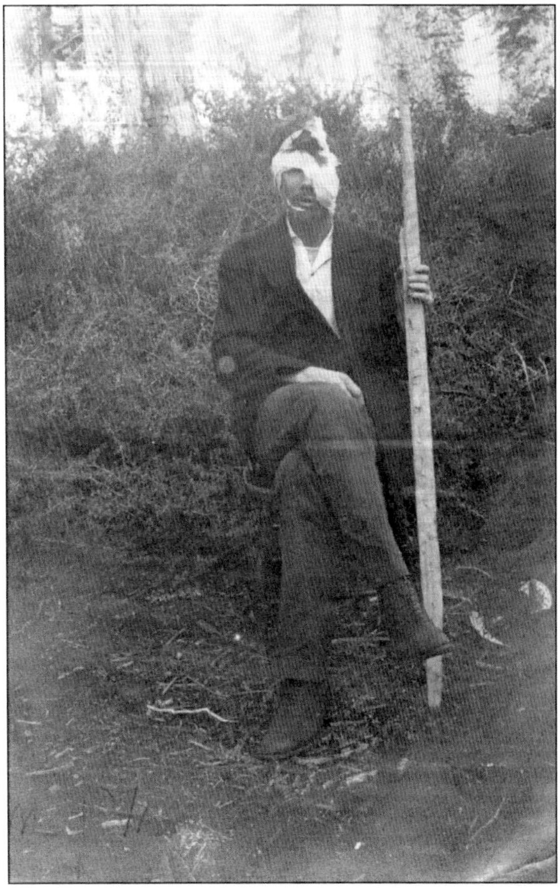

A man believed to be Harvey W. Swift (1854–1915) is shown astride his steed in this real-photo postcard by Shipp & Shipp. Swift was the brother-in-law of Charles B. Shaver (1855–1907). These lumbermen from Michigan organized the Fresno Flume & Irrigation Company in 1891. In 1912, Harvey Swift sold his interest in the company to Ira Bennett, formerly of the Hume-Bennett Lumber Company, and retired.

There is a story here in this Manley White photograph, and it is not a good one. The man seems rather calm as he poses with a long piece of wood that apparently pierced his head. Logging and millwork were very dangerous, and there were countless injuries and deaths among the workers.

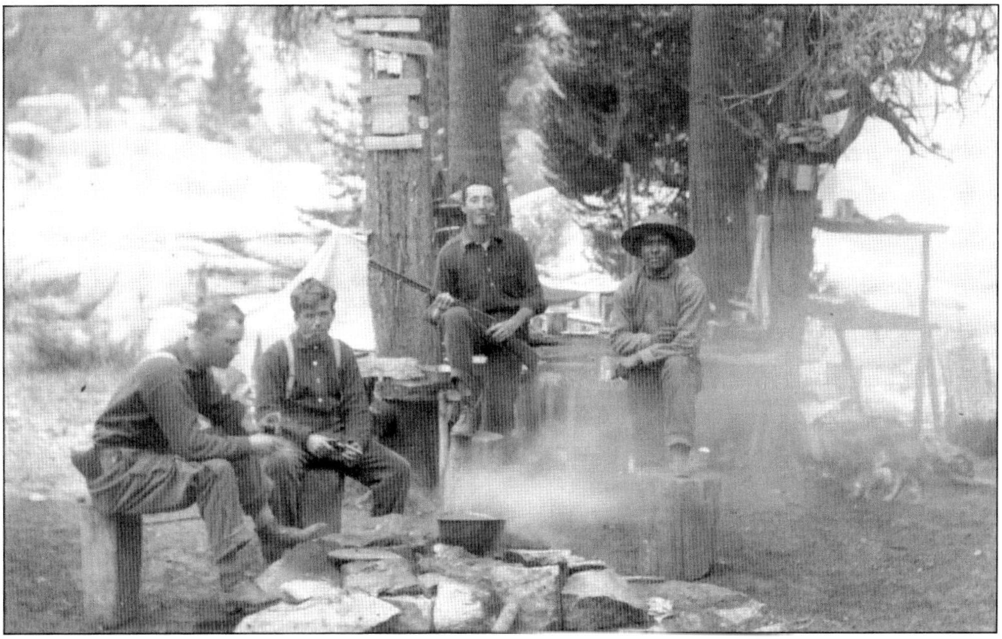

A well-established camp, probably near Shaver Lake, is shown in this real-photo postcard by Shipp & Shipp. The four well-armed men are enjoying their pipes and cigars around the campfire as they cook a meal. It is possible these were commercial hunters rather than sport hunters. There was undoubtedly a market for game—such as deer, bear, and quail—at the various hotels and camps on Pine Ridge.

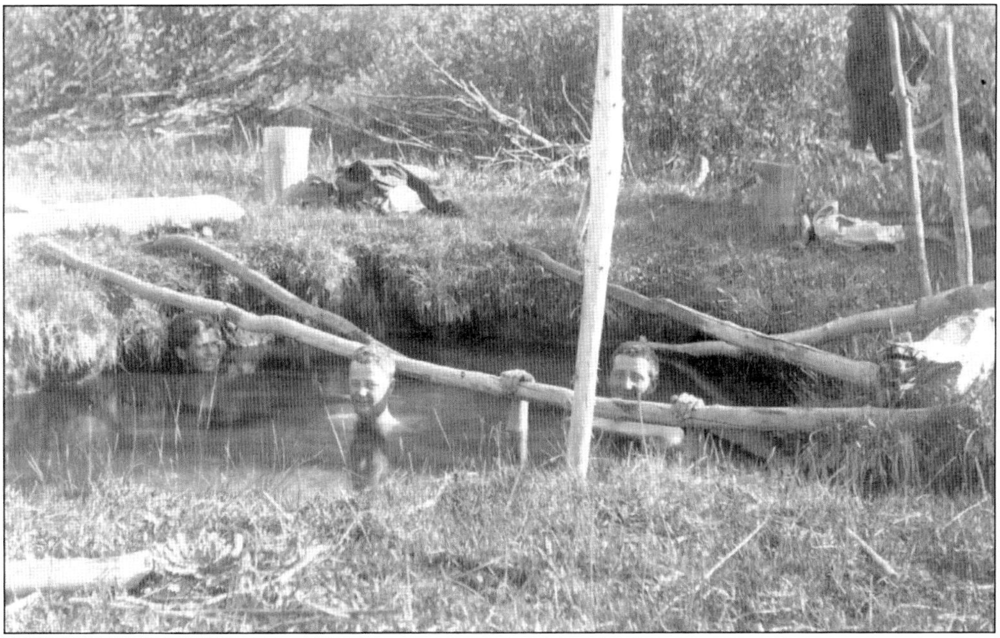

Three men enjoy a dip near the Shaver area in this photograph by Shipp & Shipp. Poles across the hole suggest it might be deep. The nearest hot springs are at Mono Hot Springs across Kaiser Pass; however, there were sulfur springs near Shaver. Bathing opportunities were probably limited in the logging and mill camps with their six-day work schedules.

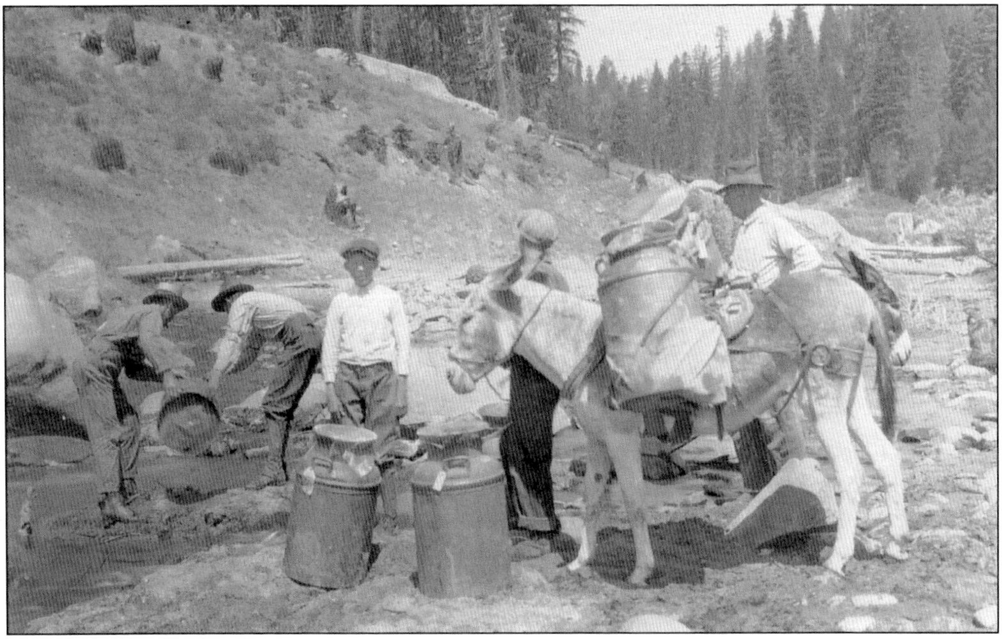

Burros carried these heavy milk cans, loaded with baby trout, into the backcountry of the Sierra Nevada near Shaver Lake. This photograph by Robert A. Parker shows the trout being planted as the men at left empty one of the cans into a stream. Later, anglers, such as the group shown below, would reap the benefit of this hard work. (Fresno County Public Library.)

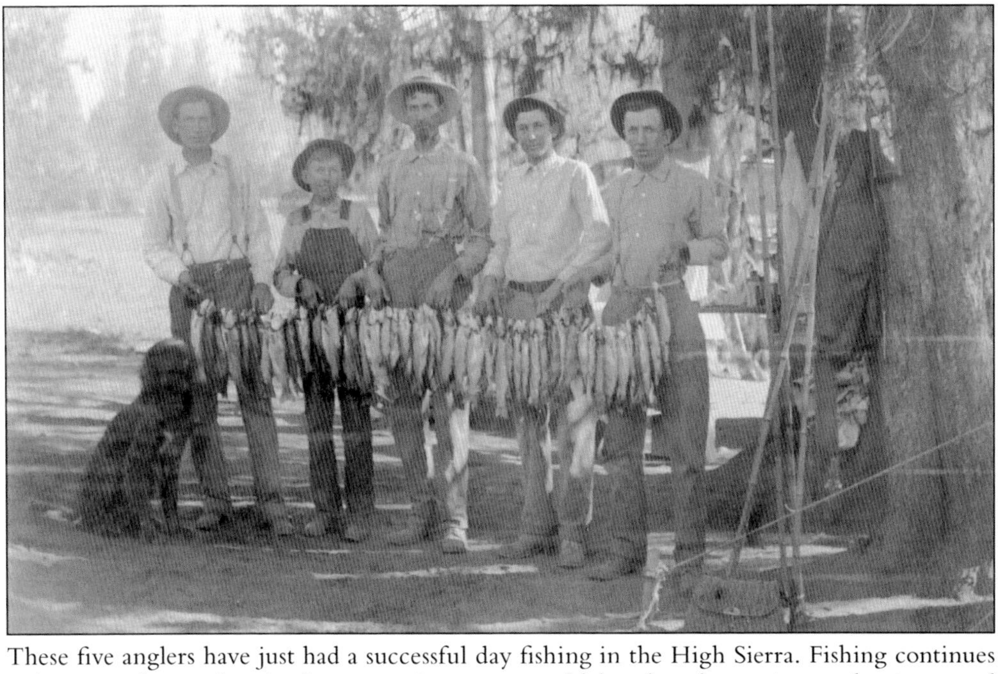

These five anglers have just had a successful day fishing in the High Sierra. Fishing continues to be a popular pastime in the mountain streams and lakes, but the equipment has improved from the cane poles seen leaning against the tree. The higher elevations have rainbow, brook, brown, and golden trout. This looks like a lot of fish, but a limit of 50 trout had been established in 1905.

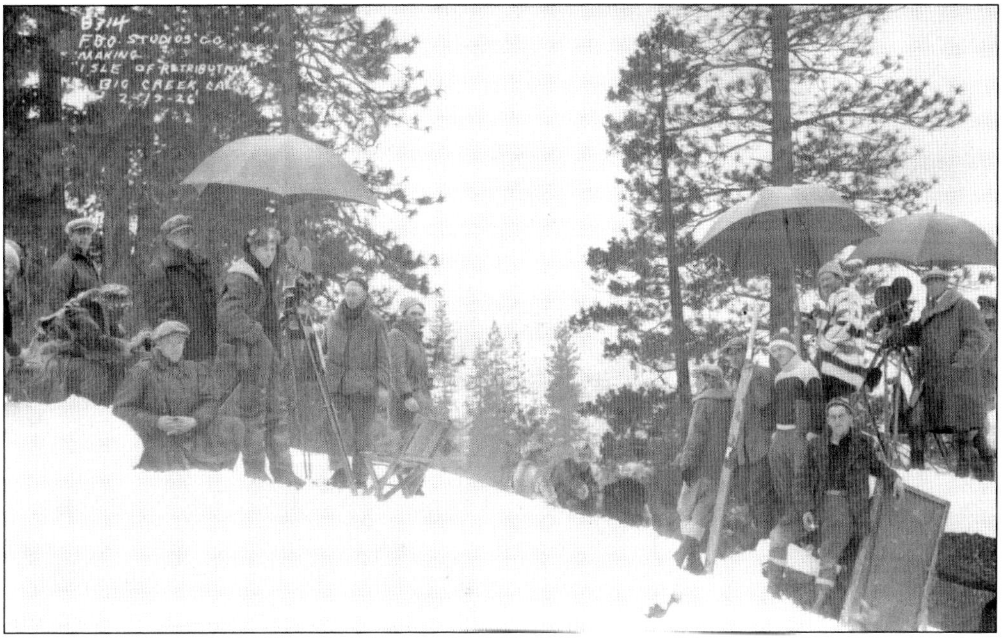

Big Creek and the vicinity were the location for several silent films and talkies. FBO Pictures Corporation filmed *Isle of Retribution* at Big Creek in February 1926. The movie centered on five people stranded on an island off the coast of Alaska, so the snowy February weather at Big Creek made it an excellent location for the film.

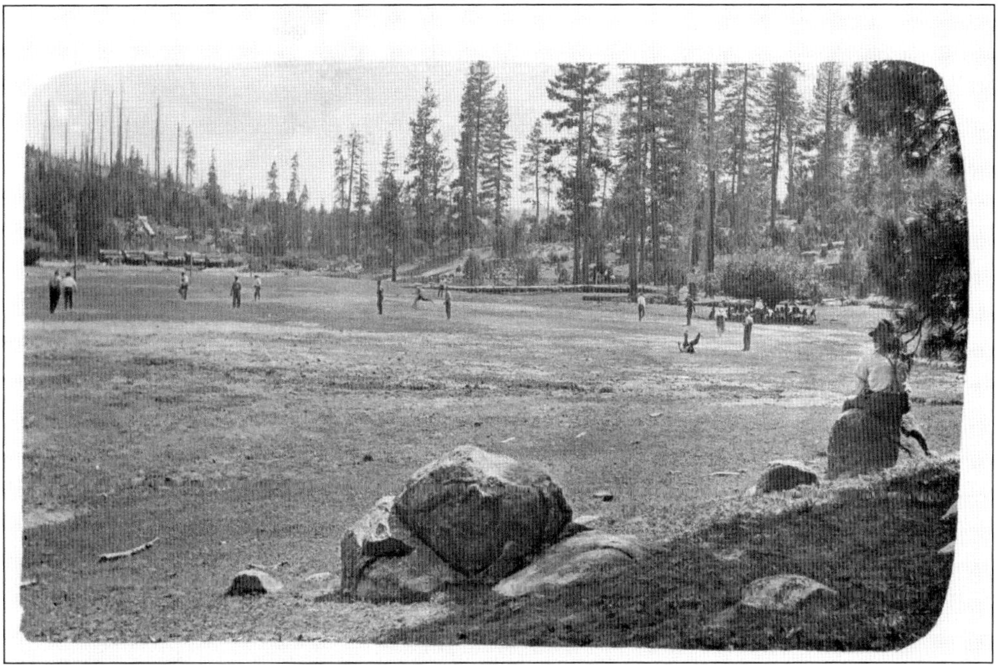

Even in the rugged Sierra Nevada, residents—mainly loggers and millhands—could find a flat location for a Sunday game of baseball. The Morgan Pine Knots, Meadow Larks, and Shaver Giants were among the teams playing in Swanson, Markwood, and other meadows near Shaver in the early 1900s. In the background is a train with logs headed for the millpond.

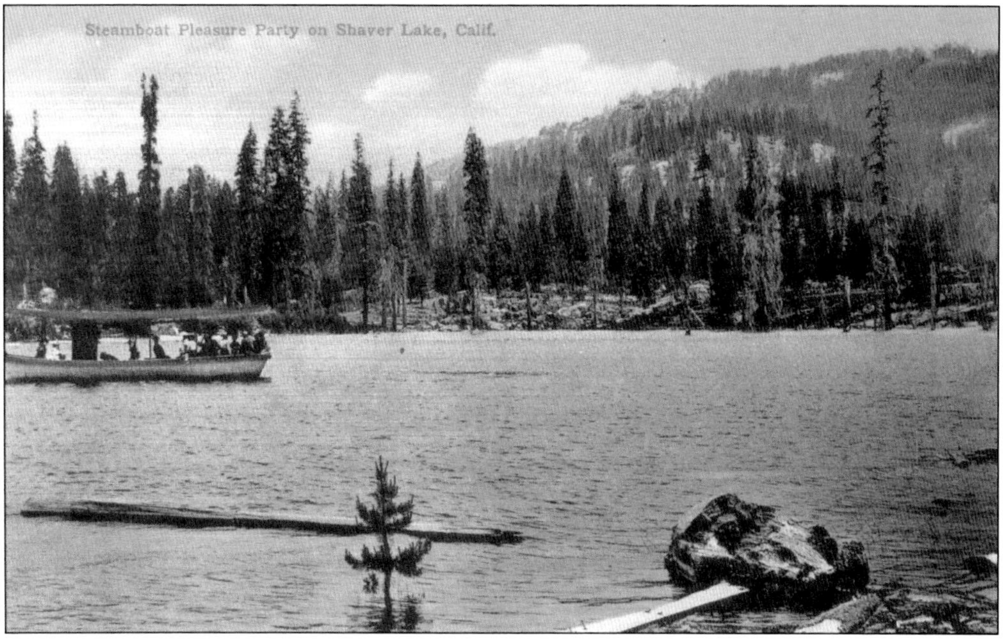

Shaver Lake has always been popular with tourists. In this commercially produced postcard, a group is seen riding in the *Michigan*, a steamboat with a vertical boiler. In addition to being used for pleasure trips on the lake, it also worked hauling logs across the lake from the log dump to the sawmill.

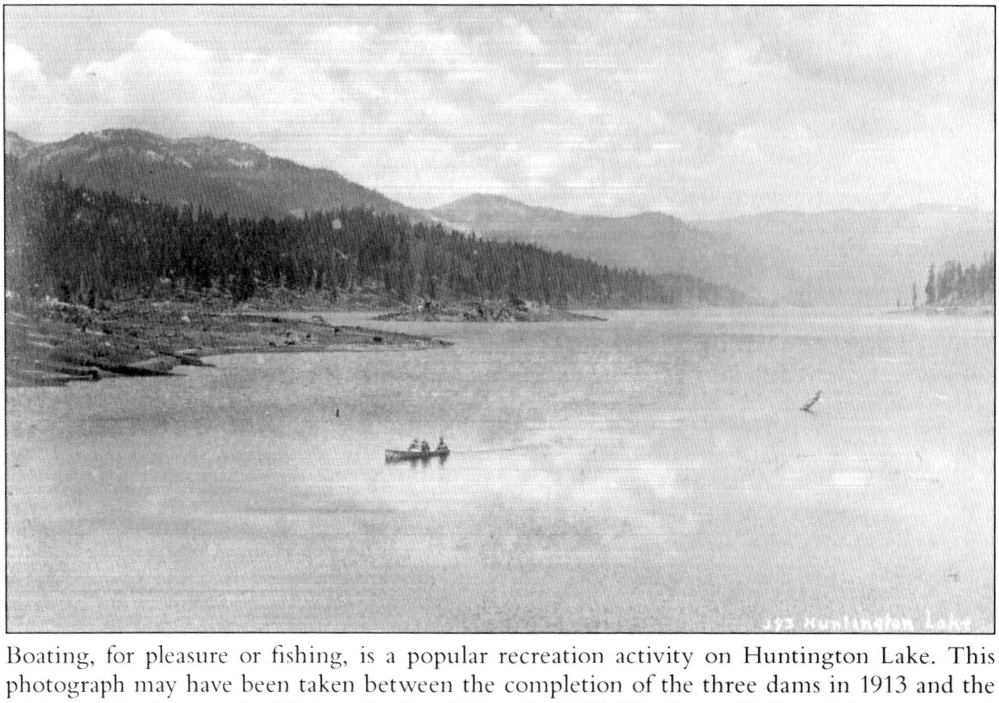

Boating, for pleasure or fishing, is a popular recreation activity on Huntington Lake. This photograph may have been taken between the completion of the three dams in 1913 and the raising of the dams and addition of a fourth dam in 1917. The five-mile-long lake was named for Henry E. Huntington, who owned both the power company and the electric railroads in Los Angeles that used the electricity.

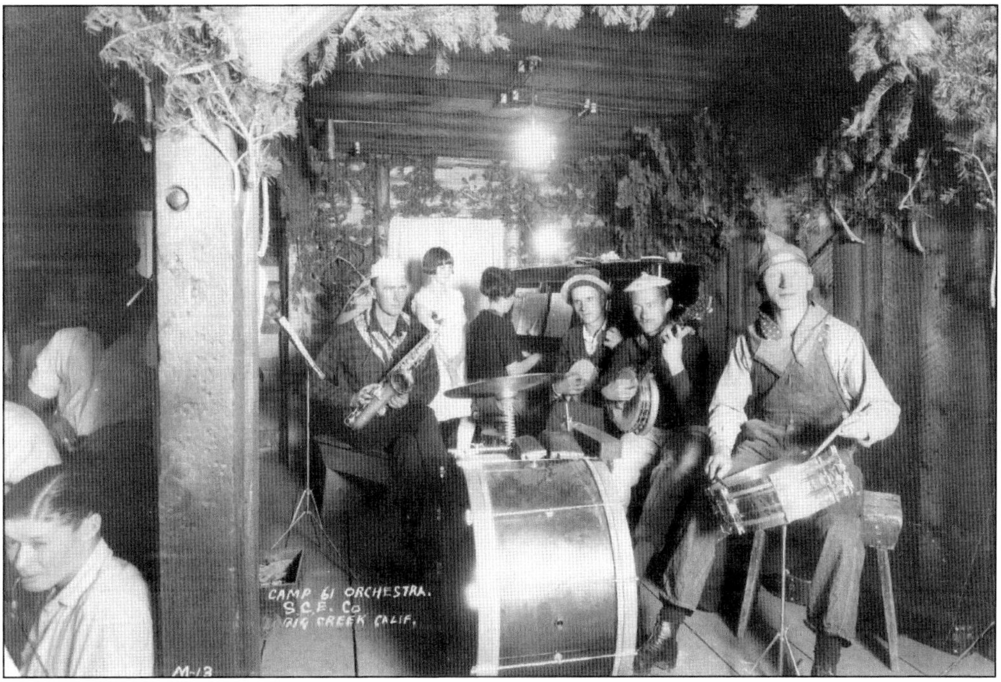

With the hard work of building dams and digging tunnels, it was nice for the Southern California Edison workers to relax and have some fun. Camp 61, at the Florence Lake end of the Ward Tunnel, had an "orchestra" with an odd variety of instruments and hats. The decorative pine boughs suggest that a Christmas party is being held.

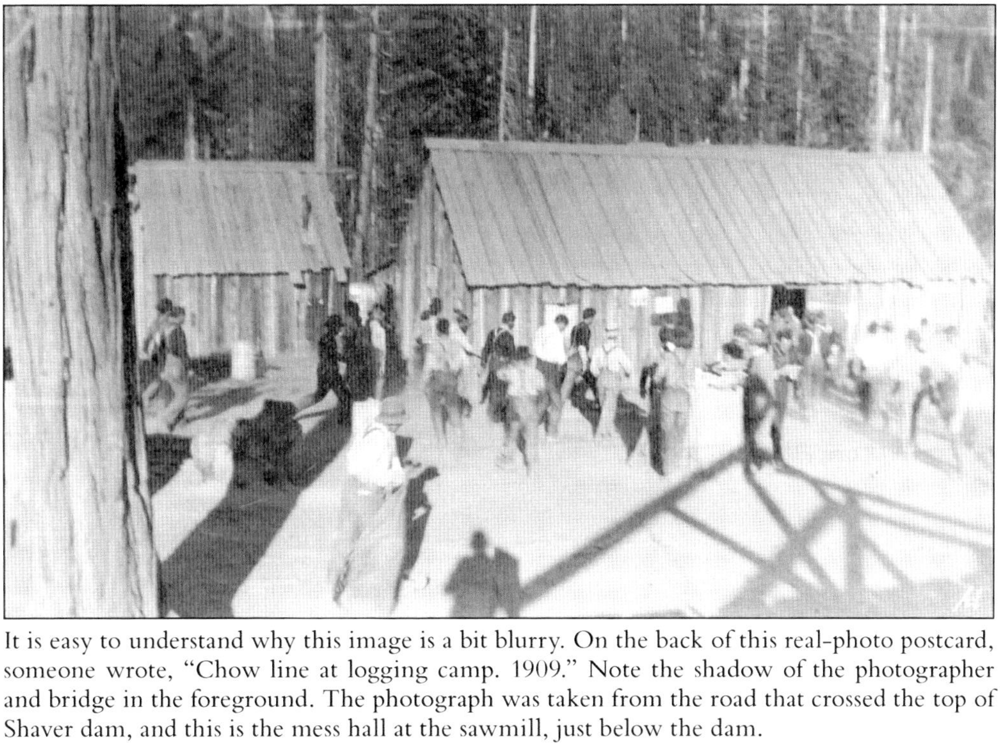

It is easy to understand why this image is a bit blurry. On the back of this real-photo postcard, someone wrote, "Chow line at logging camp. 1909." Note the shadow of the photographer and bridge in the foreground. The photograph was taken from the road that crossed the top of Shaver dam, and this is the mess hall at the sawmill, just below the dam.

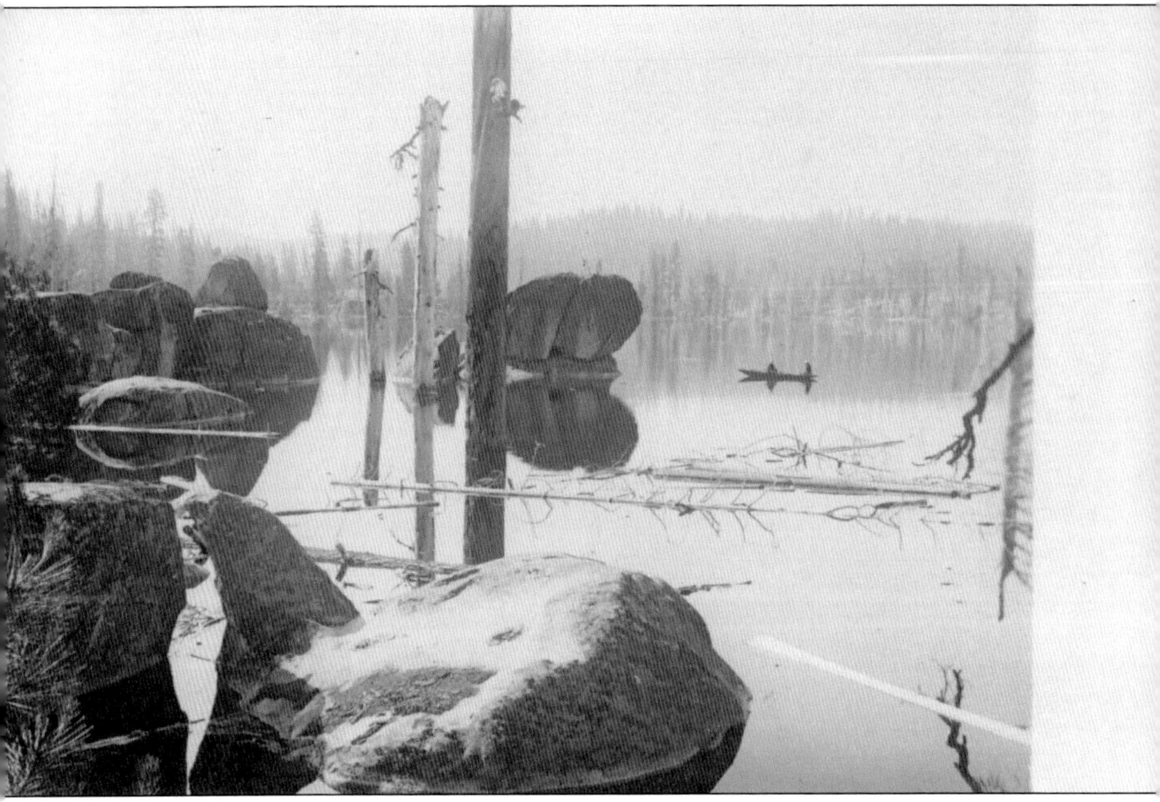

A peaceful but eerie scene on a very still Shaver Lake was captured here by Manley White. All the sounds of logging, including chopping, falling trees, steam donkeys, Shay railroad engines, and logs being dumped into the millpond or sawed into boards can be forgotten. The construction of numerous hydroelectric dams is also a thing of the past. The serenity and quietude of the Sierra Nevada has returned.

Bibliography

Hurt, Bert. *A Sawmill History of the Sierra National Forest, 1852–1940.* Washington, DC: Government Printing Office, 1941.

Johnson, Merv. *In Search of Steam Donkeys: Logging Equipment in Oregon.* Hillsboro, OR: Timber Times, 1996.

Johnston, Hank. *The Railroad That Lighted Southern California.* Glendale, CA: Trans-Anglo Books, 1975.

———. *They Felled the Redwoods: A Saga of Flumes and Rails in the High Sierra.* Los Angeles, CA: Trans-Anglo Books, 1971.

Redinger, David H. *The Story of Big Creek.* Los Angeles, CA: Angelus Press, 1949.

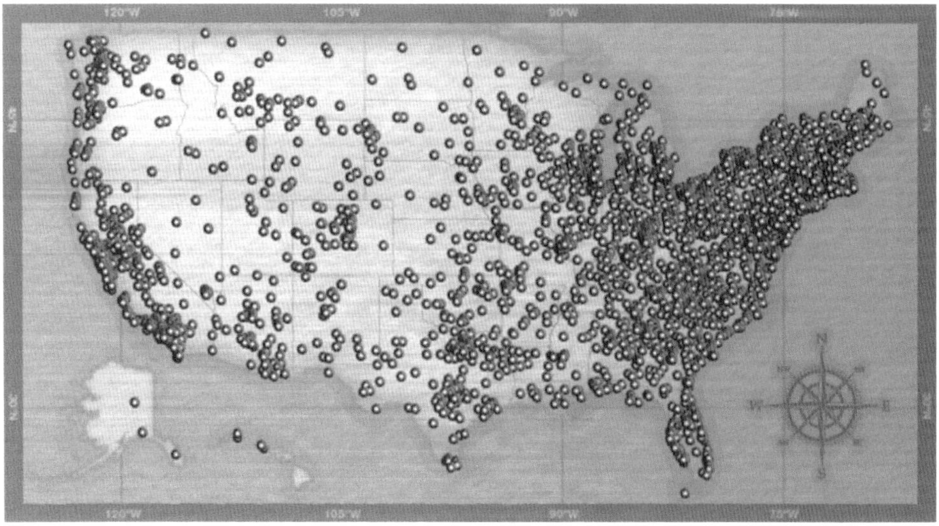